THE RACE

Other books by J. T. W. Hubbard

Banking in Mid-America: A History
of Missouri's Banks

Magazine Editing

THE RACE

*An inside account of what it's like to compete
in the Observer Singlehanded Transatlantic Race
from Plymouth, England, to Newport, Rhode Island*

c. 1

by J.T.W. HUBBARD

Maps and illustrations by the author

W·W·NORTON & COMPANY
New York   *London*

797.1
HUBBARD

Lines from *The Man of La Mancha* on page 80 used by permission, words by Joe Darion, music by Mitch Leigh; copyright 1965 Andrew Scott Inc. and Helena Music Corp.

The text of this book is composed in Janson, with display type set in Bulmer. Composition by ComCom. Manufacturing by Haddon Craftsmen. Book design by Jacques Chazaud.

First Edition

ISBN 0-393-03313-9

W. W. Norton & Company, Inc., 500 Fifth Avenue, New York, N. Y. 10110
W. W. Norton & Company Ltd., 37 Great Russell Street, London WC1B 3NU

1 2 3 4 5 6 7 8 9 0

This book is dedicated to the
memory of my father
Walter Glover Hubbard
1905–1984

CONTENTS

THE RACE

1

No Better Place . . .

"*Johan Lloyde?*"
   The shout came again, louder this time.
   "*JOHAN LLOYDE,* AHOY."
   I put down my coffee mug and pushed back the hatch. I stared across the decks of the three other boats rafted alongside my cutter in Mill Bay Dock. After a moment's search among the crowds of sightseers I spotted two men, heavily muffled in parkas, standing thirty feet away on the floating pontoon. They waved.
   "Yes?" I shouted back.
   "Inspection Team. We're coming aboard."
   "You're an hour early. I just came in from the Mayflower Marina five minutes ago."
   "Doesn't matter. We'll inspect her now, or we'll never get done."
   It was necessary for *Johan Lloyde* to pass this inspection if she was to sail in the 1984 Observer Singlehanded Transatlantic Race (OSTAR)—a contest that ran 3,000 miles across the ocean from Plymouth, England, to Newport, Rhode Island. I designed and built the interior of my thirty-two-foot pilot cutter myself. For reasons of professional pride I wanted to impress these inspectors with my handiwork. Yet at this critical moment the cabin was a shambles. The remains of breakfast still lay in the sink. Just an hour earlier I'd bolted a new stemhead fitting on to *Johan*'s bowsprit, and tools and polysulphide sealant littered the floor. My blankets lay heaped in the port berth. Piles of sweaters, old towels, and two pairs of J. C. Penney's long johns festooned the seat cushions to starboard. Copies of the London *Daily Telegraph*, the

Western Morning News, and English boating magazines were scattered everywhere.

For a moment I considered demanding ten minutes' grace in which to clean up. But as I looked around, it occurred to me that asking for a recess might not be a smart move. It was a Saturday late in May, and a very cold wind was cutting through the Devon hills off to the north. The longer I kept the inspectors stamping their feet on the dock, the shorter their tempers were likely to be when they finally came aboard. Under the circumstances, they could hardly complain if everything were not quite Bristol fashion.

"It's a mess," I yelled across to the pontoon, "but come on over."

The inspectors clambered gingerly across the foredecks of *Sherpa Bill, Moustache,* and *Crystal Catfish III*. The first to climb over *Johan*'s rail was a red-haired man in his middle-thirties. Just behind him came a shorter, older man with deep-set grey eyes. I recognized him as the Chief Inspector of the Royal Western Yacht Club. During the week it was his job, I knew, to check commercial shipping in and out of Plymouth for the British Board of Trade. Here, then, to check my homemade boat was a *professional* inspector. I'd ruffled some feathers down at the Royal Western in my efforts to enter the Observer Singlehanded at the last minute. Was this sudden appearance of the Chief Inspector, I wondered, the Race Committee's rebuke for the trouble I had caused them? It wouldn't be hard for such a knowledgeable man to prove that *Johan Lloyde* must be relegated to the sidelines for extensive alterations.

The two inspectors climbed cautiously down the companion way into *Johan*'s cabin. Even though I'd now swept clear some sitting space, both men chose to remain standing. Then, without a word, one of them leaned over and switched off my depth sounder, still plugging fourteen feet. I bustled around some more and pulled a bottle out of the cuddy.

"Would it be inappropriate," I asked, "for me to offer you a peg of whisky?"

"Yes, it would." The tone was snappish. The Chief Inspector looked as if he had me figured out: first, lame excuses, now bribery. He coughed and began to peer into the darker recesses of the cabin with an expression of polite distaste. Then he turned a page on his clipboard.

"Seacocks!"

The word was uttered with such abruptness that I jumped. "Right. Seacocks," I mumbled. "There's one here, and here, and

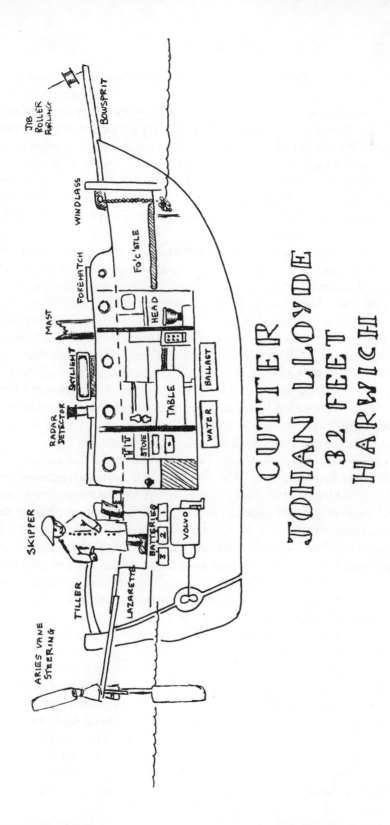

CUTTER
JOHAN LLOYDE
32 FEET
HARWICH

all through here, here . . ." As I identified each item the inspectors ticked it off in red. For the next few minutes they kept me swinging round the cabin. I began to feel myself slowing down. Once, to anticipate the next command I took a sly glance over the inspector's shoulder at the clipboard. He glared at me and tilted it away. Batteries? Gas cylinders? Ballast secured? We went down on our hands and knees and reached around in the bilges. Nothing moved. Another red check. The inspection wound its way through the rest of my precious handiwork. (See diagram, page 13.) Lights? Toilet? Stove? So far, so good.

"Do you have three or more securely installed water tanks?"

"Thirty gallons here in the bilge, another thirty here on the starboard quarter . . ."

"Are these Imperial gallons, or American gallons?"

Imperial gallons. The notion had a good, full-bodied ring to it. But, I wondered, how can you still have Imperial gallons when you no longer have an Empire? "British gallons," I replied. But even as the words popped out, I realized that my casual updating of their Great Island Story could hardly improve the mood of the Inspectors. "There's a third tank here, under the starboard berth."

"Where?" The tone was peremptory.

"There. Under the berth."

"I don't see it."

"Behind the bulkhead." I'd also heard that this inspection doubled as an oblique little exam to assess the skipper's psychological ability to survive a month alone in a small boat. Sycophancy and bluster were out. And, I'd been told, a disdain for the seriousness of the proceedings could be almost as damning. But by now I was out of breath. Perhaps the Chief Inspector would care to find it for himself? A screw cap labelled "Water" appeared. I wasn't lying after all. But clearly they believed I was quite capable of lying my head off on the next one. In a little while the men seemed to enter a new phase of their inspection. On a given signal, both of them grabbed *Johan*'s starboard berth and tried to jerk it loose from its moorings. Then, with much puffing and grunting, they tried the same stunt on the saloon table, the galley bulkheads and the other berth. Did they do this to every boat? Or was this treatment reserved for craft of amateur construction? Nothing budged, thank goodness. But such gangbuster ways served to ignite in me a spark of rebellion. Now they took it in turns to bark their questions, and it was all I could do to keep up. Perhaps they'd forgotten the old maxim: treat a man like a felon and, after a while, he'll behave like one. Two fire extinguishers? Two bilge pumps? Two buckets? Storm jib? Let's look in the bag. Weary now, I moved forward and started hauling sailbags around in the fo'c'sle. Eventually I found it.

"Open the bag."

"Yes, sir."

He examined the sail's tack. "You should be able to find it in the dark."

"Yes, sir!"

The Chief Inspector looked at me sharply. I grinned back. My psychographic profile was probably losing points fast, but I was not about to be patronized on matters of basic seamanship. Only last summer I had singlehanded this boat from Nova Scotia to Falmouth, England. The catechism continued. First aid kit? A fifty-foot heaving line? Radar reflector? Emergency steering? This was a proud moment for me. I took both men on deck and showed them emergency steering with a vengeance in the form of a fourteen-foot lifeboat oar lashed to *Johan*'s starboard rail. The Inspectors, however, did not seem to be impressed. In the days ahead, Blagdon's Oar, as it came to be known among OSTAR skippers, was destined to pass from boat to boat in an orgy of deceit. By June 2, the day of the start, it would be counted no fewer than five times by various teams of inspectors. Lifejacket? Yes, sir.

"You should put the boat's name on this."

"How so?"

"If the vessel founders, this will aid in identification."

For an instant I was struck by the image of a soggy corpse, its features eroded beyond recognition, borne up by an orange life jacket indelibly stamped with the words "Johan Lloyde."

"Isn't that getting a little morbid?" I asked. The Chief Inspector looked at me intently. Skipper questions authority—deduct six more points on the psychiatric profile. While the Assistant Inspector looked at his boots, the Chief Inspector and I glared at each other across the cabin, eyeball to eyeball.

"The boat's name *must* be on the life jacket." Now his voice carried with it a hint of exasperation. "This is no joke, you know."

"I'll be in Kingdom Come by the time that thing washes ashore."

"You have a wife, a family?"

"Yes."

"Well, perhaps they might wish to know your fate?" The note of irritation was stronger now. "This race is not a tea party. More than a third of all the boats starting never make it to Newport."

Radio? VHF? Tools? EPIRB locator? Life raft? Panic bag, with water and rations? Flares? Almanac? Charts? I had charts of everywhere aboard the *Johan Lloyde*. The starboard berth in the fo'c'sle contained eight hefty rolls of them.

"You want charts? I've got charts . . . Bermuda, Newfoundland, the St. Lawrence River, Bay of Biscay, North Sea, Ireland, the Azores, Spain, Portugal, and Greenland." The Assistant Inspector glanced at the paper logs in the fo'c'sle. He made no move to unroll and check them. Instead, he seemed surprised. Was this, he appeared to be asking himself, really what it took?

"Sextant?"

"I've got three." I pulled open a locker above the starboard berth. First out was a Henry Hughes Ltd. "Husun," top of the line in 1942. "This was my father's sextant." For a moment I fumbled with the latch. The wooden box clicked open and the magnificent instrument was revealed. Seven shades, three eyepieces, the heft of a heavy revolver, and a vernier scale accurate to ten seconds of arc. The Chief Inspector put down his clipboard, reached into the box and picked the sextant up in the prescribed manner. The inquisitorial manner was gone. He held the sextant up to the light as if he were savoring fresh sea air. He adjusted the index arm and twiddled the micrometer drum. As he did so, I realized that I was in the presence of a most reluctant landsman, someone whose memories ranged far beyond the confines of the Board of Trade.

"Very nice."

"They don't seem to make them like that any more," I said.

"It's all plastic now, of course."

"Don't I know it."

We spoke not as Inspector and Official Victim but as equals. In a little while the sextant went back into its box, and the inspection became perfunctory. A few more check marks were entered on to the forms and then it was announced that *Johan*, and her amateur builder, had passed muster. They were adjudged seaworthy enough to challenge anything the North Atlantic could dish out, head on. Later, I learned that many of my fellow skippers had not fared so well with their own inspections.

After the departure of the scrutineers, I tidied the cabin for an hour or so and then stepped across the bows of my neighbors' boats. It was time, I decided, to give myself a walking tour of the other contenders. But once I arrived on the pontoon I found I could hardly move. The British public had also come down to see the boats. Old men, old ladies, children, babes, and young parents, their eyes filled with far horizons, were packed in a solid phalanx upon the dock. TV cameras were everywhere, beaming images of crowds and exotic marine hardware into millions of British and West European homes. I slowly worked my way along the pontoon and up the steep gangway on to the stone wall of Mill Bay Dock. Spread out below me were nearly one hundred yachts, many of them flying the blanket-size *Observer* racing pennant. The mighty French multihulls, sixty feet long and thirty feet across, were moored check-by-jowl with chunky little sloops that could have been designed a century ago. The hum of power tools was all about me, and at least one mast in four had a man up it making final adjustments to the rig.

To increase the element of competitiveness, the boats had been divided into five classes, according to length. Each class had then been further divided by type into monohulls (sloops, ketches, schooners, and cutters, like *Johan*) and multihulls (two-hulled catamarans and three-hulled trimarans). Prizes were to be awarded to the first three boats home in all ten categories, and grand prizes were to be awarded to the first three boats of any size across the line in Newport. In addition, winners would acquire hundreds of thousands of dollars' worth of promotional benefits. The table below shows the final number of competitors in each category:

		Monohulls	Multihulls
Class I	(45'–60')	5	19
Class II	(40'–45')	10	6
Class III	(35'–40')	11	5
Class IV	(30'–35')	17	3
Class V	(25'–30')	14	2

This then was the order of battle, the firmament according to OSTAR. While *Johan Lloyde* made ready to do combat against sixteen other doughty monohulls in Class IV, the titans of Class I—sailing $500,000 boats at speeds in excess of twenty-five knots—prepared to clash and grapple their way across the heavens like the gods of old. The role of Thor undoubtedly fell to Eric Tabarly, the iron-grey French naval officer who had won the race in 1964 and again in 1976. In 1984, he planned, with the help of huge sponsorship by the French apéritif Paul Ricard, to go for a third victory. The crown, I learned, was also sought by two of his former protégés, Marc Pajot and Philippe Poupon, both sailing very fast boats and both well versed in the wily strategems of the master.

However, Thor, now fifty-two years of age, had more to contend with than upstart sons. There were disturbing rumors of a stranger from across the water, clad in dark leather and reflector shades and armed with exotic technology, who had designed and built a space-age sloop named *Thursday's Child*, which was capable of speeds that might smash the multihulls' long domination of Class I. Warren Luhrs, aged forty, was the president of a boat manufacturing company in Alachua, Florida. His entry in the previous OSTAR had been forced to retire with serious keel problems. Now *Thursday's Child*, replete with water ballast, rotary boom vang, and pendulum rudder, had returned to set the record straight.

It was clear to everyone in Mill Bay that the Ricard company was prepared to spend millions to get Tabarly to Newport first. The boat, notable for its flared decks and white hydrofoils angled down and inward from each float, was under the constant care of a dozen uniformed technicians (see picture p. 19). They were backed by the services of two panel trucks, three automobiles, and a large helicopter, all tricked out in the distinctive Ricard colors of blue, red, and goldenrod yellow. Two other Class I French tris lay against the dock wall at a point exactly opposite *Johan*'s place on the pontoon. They were *Umupro Jardin V*, captained by the affable Breton Yvon Fauconnier, and the 56-foot *Fleury Michon*, piloted by Philippe Poupon, the twenty-nine-year-old professional navigator who was once a protégé of Tabarly.

Another major threat to Ricard's chances was the "swing wing" 60-foot catamaran *Elf Aquitaine II*, skippered by Marc Pajot. *Elf* was so delicate and revolutionary in design that she could not enter Mill Bay with the other boats. Instead, she remained moored off the Royal Western clubhouse, where her airplane-wing mast kept her zigging and zagging around her buoy. Skittish to be off, said some savants in the club bar. Others pronounced the boat downright unseaworthy.

Of the nineteen multihulls entered in Class I, no fewer than sixteen were French. Only the 60-foot American cat *Fury* (skippered by Hugh McCoy, a former U.S. Navy fighter pilot from Colorado) and two British tris, *Colt Cars GB* and *Travacrest Seaway*, were there to challenge the French. A little further away, the sloop *Thursday's Child* sat in the water like a large, elegant swan. It was rumored in the pubs and bars around Mill Bay that this essay in

The boat to beat—Eric Tabarley's 60-foot trimaran, Paul Ricard.

high-tech had on several occasions on her way over from Florida
come close to speeds of thirty knots.

The crowds were thrilled by the chance to see these speed
machines up close. But as I worked my way down the pontoons
it was clear that few visitors had noticed the presence of a small
green folkboat moored on the outside of the pontoon. She was
junk-rigged and displayed a big "27" on her side. This was *Jester*,
twenty-six feet long, and the only boat to have sailed in all six
previous OSTARs. In 1960, she had been sailed by Colonel Blondie
Hasler against Sir Francis Chichester's boat and three other vessels. She had subsequently been bought by Michael Richey, an
Anglo-Irish gentleman of distinguished mien, who had entered the
boat in the last four races. However, in 1976 and in 1980 he had been
disqualified for failing to finish in the fifty-day time limit imposed
by the Race Committee. There was no way this piece of floating
history could win. There was only a remote chance she would
make it under the limit. Yet, quixotically, Mike Richey, now aged
sixty-seven, was going to try. The boat's cabin was just four feet
high and eight feet across. I wondered how anyone, even an an-
chorite monk, could survive a voyage of two months in such a
coracle.

The sight of *Jester*, demurely moored in the center of that noisy
multitude, led me to review my own chances in the Observer
Singlehanded. *Johan Lloyde* had some obvious shortcomings, but
she also had some notable strengths. Her eleven-foot beam and her
19,000-pound heft made it hard for her to point high into the wind
in a sharp chop. But then, the North Atlantic had few sharp
choppy seas and when you were sailing 1,000 miles from land, a
half-point off the wind could always be made up riding another
wind later on. *Johan's* long pilot-cutter keel made her most competitive sailing close-hauled in gale-force winds. While other boats
were hove-to she continued to charge ahead, two reefs down, at six
knots. She did not carry a spinnaker but had a surprising turn of
speed in light winds. Though her hull was only thirty-two feet
long, her bowsprit and boomkin gave her the effective sail area of
a small forty-footer.

Such qualities, if handled properly, could serve me well in a
race like OSTAR. I realized that—short of weather apocalyptic
enough to rip the gods out of their heavens—I had no chance of
of reaching Newport first. I could not out-maneuver the big boats
on an ocean 3,000 miles wide and I certainly could not out-run
them. But, given the special meanness of the North Atlantic

weather, perhaps I could manage to out-last quite a few gaudier titans in Class I and Class II. I recalled a conversation had with an American skipper on the docks a few days earlier, had entered and done well in the OSTARs of both 1976 and 198 "Being first, or second, or third is not important in this crazy race," he said, standing in a cockpit full of unstowed provisions. "If you make it to Newport you're a winner."

That thought was worthy of my old Thames bargemen. But it had an ominous undertow. Despite the diligence of the inspection teams now combing their way through the fleet, more than one third of all the vessels rafted up below me would not make it to Newport. Who, I wondered, would be dismasted? Who would capsize? Who would be run down by a freighter? Who would be attacked by whales and who would abandon ship? I looked around Mill Bay, sniffed the north wind and experienced an unexpected surge of confidence. The path of my life, like that of almost everyone else, had contained its share of false starts and blind alleys. But as I stood on that grimy dock in Plymouth, I knew that I had not sailed 4,181 sea miles down the St. Lawrence and across the North Atlantic in vain. I knew, so far as my own life was concerned, that I could not be standing in a better place at a better time.

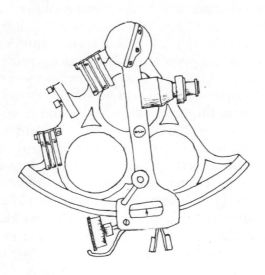

ntategy

*P*lymouth is one of the great naval ports of the world. The city and its stone citadel lie on the south coast of England at the junction of two rivers. Sir Francis Drake pitched his famous game of bowls on the grassy heights of Plymouth Hoe while awaiting the Spanish Armada in 1588. The Pilgrim Fathers stepped aboard the *Mayflower* from a little dock on the west side of Sutton Pool. The tidal reaches of the Cattewater and the Hamoaze succored Nelson's fleets in their epic struggle with Napoleonic France. And Plymouth formed a major jumping off point for the forces that landed in Normandy in 1944. As a return favor, the German air force bombed its downtown and dock areas quite flat.

The center of the city has been rebuilt into a post-nuclear mosaic of roofless churches—preserved as monuments of Nazi brutalism—and spanking new towers of prestressed concrete. But for all the bad memories, Plymouth was still very much a garrison town. The surrounding hills were still studded with huge gun emplacements, most of them trained upon the entrance to Plymouth Sound. Columns of grinning Royal Marine Commandos, bronzed from summer service in the Falklands, loped through the streets. Every other corner was occupied by pubs bearing such martial names as The General Moore and The Master Gunner. *Johan* had first sailed into Plymouth in August 1983. Her arrival was the culmination of a voyage that had really begun nine years previously, when I had traded in my 23-foot O'Day sloop for a Westsail 32 "Sailaway Kit" that was soon christened *Johan Lloyde*.

In the eight summers that followed, our dock on the upper St. Lawrence resounded to the screech of saber saws and power sand-

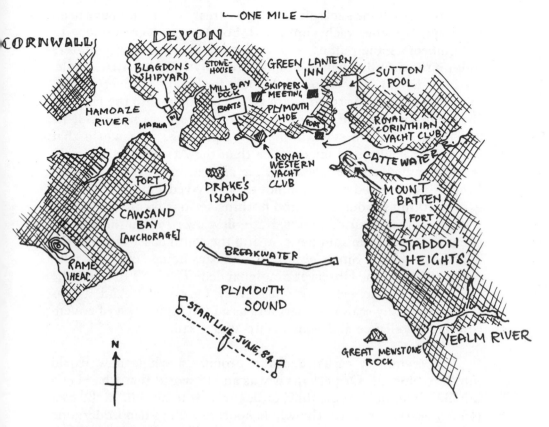

OSTAR's Plymouth.

ers. I planned and constructed the deck layout, the interior plumb-
ing, and the electronics. I am a native of Suffolk, England, and
Johan's accommodations—with their bronze portlights, varnished
mahogany, and heavily gimballed lamps—came to resemble those
of the sailing barges and old wooden cutters and yawls that I'd
sailed in as a child on the Thames Estuary. Seaworthiness and snug
comfort down below were paramount.

In the spring of 1983, my fifteen-year-old son, Rufus, and I
loaded an extra measure of stores on to the completed *Johan* and
sailed her 800 miles down the St. Lawrence to the sea. Below
Quebec City most days were spent tacking into gale-force winds
straight out of Labrador. First came rain like frozen sand, then fog,
then snow. Nights were passed huddled around a red-hot cabin
stove, while the cutter tugged at her anchor chain in a succession
of unnamed bays set at the foot of unnamed mountains. The poet's

description of "lone keels off headlands drear" could not have been
more apt. No other yachts appeared. For days we were alone with
the guillemots, the puffins, and the brant. There were no hunters
to hunt them, and, when it was blowing anything less than a gale,
the birds would gather around the boat for breakfast. Every night,
without fail, we'd tie the huge brass anchor light into the rigging.
It would not warn off other vessels, for there were none. But its
dim glow became a symbol of *Johan*'s presence in a world that
seemed far colder and far emptier than the Atlantic ocean itself.
After many adventures, *Johan Lloyde* arrived in Nova Scotia, and
I then singlehanded her to Falmouth. I survived a mighty five-day
gale. Nothing serious broke and nothing serious went wrong. My
wife, Susan, and our daughter, Kate, flew over to join me and we
spent the rest of the summer cruising the south coast of England.
Then it struck me. Since *Johan* must sail back home next year, why
not enter her in the Observer Singlehanded? The OSTAR, like the
Olympics, was staged only once every four years. And it was
viewed by many seasoned mariners as an Olympian test of adventurous self-reliance and seamanship under sail.

   Why not?

   This seemingly casual decision brought a whole new world
into focus for me. Or perhaps it was an old world that I had been
inhabiting for quite some time, unbeknownst to myself. In the past
twenty years, I realized, the whole sport of sailing had undergone
a radical change. Yes, of course the materials and the techniques
were different (as an amateur shipbuilder, I knew that as much as
anyone) but it seemed that an important part of the spirit of sailing
had been lost in the process. Many of the newcomers to the sport
spoke of it as if it were like driving a car. "When I learned to sail
. . .", they would say of some week-long course in a Caribbean
school. I was, I realized, bored of being lectured about the merits
of plastic-rope anchor rodes, alcohol stoves, and "weathered" teak.
I was weary of the way modern racing skippers hoisted perpetual
protest flags and bellowed at their crews. I was, like the Chief
Inspector, fed up with plastic both in substance and in spirit.
There had to be a better, quieter way. By entering OSTAR, I
could, perhaps, restore a piece of my own soul and reaffirm some
of the good-humored verities that I had learned as a boy among the
commercial sailors and the tides and fogs of England's East Coast.

   One great difficulty, however, stood in my path. When I arrived
at the clubhouse of the Royal Western Yacht Club in Plymouth in

the third week of August 1983, I received some disquieting news. The sailing secretary, a former Royal Navy commander immaculately attired in club blazer and tie, was amiable but adamant. "Sorry old chap. No can do. Try again in 1988." I tried to be philosophical. But as I walked out of the plushly carpeted offices I began to wonder how any race across an ocean as vast as the Atlantic could be called "full." And how could any organization, even the lordly Royal Western, choke off entries almost a year before the official start? This ultimate symbol of rugged independence was, it seemed, succumbing to a near-lethal attack of regulation. At first I was tempted to write off the whole idea and chalk up another triumph for bureaucracy. Early in September, we laid up *Johan* for the winter at Blagdon's Shipyard in Plymouth and flew back to upstate New York, where my wife and I both served on the faculty of Syracuse University. Then I began to think about it some more. If I had the enterprise to compete effectively in the Observer Singlehanded, then surely I had the enterprise to get my boat on to the starting line in 1984! The old East Coast sailors, with their shifting shoals and muddy tides, were nothing if not sly. Perhaps I could steal a leaf or two from the log book of those Suffolk marsh rats and somehow finagle my way past the scores of boats on the official waiting list.

For months, *Johan* and I tacked back and forth in a very narrow channel, and bumped into our share of bureaucratic shoals. But we also encountered a few old-time seadogs who caught our drift and helped us on our way. As the months passed, I learned that several other skippers—mostly heavily sponsored French professionals— were also seeking to push their way into the race at the last minute. The entry of my own home-built *Johan*, unfortunately, became increasingly entwined with those of the diehard professionals. One megafranc sponsor even prevailed upon the French ambassador to call Commander Lloyd Foster, RN (Retd.), the sailing secretary, from London. The high-powered stratagems of the French, however, only served to stiffen the club's resistance. No more entries, said the Royal Western. Finis.

When my son and I returned to Plymouth on May 11, 1984, *Johan Lloyde* had yet to secure a place in the starting lineup. Railings and shop windows were already blossoming with posters advertising the start of OSTAR. Banners, strung across the major downtown streets, announced to shoppers in big blue letters "Observer/ Europe 1 Singlehanded Transatlantic Start June 2."

On May 18, just two weeks before the start, the Race Committee
held its final meeting. The mood was bitter, the discussion explosive. The *Observer* and its fellow financial backer, the French all-
sport radio station *Europe 1*, believed that they, too, should have
some say in the number and the identity of entrants. The Royal
Western responded that either it was managing the race or it was
not. When the meeting was over, and the dust settled, it was
announced that three professional skippers and myself had been
admitted to OSTAR 1984. *Johan* was presented with the official
indentification number of "11." By way of celebration, Rufus
(who'd skipped two weeks of high school to help *Johan* get started)
and I painted this, in black characters one foot high, on the foredeck and on each side of *Johan's* bow. The two "ones" did not look
good on their own, so we circled them with a big black ring, two
inches thick.

Now I was one of the gang, an accepted member of the group
of four women and eighty-eight men from seventeen nations who
would sail across the start line just beyond the Plymouth breakwater on June 2. Our chief patron, I noted from my bright new
rulebook, was no less a personage than His Royal Highness the
Prince Philip, Duke of Edinburgh, KG, KT, OM, GBE.

Between the inspection and the start one week later the skip-
pers were subjected to a dizzying round of social events. The Lord
Mayor of Plymouth, adorned in a handsome gold chain, invited us
to a glass of champagne down at the city's modernistic Council
House. The Royal Corinthian Yacht Club, arch rival to the Royal
Western, put on an "At Home," and a reception was held at the
Royal Navy's Engineering College at Manadon. Back in our floating village in Mill Bay a carnival atmosphere quickly took hold.
The cobblestone wharves were soon dotted with booths selling
everything from sweatshirts and commemorative posters to baked
potatoes and official race programs—only a pound, luv. Captain O.
M. Watts, the fashionable London ship chandler, opened a store in
the back of a trailer truck. Caravans of men and women from
various equipment manufacturers—Barlow winches, Brookes and
Gatehouse, Lokata radios—arrived to give free service to any competitor who needed it. Plainly, they were anxious to see their gear
give a good account of itself. But there were some discordant notes
amid these merry scenes. At the northeast corner of the dock, the
Observer/Europe 1 Courtesy Pavilion opened for business. It was
shaped like a sheik's palace, with glass walls and a high, bulbous

white roof. The skippers quickly learned, however, that it was not put there as a courtesy to them but as a convenience for the visiting media. On one occasion, I watched an American skipper stopped at the Pavilion door by a French-speaking official. *Fermé. Interdit de séjour.* The American, with the help of one of the French skippers, patiently explained that he'd just completed a 5,000-mile voyage across the Atlantic and that his mail was being held in the Pavilion. *Non, non. Fermé.* Come back later. The American argued patiently for several minutes. But the functionary stood his ground. "Aw, shit," said the American finally, and just pushed his way past the outraged official. Never stand between a man and his mail. . . .

In the days ahead this little scene came to symbolize, for me, the presence of a wider malaise. The Observer Singlehanded, begun in a spirit of good sportsmanship and high adventure, was clearly acquiring a thick veneer of commerce. Some of the gimmicks were harmless, even comic. Many skippers, to defray costs, found themselves touting high energy drinks, freeze-dried food, oilskins, coffee, sealing compounds, and beer. In their next commercial, the manufacturers could add the kicky line "as used in OSTAR 1984"—even if their intrepid tillerman sank ten minutes after the race began. With some misgivings, I accepted my share of freebies, including some dried eggs, a sun visor, and a pack of fiberglass that claimed it could be used to repair leaks under water. The *Observer* itself, as a hint of things to come, presented me with a little monogrammed scarf to stop seawater running down my neck.

After a few days out there in the spotlight, some of the competitors, I noticed, began to behave in a markedly different fashion. A few swaggered through the crowds of spectators like an assistant director on the night of the school play. Others surreptitiously pocketed their red "Competitor" badges and nipped about their business as inconspicuously as possible. A couple of contestants even sought to use the publicity to raise money for various pet causes. A standout in the realm of OSTAR fund-raisers was Dr. Christopher Smith's 30-foot cutter *Race Against Poverty*. The first time I walked by I noticed that this vessel had a number of posters attached to it depicting cattle that were either dead or dying. Three or four coin boxes, also adorned with pictures of dead cattle, were attached to the boat's rails. Not quite knowing what I was getting into I plunked two ten-penny pieces into the sternmost can. I was about to walk on when I saw Dr. Smith, an Englishman, step into his cockpit.

Blondie Hasler's Jester *was the only boat to have entered every race since OSTAR began.*

"If you're competing in OSTAR," I asked him, "shouldn't it be Race *Into* Poverty instead of Race *Against* Poverty?"

"No, no. It's Race Against Poverty," replied Smith as he scanned the crowd beyond my left shoulder.

"You mean Poverty has entered a boat and you're racing against her?"

"Of course not." The eyes glazed over. This was the public—his public!—talking to him. He had no way of knowing that I, too, was in the race.

"I mean, are we talking about personal poverty," I persisted, "or poverty in general? Surely this race must be making all these fellows" (I swept the horizon with my arm) "kind of impoverished?"

"You Americans never get it, do you?" said Smith, focusing on me for the first time.

"I guess not." I should've set him straight about my origins. But he must take me as he found me. "What's with all these dead cattle, anyway?" I asked.

"What we are talking about is Third World Poverty," said Smith in a slow, rather pedantic tone of voice.

"Ahhh . . . you guys are racing against Third World Poverty . . . ahhhh." I began to walk backward down the dock, flapping my arms as I went. "Now I get it, Third World Poverty . . . ahhhh." Dr. Smith said nothing, but a tight, perplexed little smile remained on his face as I vanished into the crowd.

* * * * *

"What's your strategy, Mike?" Half a dozen OSTAR skippers were sitting around one evening in the cockpit of the 31-foot cutter *Crystal Catfish III*. Their host, John Hunt of Birmingham, Alabama, was dispensing cheap Azorean wine out of a five-liter wicker bottle. The question was directed at Michael Richey, master of the legendary *Jester*, veteran of four OSTARs, and, for most of those present, something of a singlehander's guru. Everyone wanted to know Richey's plans for the race. His answer would be laced with the threads of a special karma, for Richey had never brought *Jester* in under fifty-seven days, and in the last two races he'd been disqualified for failing to finish in the maximum time permitted by the Race Committee.

"You know I can't push *Jester* hard to windward," replied Richey. He was a smallish man, with iron-grey hair and a big, sunburned nose. "I'll decide which way I'm going when I get out there." His tone was that of a man trying to decide which store to enter in downtown Plymouth. But in fact the strategic questions confronting Richey and all the other skippers were of sizable proportions. Unlike other sailing races, OSTAR did not prescribe a course for its competitors. Instead, the race would be fought out in an open space a dozen times bigger than that in which Napoleon and Hitler had maneuvered in their struggles to capture Moscow. And, as in those bitter campaigns, no competitor could formulate a plausible strategy that did not concede a decisive role to the weather.

However one looked at it, in the final analysis there were only about four and one half ways to get to Newport. True, a competitor could sail out of Plymouth in almost any direction he chose, but the last 1,500 miles to Nantucket Lightvessel compressed all campaign strategies into a limited number of scenarios, each of which was no more than an attempted solution to problems created by such interlocking variables as the Gulf Stream, wind, the presence of fog and ice, and the statistical validity of a curious outpost called Waypoint Weld.

The 1980 OSTAR had been won by a Massachusetts newspaper publisher named Philip Weld, who sailed his 51-foot trimaran *Moxie* home in the record time of seventeen days and twenty-three hours. Before leaving for Plymouth, Weld ordered up a computer analysis of all North Atlantic weather patterns over the previous twenty years and found that the centers of the fiercest storms all ran north of a point 45°N, 35°W. This place, some 400 miles north-west of the Azores, was in the middle of nowhere and came to be known in OSTAR circles as Waypoint Weld.

Another key variable was the Gulf Stream. This was not, as many students of the pilot charts imagined, a great oceanic river of warm water flowing majestically from southwest to northeast. It was, in fact, a giant serpent whose unchartable curlicues and whorls varied their speeds and directions from one day to the next. "Mixing it up with the Stream," as the skippers phrased it, was not deemed to be pleasant work. A boat could be subjected to thunder squalls and five radical wind shifts and be bumped sixty miles off course all in the space of twenty-four hours.

Where the warm Gulf Stream water collided with the frigid water of the Labrador current along the banks of Newfoundland and Nova Scotia, it generated vicious gales and a semipermanent overcast of fog—and it was these foggy banks, extending hundreds of miles from land, that became the favored haunt of fishing vessels. Trawlers, for all their service to *haute cuisine*, formed one of the greatest menaces to singlehanded sailors. Besides lurking in fogs, they seldom kept a lookout and, because of their nets, were almost unmaneuverable in any approaching collision. The noted circumnavigator Robin Knox-Johnston had been run down by an unlighted vessel the previous summer, and Chay Blyth, another iron man of the sea, had withdrawn from OSTAR 1984 because of the chance of such collisions. His discarded number was now painted on either side of *Johan*'s bow.

To the strategical stewpot of blind trawlers, arbitrary squalls, and month-long fogs must now—in the harsh spring of 1984—be added the threat of hundreds of icebergs sweeping, like a great Soviet tank charge, down the whole western shore of the North Atlantic. It was, said the Newfoundland Coastguard, the worst year for ice in recorded history—and that took us back past the sinking of the *Titanic* in 1912!

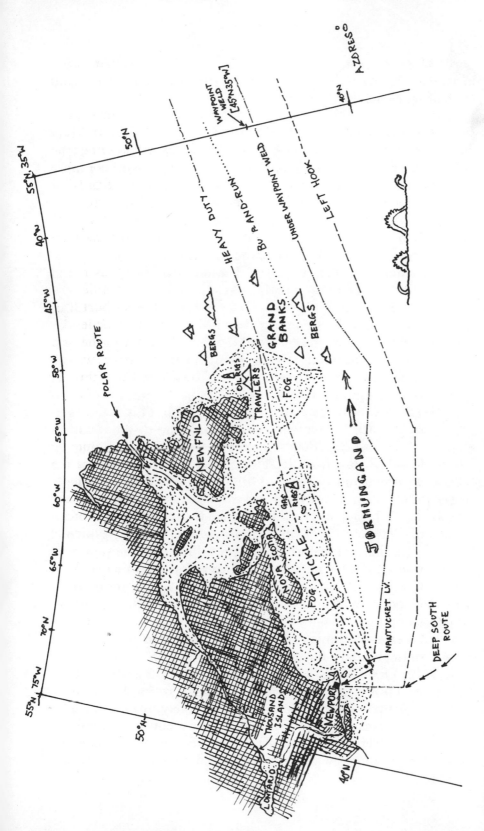

Only four and a half ways to go.

All these variables, active in their particular combinations, thrust the Observer Singlehanded competitors into these four and one half scenarios (see map):

1) *The Heavy Duty or Rhumb-Line Strategy.* The most direct route between Land's End and Newport lay over the Grand Banks, a mighty claw of foggy shoal running more than 300 miles out into the North Atlantic. Bad: *Johan* would have to mix it up head-on with trawlers, fog, ice, and the Gulf Stream, which can flow at speeds of up to two knots. Good: *Johan Lloyde* was a pilot cutter whose strongest suit was in crashing to windward in fierce gales. Comment: How badly do I want to see my wife and children again?

2) *The Bump-and-Run Strategy.* This route headed south of the rhumb line, bumped the Beak of the Grand Banks, and then went straight for Newport. Bad: Still mixing it up with the Gulf Stream, plenty of fog and ice. Good: Fine beat to windward, and few trawlers. Comment: A straight, gung-ho way to go.

3) *The Under-Waypoint-Weld Strategy.* Bad: This meant getting south earlier and lengthening the distance sailed, while sloshing down some major transatlantic ship lanes. Good: Boat can scallop along, nudging in and out of the weather, and cross the Gulf Stream at a more oblique angle. Comment: Flexible, and I survive to tell the tale.

4) *The Left Hook Strategy.* This called for swinging well south of Waypoint Weld to a point somewhere off Norfolk, Virginia, and then using the prevailing southwesterlies to slice straight across the Gulf Stream in a day or two. Bad: Quite a bit more mileage and a fair risk of tropical calms. Good: The boat stayed in the sunshine, missed the heavy shipping and side-stepped the war of attrition with the Stream. Comment: A long shot, but can lead to some dramatic dark-horse finishes from out of nowhere.

4½) *The Tickle Tactic.* This comes from a Newfoundland word meaning a narrow channel between rocks. It gets only half a point because it can be used solely by sailors applying strategies (1) and (2). It calls for a cut north between Sable Island and the coast of Nova Scotia. Bad: Much fog, rocks, and a good chance of a dead beat up to Nantucket

Lightvessel. Good: Used counter-current against the Gulf Stream. Comment: *Johan* sailed through here on her way over. Never again.

The plastic glasses were filled and filled again with red Azorean wine as the skippers in *Crystal Catfish*'s cockpit continued to gnaw on their strategical options. Some of those present pointed out that there were other, more radical, solutions to the problem. In a little while, John Hunt, our host, began to expound his Deep South strategy. He and his shipmate, Paul Porter, had just sailed *Catfish* more than 5,000 miles from Mobile, Alabama, via Bermuda and Fayal to reach the OSTAR start line. Hunt held a Ph.D. from Harvard and had given up his position as superintendant of schools in Birmingham to enter this race for the second time. He was tall, dark, and a reasonable facsimile of Rhett Butler. This evening a huge Confederate flag fluttered gently from *Catfish*'s starboard crosstree. His strategy, it appeared, was a long shot to end all long shots.

"Basically," said Hunt, with an air of quiet confidence, "you could say I'm drawing to an inside straight." It was his plan to ride the Northeast Trades almost down to the Madieras and then sweep up past Bermuda into Newport from the southeast. He believed this might win him the whole OSTAR if weather conditions off to the north were vicious enough to force a whole fleet of retirements. Some skippers told him he was dreaming. Others expressed fear that this quixotic plan might leave *Catfish* becalmed for weeks in the Doldrums.

"And then there's the Bermuda Triangle, Jack. What about that?"

"You guys don't have the right attitude," drawled Hunt, without rancor. "I want to show how one man on a regular cruising boat can do well—even win—on reasonable expenses." Then he beamed a big smile at the assembled skippers and went below for more wine. The Stars and Bars flapped softly in the breeze above.

Sitting in the cockpit on my left was Dr. Robert Scott, a grizzle-faced computer engineer from Maryland. He commanded the 40-foot cutter *Land's End,* sponsored by the mail-order house of that name. To my right was Bob Lengyel, a fifty-seven-year-old former Marine who worked as a ship's radio officer. Lengyel had been jogging, and a piratical red bandanna now adorned his head. The North Atlantic pilot charts put out by the U.S. Defense Mapping

Agency showed that the winds in the higher latitudes might be more favorable to westbound boats. In 1976, Lengyel had taken his sloop *Prodigal* so far north in search of those winds that she had to sail round the further side of Newfoundland to reach the finish. The gamble, alas, had not worked, and *Prodigal* came home seventy-third in fleet, making Newport just a few hours inside the fifty-day limit. Now he was about to try again. I shivered and thought of ice in the crosstrees and the J. C. Penney long johns aboard *Johan*.

We sat and sipped our wine in silence. As we did so, the mythic dimensions of this whole adventure began to overwhelm me. The old Norse sagas spoke of the Creation as the fusion of a great wave of fire from the south and a great wall of ice from the north. Midgard, the sphere of existence inhabited by living men and women, was surrounded by a vast ocean in whose depths lurked a treacherous serpent named Jormungand. This monster was so gigantic that, even though his folds coiled grotesquely back on themselves many times, he still managed to stretch all the way around the known world. It was whispered that from time to time Jormungand dined upon his own tail.

The wine party in *Crystal Catfish*'s cockpit continued into the dusk. I didn't kid myself that I could win the whole thing, but Jormungand or no Jormungand, I thought *Johan Lloyde* had a pretty good shot at coming in first in Class IV. I asked myself what Napoleon would do. Or, more to the point, what would Lord Nelson—my fellow East Anglian—do in such a strategic situation? I was prepared to exercise any of the first four options. But unlike my fellow skippers I felt uneasy about choosing any particular route while parked here in Plymouth. I'd let the weather show the way. That would be my strategy. I would wait, like Richey, until I got out there, alone with the wind, the sun, and the stars. Then I'd decide. Eventually the party broke up, and clumps of skippers —still debating like seminarians—wandered out of Mill Bay Dock down to the bar at the Royal Western.

Only one other man had ever raced a Westsail 32 like *Johan* in an Observer Singlehanded race. In 1976, the American David White brought *Catapha* to Newport in thirty-nine days. As luck would have it, White—a blond giant of 6′ 6″—was now in Plymouth with a new boat, a 55-foot Class I sloop named *Gladiator*. He had already campaigned this boat in the BOC Round-the-World Race, which he had helped to establish. One afternoon, I decided

I pay White a call. I knocked on *Gladiator*'s crimson hull, and White came up through the hatch, a man-mountain with a voice like a bullhorn.

"What's my best strategy?" I said, asking the inevitable question.

"In a Westsail?" boomed White. "You just keep going. In '76, when other boats were hove-to, I was steaming along double-reefed at six knots. I got half way across the Atlantic in ten days." White's overall time was subsequently spoiled by a series of calms encountered almost within sight of Newport. Later that day I heard White counselling another newcomer, Hugh McCoy, who was in command of the 60-foot catamaran *Fury*. The two men were standing on the Mayflower's central pontoons. I nodded and squeezed past them. As I did so I heard White sonorously declare ". . . the big thing to remember about OSTAR is that IT'S ONLY A SPRINT." This assessment of one of the most arduous endurance tests in the world of sport seemed, at the time, to be an understatement worthy of Dr. Pangloss himself.

Whenever large numbers of people are confined in small spaces, strange stories begin to circulate. In Mill Bay Dock, rumors now began to flow in and out with the tides. Someone said . . . Someone said the 25-foot home-built *Nord* from Bulgaria needed major surgery. Someone said Florence Arthaud, the angelique Parisienne, had been in no fewer than three pre-start collisions in her 60-foot trimaran *Biotherm II*. Someone said Mike Richey would receive the Last Rites before embarking on his fifth (and final?) OSTAR in the 26-foot *Jester*. Someone said the French were plotting to hold their own private French weather briefing. Someone said that Commander Lloyd Foster, the sailing secretary of the Royal Western, had resigned his post in the last explosive meeting of the Race Committee on May 18. He would see this last OSTAR through, then retire. For many of the veteran skippers, Foster, with his clipped diction and no-nonsense Navy ways, had come to represent the race's chief custodian of good sportsmanship and fair play. Some details began to leak out. The *Observer*, at the instigation of *Europe 1*, had stuck it to the Royal Western: Either accept the three French boats as late entrants, or see the Observer Single-handed go to another club in 1988. Despite these strong-arm tactics the Race Committee balked. A straw vote came out four in favor of admission and four against. At this point, Commander Foster bluntly declared that if this decision were imposed on the Committee in this fashion, he would resign as sailing secretary. Either the Committee was running this race or it wasn't.

In an effort to break the deadlock, one Committee member brought up the candidacy of Hubbard. "If we approved the motion," this stalwart observed, "then Tim Hubbard, a true amateur, could now be allowed in." This talk of amateurs kindled a flame in the hearts of the Committee, and when the formal vote was taken, the motion to admit carried 5–3. The three French heavyweights were accepted, towed into the race by the candidacy of an unsung cutter named *Johan Lloyde*. But a sobering irony lurked behind the public announcements: if I had not been so eager to get on to the start-line in 1984, the estimable Commander Foster might today still be club sailing secretary.

* * * * *

Down in Mill Bay, *Johan* and her crew were experiencing their own troubles. Under race regulations the boats could not leave the dock after inspection. The trapped feeling was further strengthened for me when a team came aboard *Johan* to seal her engine in neutral. The Volvo diesel could still be used to charge batteries, but not to propel the boat through the water. I might break the seal in an emergency, but then *Johan* would be out of the race.

Next morning was sunny. But officialdom had not finished with me yet. Two T-shirted French technicians, driving a rubber dinghy, boarded *Johan* without ceremony and began to install an Argos satellite transmitter, a flat white disc about 4″ deep and 18″ across. It quickly became apparent that we had a language problem. I steadfastly refused to let them drill holes in my teak lazaret hatch. Finally, after I came close to ordering the men and their electric drills off the boat altogether, they were persuaded to attach the Argos to the floor of the cockpit.

The president of the company that marketed the system—a white-haired, portly gentleman known colloquially as "Monsieur Argos"—now bustled aboard *Johan* without even a nod. True, he couldn't spend his day fretting about the niceties of protocol. But for me the episode was a disquieting violation of *Johan*'s private space. No longer was she a kingdom unto herself, roaming across oceans as she chose. Now she'd been shut in this dock, had her engine "fixed," and been tagged like a goose. Obviously this Monsieur Argos saw her as just another floating platform for his precious equipment. In the weeks ahead Big Brother in the sky would track *Johan's* every move, night and day. The transmitter would report her speed and course and the weather conditions nearby. But the one-way rules of this particular game decreed that none of this information could be returned to its source, the sailor himself. As each day passed, I was becoming impressed by the extent to which OSTAR skippers—surely the very heart of the race—were deemed close to irrelevant. In a little while I looked over to *Moustache*, where Lloyd Hircock, parsing schoolboy French, was now fighting his own duel with the drill-happy emissaries of Monsieur Argos.

"Hang in there, Lloyd," I yelled. "It's your boat and they have to put the damn thing where you say." The vehemence of my tone surprised both me and the men in the T-shirts. I went below to *Johan's* cabin, not particularly pleased with myself. I wondered if all this talk of safety was beginning to get to me. Others were also showing the strain. Perhaps the singlehander's worst fear was that of falling overboard. There was no hope of rescue. All he could do was to dog-paddle in 3,000 fathoms and watch his boat sail herself serenely over the horizon. Even Monsieur Argos had no remedy for that one, unless he installed a kind of foot pedal that activated an alarm if it were not depressed every hour on the hour. In its present mode, the transmitter would go on beeping up the boat's position until she ran herself ashore somewhere along the eastern seaboard, sans pilot.

In addition, most competitors nursed their own special apprehensions. Some feared becalming and the exhaustion of their food and water. Others worried about the effects of loneliness and were tormented by the thought that they might go mad and throw themselves over the side, as Donald Crowhurst had done. A few fretted about sinister hallucinations, of being strangled by barnacled mermen who boarded the ship at night. A good skipper, I had learned, must have the imagination to foresee, and to forestall, every kind of disaster possible. Yet, at the same time, he must be able to impose a damper on his mind if he is not to drown in an ocean of phantasmagorical horror. Once, just north of the Azores on my voyage over the previous summer, I had myself been lured into the garden of Edgar Allen Poe. It was about 1 A.M., and the waves reflected the fullest moon in a thousand little cups, and I was reminded of those Gothic paintings that depict gloomy battlements upon high crags. As I came through the hatch, a furry thing making a growling noise flung itself at my face. Grrreeech! I jumped back and downward, and slammed the hatch shut, my adrenalin pumping. I must have surprised a bird perched on the boom gallows, but for an instant I had experienced the full, raving terror of a maniac.

Most of the professionals, men who had sailed the Atlantic alone half a dozen times or more, were more down-to-earth in their apprehensions. The chief fear seemed to be of a personal injury so severe that they could not summon help. Of the more fanciful terrors they were able to somehow say enough is enough, and switch out the basement light. If they experienced any tension at all, it was generally displayed in an eagerness to be off.

"This is our wind, baby," yelled Luis Tonizzo to me one sunlit morning as a brisk northeaster blew across the docks. A merchant marine officer from Louisiana, Luis (pronounced Lewis) was generally deemed to be one of the hardest-driving skippers in the entire fleet and his 35-foot sloop *City of Slidell* was expected to beat a lot of bigger boats. Much of the time I had trouble comprehending Tonizzo's rope-a-dope manner of speech. But today his meaning was clear. "Shit, man, we gotta get goin'." He gestured impatiently at the forest of masts in Mill Bay Dock. "This is like Stalag 17. Here, this is yours." Tonizzo dipped one of his almost square hands into a brown paper bag and presented me with a monstrous onion.

"Thanks," I said, "This'll last me past Waypoint Weld."

But other, less professional, skippers were not so lucky. A couple, neither of whom had sailed an ocean before, spooked themselves quite badly. One, the owner of a 36-foot sloop, seemed obsessed with the idea that an unfriendly doppelganger would take command of his boat while he slept. Another, a Dutch skipper with several university degrees to his name, was haunted by the fact that he was about to sail over the graves of thousands of ships sunk in the great U-boat battles of World War II.

As the start approached, I had to wrestle with some of my own apprehensions. The struggle was not made easier by certain circumstances in my personal life. Just a few weeks before I sailed *Johan* into Mill Bay Dock my father had died in a London hospital after a long bout with cancer. Back home in Syracuse, my wife, Susan, was five months pregnant with our second child. Clearly this was not the best of times to launch oneself into the middle of an ocean. In their separate ways, both my father and my wife had given my entry into OSTAR their blessing. Yet, on occasion, the sense of failed responsibility weighed heavily upon me. I suppose, too, that I was frightened of going up against the North Atlantic once more, alone. Sometimes I was able to drown my misgivings in English beer. But on many occasions they just bobbed back up again. One blustery afternoon I was plodding around the docks when I was hailed from forty feet away by Bill Homewood, the skipper of the little trimaran *British Airways II.*

"I say, mate, are you okay?"

"Oh yes, Bill, thanks. Just a bit cold, that's all."

"The worst thing you can do is take a cold to sea. Come and have a cup of tea."

I dithered in the cutting wind, and then accepted. My condition, so opaque to myself, was gruesomely apparent at a distance of forty feet to a veteran singlehander like Homewood. *British Airways II,* thirty-one feet long, was a famous boat. Under the name of *Third Turtle,* she came third in OSTAR 1976—a particularly brutal year when more than fifty boats dropped out or sank. She weighed only 3,000 lbs and her "cabin"—really a little hutch three feet by eight feet—was so small that I had to sit outside in the cockpit while Homewood brewed two very strong cups of tea. The only thing preventing every sea from washing through this cabin was a zip-up shield made of sailcloth. As we talked, it became clear that Homewood's life had run an eerie parallel to my own. We were both forty-nine years old. We both grew up amid the blitz of Churchill's war-time England. We both performed our National Service in the British Army—Homewood in Europe and Hong Kong and I with the Middle East Land Forces in Egypt. We both emigrated as youngish men to the United States, where we both had children and had both been married twice.

"Remember the radio show ITMA?"

"I cried the day Tommy Handley died."

Homewood had a veteran's solution to the problem of nerves. "Just imagine the worst, mate. Imagine you'll drown three weeks from today, and go from there." The advice seemed crazy, but I tried it. I assumed I'd end up floating around the Grand Banks, an eyeless carcass in one of the Chief Inspector's carefully labelled life jackets. My present doings acquired a new significance. This, then, was the last time I rode upon a double-decker bus, browsed in a bookstore, or bought a tube of toothpaste. Surprisingly, it worked. By trivializing death in the pleasant sunlight of Plymouth, I suc-

ceeded, for myself at least, in bluntening its sting. Taking things
head on was not so bad. Perhaps that's what this race was about.
One rainy day I donned my oilskins and walked to the top of
Plymouth Hoe, and stood there for a while amid the rippling
daffodils. I looked out across the white caps in the Sound and
wondered how Drake, Hawkins, and the Pilgrim Fathers felt
when they gazed down upon this same scene at the outset of their
great voyages. Even Drake must have been a little scared. Then the
words of the old Norse saga came into my mind. "The length of
my life," wrote the ancient chronicler of *For Scirnis*, "and the day
of my death were fated long ago." This simple pagan thought, I
decided, offered more comfort to those about to set forth on a long
sea voyage than most of the teachings to be found in the Holy
Bible.

3

The Half Crown Club

*A*s the day of the start approached rumors of ice on the tracks ahead gained substance. Then one morning late in May the official word came through to Mill Bay. A letter from Commander N. C. Edwards, USCG., dated May 18, was pinned to the noticeboard of the Courtesy Pavilion. It stated:

The International Ice Patrol is currently in the midst of possibly the worst ice year, in terms of the large number of icebergs coming south, in recorded history. The below numbers will help emphasize the severity of the iceberg hazard this year:
   1976—a total of 151 icebergs were reported south of 48°N.
   1980—a total of 20 icebergs were reported south of 48°N.
   1984—1054 icebergs have been reported south of 48°N as of May 1, 1984.

The report went on to declare that "it is not anticipated that the situation will improve, i.e., the number of icebergs along your track decreasing by the time you transit the area near the Grand Banks in mid-June." An accompanying chart showed the Plymouth–Newport rhumb-line knifing through a frigid cordillera of little black triangles, each representing a major berg. The press, sensing blood, gathered round. What did it mean? Was this a suicide mission? Perhaps the *Observer* should consider delaying the start?

The public relations men creased up their smoothest smiles . . . nothing to worry about . . . just a quirk in the weather . . . all the ice is 2,000 miles away . . . go the Azores route instead. Everyone relaxed. Then in marched man-mountain David White, master of the 55-foot *Gladiator* and a BOC Round-the-World contender. He took one look at the chart and, in a voice that shook the Courtesy Pavilion, declared: "Holy Mary, Mother of God, WE'RE ALL GOING TO DIE."

As the cameras and tape recorders whirred, the sleekly groomed flacks rolled their eyes heavenward. White was undoubtedly stirring up a bit of dust for the hell of it. But another thought began to form in my mind. Could it be that the London *Observer*, having ridden roughshod over Commander Foster in the final meeting of the Committee, was now deciding critical questions concerning the very lives of the skippers with unseemly haste? How could they know what was out there? Maybe I was missing a beat. But it seemed to me that the *Observer*, Monsieur Argos, and the big buck sponsors whose colored cars sent dockside spectators jumping, had convinced themselves that they somehow OWNED this race. The skippers, the people who actually sailed the boats, had become for them little more than errand boys hired to deliver the corporate groceries. Below the errand boys stood the amateurs. These, in the entrepreneurial mind, were probably viewed simply as entrants too lackluster to acquire sponsorship.

What had happened, I wondered, to the spirit of independence, good humor, and high adventure that had inspired Sir Francis Chichester, Blondie Hasler, and three other voyagers to embark on the first race in 1960? In that contest, Chichester bet Hasler half a crown (about fifty cents) that he would get to America first. Now companies staked millions on the outcome, and people were tearing each other's eyes out.

"I just don't get it," I said later that night, seated in a pub that lay somewhere in the hills to the west of Plymouth. "I don't understand how anyone can impose a time limit that prevents *Jester*, the only original boat, from being a qualified finisher. It's happened twice now."

"Yeah. In the land of the bureaucrat, bullshit is king."

"We gotta make a point."

"Yes, but how?"

This pub was the secret hideaway of Alan Wynne-Thomas, a Welshman with a square face and a nose somewhat flattened by many games of Rugby. His sleek 40-foot cutter *Jemima Nicholas* was given a good chance of winning Class III. Wynne-Thomas was also a power in the land of computers. *Jemima*'s bulkheads were decorated with many greeting cards. One was from Neil Kinnock, the Leader of the Opposition in the House of Commons. The inscription read: "If you drown I shall kill you." Also seated at the table with us was Lloyd Hircock, a great moustachioed bear of a man and the only Canadian in the race. Lloyd and I, we discovered some time back, had attended the same university in Canada. The Observer Singlehanded was Hircock's big shot. At the age of forty-three he had quit his job with a spar manufacturer and put his life savings into the thirty-foot sloop *Moustache*. If he could do well in Class V, he figured he could become a full-time professional racing skipper.

"Why not start a group? Call it the Half Crown Club."

"We're cooking. How about a T-shirt?"

"Great. What shall we use for a logo?"

The pints flowed, and the skippers pondered. Hircock and I had no idea as to our whereabouts, except that we were somewhere high in the hills of Cornwall. The elderly men at the next table were dressed in shepherd's smocks and spoke in a dialect we did not understand. Around the fourth pint our thoughts began to coalesce. How about . . .

GO FOR BROKE
WITH THE
HALF CROWN CLUB

That's it! And on the back of the shirt will be David White's immortal word's, IT'S ONLY A SPRINT. The tone would be informal. No rules, no dues, no by-laws, no meetings, and no minutes. Oh blessed club! If the *Observer* and the Race Committee got too oppressive, members could just opt out of OSTAR all together. The Half Crown Club could stage its own race from Plymouth to Newport, starting on the same day. After all, the ocean was free. Its surface was not, as the officials seemed to imagine, etched into one hundred—and only one hundred—distinct tracks! There must be room for all.

Perhaps the two fleets, the official fleet and the shadow fleet, could go across the line at the same time? Professionals versus amateurs. Now there's a race! The *Observer* charged £300 in entry fees. But the Half Crown fleet would have no fees, no dues, no rules, no safety inspections, and no oblique little psychiatric tests to weed out the wild men. True, with all those boats starting at once there would be an element of chaos. But had not a recent newspaper article described the Royal Western as being "past masters at the business of race organization"? Such a multifaceted event would certainly test their abilities to the limit.

A few pints later we piled into Wynne-Thomas's Audi Quadram and howled back into Plymouth. By the next afternoon the chests of thirty-two skippers (more than one third of the total lineup), from eight nations, were illuminated with exhortations to "Go for Broke" in plump red letters on a dark blue shirt. They included in their number David White, Mike Richey, and Luis Tonizzo, skipper of *City of Slidell*, one of the most heavily sponsored boats in the fleet.

That night, in the Corinthian Club's "At Home," Alan Wynne-Thomas and I joined a circle drinking scotch whiskey at the cash bar. Included in the group was Vasil Kurtev, a short, stocky dentist from Bulgaria who had built his 25-foot sloop *Nord* from scratch on the shores of the Black Sea. He was accompanied by a heavily muscled man from the Bulgarian embassy in London. This must be the baby-sitter here to help Dr. Kurtev with his already excellent English.

What's it like sailing in the Black Sea? Is there much racing? Any big yachts? What are you drinking? I stood the Bulgarian a double Dewar's and consulted briefly with Wynne-Thomas. By all means, let's do it.

"On behalf of the people of Great Britain, Canada, and the United States"—the muscleman was translating furiously into Bulgarian—"we wish to present you with this T-shirt and invite you to join our informal association of transatlantic captains."

Kurtev started to reply, but before he could get a word out, his mentor grabbed the T-shirt, and spelled out the words thereon.

"Go for Broke . . . what this mean?"

"That means to spend everything, to hold nothing back."

"To go broke, to go bankrupt?"

"Yeah, that's it."

"American slang?"

"Yeah, don't worry, it's not political."

The goon pouted skeptically. I could see the hair growing out of his ears and remembered that his bosses were the savants who had contrived to fire a couple of revolver bullets into the Pope. The Bulgarian turned the T-shirt around.

"And what this mean? It's Only a Sprint?"

"It's a capitalist joke," I said. "Look, if you don't like the shirt we'll take it back . . ."

"What's a sprint?"

"It's a short, very fast run."

"Across the Atlantic?" Again, the incredulous pout. Attempting to knock off world leaders was one thing; coming here into the sacred and slightly drunken precincts of the Corinthian to impugn the ideals of the Half Crown Club was something else. The Dewar's began to stir in my blood. Alan Wynne-Thomas, fearful that an international free-for-all might tarnish the name of the newborn club, took up the task of explaining what a joke was to the Bulgarian secret police. Kurtev, quicker on the uptake, was staring off into space. Finally Alan convinced the gorilla, now turned sullen, that the Half Crown Club was not a subchapter of the CIA. All ended more or less amicably with another round of scotch, which the skippers belted down vodka-style.

Other skippers fought regimentation in their own special ways. One evening there was a loud rap on *Johan*'s hull. I went on deck to find Jack Hunt and Paul Porter swaying gently against the rail; they were drinking gin and tonic on a grand tour of all the boats in Class IV. They came below and I replenished their glasses.

"This race is getting too goddam formal," said Porter, a schoolteacher from Maine. "So we're having a class party."

"Sounds great."

"We're trying to get the upstairs of the Green Lantern," chimed in Hunt. This was a tavern restaurant in the Barbican, the only part of the old waterfront not destroyed by the German bombs. Everyone sipped his gin for a while.

"We were wondering . . ." Hunt shifted in his seat. "We were wondering whether we should ask your nemesis, Lloyd Foster down at the club, to join us?"

"He's not my nemesis. He might have voted against me but he was trying to stop the race from becoming totally commercial. We see eye-to-eye."

Porter totted up his list of names. We discussed arrangements and dates, and then the talk drifted back to the inevitable topic: Strategy.

"Did you hear the latest about Tonizzo?"

"What?"

"Luis is competitive, right? He's going straight down the rhumb-line."

"Straight through the ice? Jesus."

"Hey diddle diddle, straight down the middle."

"But they say icebergs don't show up on a radar plot."

"No problem."

"What do you mean, no problem?"

"Tonizzo doesn't have any radar."

Right. Such exchanges were only the beginning. Soon all the residents of Mill Bay developed a palate for gallows humor. But sometimes the jokes were not so funny. Not long after the conference on the class party a photographer from the *Western Morning News* turned up to take a mugshot of me, "Just in case you win."

"What, in this lady?" I asked. But I was nonetheless quite flattered. Then, one day later, another photographer appeared. This one was from the London *Observer*.

"Must take a couple of shots."

"In case I win?"

The lensman was not amused. "We're told to take all the contestants. Smile, please." The camera clicked, and clicked again. But wait a minute. All this coverage could not be for my victory parade. The snaps had a better chance of appearing with my obituary. I gave the photographer my most radiant smile. But that was not enough. One more, please. Snap, snap. The photographer would not finish. As the camera continued to click, I began to feel the mark of death upon me. Have the dockside tipsters singled me out as most likely to sink? Snap, snap. Just one more. Snap, snap. The last few frames depicted a skipper with an unholy scowl.

Later, another incident confirmed my deepest misgivings. One afternoon I looked up to see a glum-faced man working his way across the decks of the rafted boats.

" 'Scuse me, sor. 'Ave ye filled in this 'ere next-o-kin form?" The melancholy visitor, speaking in the broadest of Devon accents, held out a mimeographed questionnaire that was drawn up like a will. I glanced at it.

"No."

"Ye 'ave to fill it in, sor. I'll leave it wid you."

I stared into the simple face. The sun was shining. There were people all around. Yet there was a coolness in the air, and I began to wonder. Why was the Royal Western sending such a rustic? Could he be more than he seemed, perhaps even the Great Messenger Himself? Often, I had heard, visitors from the Beyond appear plainly clothed and plainly mannered.

"You say this is mandatory?"

"Sor?"

I looked down at the paper again and wondered dully why they were handing out *mimeographed* sheets. You'd think the Summons, even for those in the humbler walks of life, would command a better grade of stationery. At first I was frightened. Then I felt my gorge beginning to rise. Was this all I rated, just a fucking *mimeo* sheet? Anger swelled up and pushed me into a dangerous bravado. I looked up at the messenger.

"You should be wearing a black suit."

Cheeky, that, in the circumstances. I looked for a glint of hatred —or appreciation—in the eye of my beholder, but all I got was a pitying stare. Perhaps the fellow had heard that particular jest too many times before. A few seconds passed. "Wal, sor. I'll leave 'ee to it."

I stood on *Johan*'s deck, mimeo paper in hand, and watched this harbinger as it stalked off through the crowds. Why, I wondered, was he not stopping at other boats? Had he already distributed his grim notes among them? Or perhaps J. T. W. Hubbard was the only one to be handed his sailing orders? Truly, an appointment in Samarra. It was as if a cloud had passed over the face of the sun. I sat down heavily in the cockpit and found my chest pressing down against my knees. Holy Mary, Mother of God, I alone am going to die!

*　*　*　*　*

On the eve of the Committee's final briefing to competitors, twenty-two skippers in Class IV (and some in Class V) gathered at the Green Lantern. The old inn, built of wooden beams and panels of wattled plaster, had an overhanging second story and must have been all of three centuries old. Perhaps the Pilgrim Fathers put down a pint or two here before they stepped off the wharf at Sutton Pool, just a hundred yards to the east. The Green Lantern's ceilings were low, and the staircase was so narrow that the burlier skippers had to mount its creaking steps sideways.

Commander Foster and his wife, Eve, had cancelled another dinner appointment to attend. The group included skippers from Holland, France, Britain, Canada, New Zealand, Ireland, and the United States. During an Elizabethan repast of oxtail soup, roast duckling, carrots, and spring potatoes, many speeches were made, and many toasts were proposed and drunk. Finally, Lloyd Hircock, the Canadian, climbed to his feet and, with a nod to the native-born Britons, proposed a toast.

"To Her Majesty, the Queen."

All stood. To the Queen, God Bless Her.

Then one of the Dutch skippers rose, somewhat shakily, to his feet and proposed a toast to Queen Beatrix of the Netherlands. The skippers rose and drank again. These salutations were followed by a pregnant silence. Would the representatives of those two great

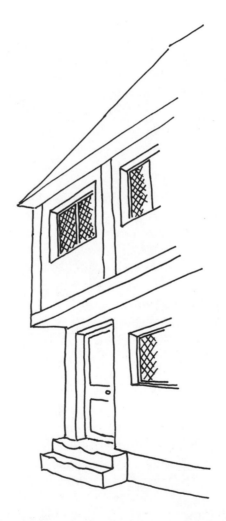

The Green Lantern. Did the Pilgrim Fathers put down a pint or two here on their way to Cape Cod?

republics, France and the United States, also call the assembly to order? The silence lengthened. Two Americans, both well laced with wine, were mumbling to each other down the table. "The French can't call Mitterrand and, for Chrissake, we can't call Ronald Reagan."

"We could try George Washington?" said the drunker of the two, in a stage whisper.

"And who will they go for, Napoleon? Jesus, the guy tried to invade this place!"

"That's *their* problem. If they don't like Napoleon, they can go with Robespierre or Louis XIV."

"Robespierre!" said the first mumbler with an expression of genuine shock. "I ain't gonna drink to Robespierre."

"So siddown."

Washington, Napoleon, Louis . . . the silence stretched on. Nobody moved. The citizens of the world's two noblest republics stood mute. Perhaps, I mused to myself, that was entirely appropriate. A long toast to silence.

Small local conversations started again around the room. I glanced at the ring of faces. Homewood, Tonizzo, Rachael Hayward, Tony Lush, Jack Hunt, with his wife Sue, Hircock, Jack Coffey, John Mansell, and Alain Veyron, a shipbuilder from Brittany, with his younger brother Thomas. In a few hours this happy crew would sail, each entirely alone, into the North Atlantic. Now Paul Porter, the organizer of this dinner, was on his feet.

"I shall not be accompanying you on this great race," he said, pushing a grey lock back from his eye. "But believe me, I and those others who remain behind will be thinking of you. Not every day, but every hour we shall look at the clock and wonder, 'Where are they now?' A few days ago I went a little north of here to Buckland Abbey, which, as you know, was the home for many years of that most famous man of Devon, Sir Francis Drake. There are many interesting things at the Abbey, but one struck me as of special interest to you who will be alone for so long and travel so far upon this great ocean. These are the words of Francis Drake's Prayer as they stand framed upon the wall of the Abbey. They read . . ." Here Porter fumbled for his spectacles, put them on, held up a tattered envelope and began to read:

There must be a Beginning of any great Matter, but the Continuing unto the End until it be thoroughly Finished yields the True Glory.

There was silence. It was as if, for one fleeting moment, the Great Adventurer himself had stood in our midst, urging us to the voyage ahead. Porter looked up from his notes and grinned. "There you have it folks. Continue unto the End. Hang in there, and come back safe. God bless." He sat down amid applause and not a few claps on the back.

4

Twelve O'Clock High

J ust a little before noon on the morning of June 1, 1984, about ninety OSTAR skippers walked up the stone steps into the front lobby of the Duke of Cornwall Hotel. The Race Committee was about to give them its final briefing. Though the Luftwaffe had launched more than 600 bombing raids against Plymouth in World War II, the hotel had refused to buckle under the blasts. Its granite towers, steep slate roofing, and crenellated stone gables gave it the appearance of a Victorian chateau, transported from some Highland glen to the shores of southern England. Now, even though much of the city had been rebuilt, it stood alone, like a great beached brontosaurus, on the western slopes of Plymouth Hoe.

It was a splendid June morning, with a cool dry wind blowing gently from the northeast. I was halfway up the steps when a voice behind me said, "There's Phil Weld, now." I turned to see a dark, craggy man of about seventy years loping across the road alongside Hugh McCoy, skipper of the 60-foot catamaran *Fury*. In OSTAR circles, Weld—discoverer of the mid-Atlantic weather mark Waypoint Weld—was a figure of heroic proportions. As a young man, he had been decorated several times while serving with the U.S. Rangers. Later, he made a fortune as a newspaper publisher and in 1980, sailing his elegant 51-foot tri *Moxie*, broke the Atlantic speed record and became the first American ever to win the OSTAR. This year he was not campaigning a boat of his own, but it was clear that he and McCoy were deep in discussion about routes and strategy.

"Hi, Tim, great to see you. I was asking for you down at your boat earlier." The welcome was effusive, the handshake firm. For a few seconds we stood in the sunlight at the top of the steps. Other skippers filed by, clipboards in hand, like unusually grizzled undergraduates on their way to a lecture. A gratifying number had T-shirts that exhorted the beholder, in bold red type, to

GO FOR BROKE
WITH THE
HALF CROWN CLUB

As the skippers trooped on by (IT'S ONLY A SPRINT, IT'S ONLY A SPRINT), I found myself at a loss for words. Weld was the friend of a friend. He was one of the seadogs who had advised me in my attempts to enter the race. Yet he was also a member of

Entering the beached Brontosaurus for the skipper's conference, June 1, 1984.

the official Race Committee and could thus find himself judging my conduct in matters connected with OSTAR. I could not say "Thanks for everything," for it somehow implied that he had played favorites. Nor could I pretend we had never corresponded. I tried to walk down the middle and said, "Thank you for all the pointers you gave me." There was an awkward silence, then Weld replied, "You did it all yourself, Tim. It would have been very hard for them to say No to a real diehard amateur like yourself."

"Well," I replied, "they were very convincing with their Nos for quite a while there . . ." We both laughed and followed the other skippers down a dark hallway into the stone bowels of the Duke of Cornwall. As we turned right into the main ballroom, I had the odd impression of stepping back in time. The air was stuffy and heavy drapes had been pulled across the windows. In fact, the drapes did not look as if they'd been drawn back for several decades. Had the antiquated staff, I wondered, ever received the word? Did they imagine the wartime "black out" was still in force? Perhaps that noise was not a passing truck but the drone of yet another Flieger-Korps overhead? Perhaps this whole gathering had passed through a time-warp and returned to England as she was in her Finest Hour.

The Race Committee, composed primarily of retired military officers, sat overlooking the skippers from a small stage. Their demeanor did nothing to dispel the impression that the assemblage had somehow marched back into 1944. The old men-at-arms stared balefully down at the boistrous lads below. What, I wondered, could be passing through *their* heads? Perhaps they were recalling the O-Groups that preceded some of the great skirmishes of history. Did they dream of the flaming oil tanks at Narvik, or of the main lock gate hanging on one hinge at St. Nazaire? Did they fly with the Lancasters into the fire-storm over Hamburg? Or perhaps they were recalling how things stood on Sword or Juno beach in Normandy almost exactly forty years ago today?

Then I had a disquieting thought. Could it be that these old buffers on the podium were seeking to recreate the scenes of yesteryear and replay there own tunes of glory? In truth, the present gathering bore a remarkable resemblance to the briefings in the movie *Twelve O'Clock High*. Maps were projected onto a screen, with assembly areas marked off in heavy crayon. The skippers— the guys who flew the kites—slouched in their chairs, feckless youth exchanging wisecracks as they scribbled down the courses to be steered. Instead of Gregory Peck on stage ordering his crews to bomb Berlin, the skippers had their own air force general to brief them. He was Air Commodore Thomas R. Pierce, CBE, RAF (Retd.).

Welcome to this, the final skippers conference of OSTAR Seven . . .

The Committee's first item of business neatly expanded the gap between the podium and the audience. The roll call, a routine device of those wishing to impose order, was read in clipped tones by Commander Lloyd Foster, RN (Retd).

Arthaud, Austoni, Bates, Bernardin, Boucher, Boye, Brand, Bullimore . . .

At first, most skippers acknowledged their presence with a curt "Here," "Present," or simply "Yes." The singsong catechism made me feel like a raw recruit back in the service, then it carried me even further back to the days at school. The psychological warfare began. The French, who'd started off by saying "Yes," quickly switched to "Oui." Then the Americans, piqued perhaps by the martial demeanor of the Committee, began to respond with markedly laid-back "Yeahs."

Unlike many of those present, I was thrilled by the roll call. I felt my entry, too recent for any printed list, would be validated if my name was called in its rightful place in the roster. But I was in a quandary. I wanted this moment to be just right. Should I respond with the word "Present"? (But wouldn't that be a shade too pompous?) How about "Yes"? (Good, but perhaps too abrupt?) In the end I blurted out the word I'd learned as an eleven-year-old boy in boarding school.

"Hubbard."

"Here."

With a marked effort I bit off the "Sir" that forty years ago would have accompanied the utterance. The deed was done. I was now aboard, a bona fide contestant, an acknowledged chevalier of the deep. My name would be entered in the record books. In big type if I won—praise be—and in much smaller type if I were dismasted, capsized, rammed, or sunk. For one shining moment my own name had hung, alone, on the stuffy air of the Duke of Cornwall's ballroom as ninety-one distinguished adventurers from seventeen different nations awaited my response.

Here, Sir! Here I am. Ready, Aye, Ready.

The games continued. The name of Philippe Jeantot was called. As the winner of the BOC Round the World Race, he is a figure of renown. Perhaps he sought to administer a mild rebuke to his compatriots for their emphatic use of French while in England.

"Jeantot."

"Here."

The hard H was pronounced with the colloquial ease of a world traveller. Soon it was the turn of Mac Smith, master of the elegant and very swift 44-foot monohull *Quailo*. Smith, from Daytona Beach, had won many stateside races with this boat and he was given a fine chance of making her the first monohull home. With a little bit of luck he might even clip the wings of a couple of 60-foot French trimarans in Class I. The gauntlet went down.

"Mac Smith."

"Oui."

Hmmm . . . The laughter began, surged, and then faded away into soft chuckles as the next name was called. Finally, the list was done. Commander Foster shuffled his papers, looked owl-like over his glasses, and prepared for the next phase of the briefing. Just as he was about to speak, Air Commodore Pierce looked up. His normally amiable and rather florid mien held an expression of ferocious puzzlement. "Was Timothy Hubbard's name on that list?"

I froze in my seat. What was happening? Were the Committee's internal disputes now boiling out into the open? Was I about to be thrown out as abruptly as I had been invited in? I thought of the big number 11 on *Johan*'s bows and deck. I'd paid my entry fee, passed their inspection, even messed up my boat with their numbers . . . now they were going to jerk me around some more.

Commander Foster was on his feet again, checking the roll. "Yes, Hubbard's name was called." Several skippers murmured agreement. Commodore Pierce's scowl turned slowly to a smile.

"Just want to make sure his name was there." The smile beamed out across the meeting. I sat back in my seat, feeling like teacher's pet. My ears began to go red. Commander Foster moved on to other business. Every statement made in English was translated into French by Christine Menzies, the Parisian wife of Bob Menzies, the skipper of the 37-foot sloop *Dancing Dolphin*. In the jabber of tongues, I turned and quietly introduced myself to June Clarke, who sat on my left. She was sailing the 40-foot trimaran *Batchelor's Sweet Pea*, and had been recruited by Alan Wynne-Thomas into the Half Crown Club. An ominous note, however, was struck. Clarke had to shake with her left hand because her right had been caught in a car door. How could you handle a boat that big and that fast, I wondered, with one hand wrapped up in a bandage?

The conference rumbled on. The start was to be at 12:10 P.M. tomorrow. To circumvent the collisions of 1980, the multihulls would pass to the left and the monhulls to the right of the Royal Navy guardship anchored in the center of the line. Spectator boats, another prime source of collisions, would be banned from a two-square-mile area behind the line. The guardship would fire a five-minute-warning gun, followed by the starting gun. Philip Weld, the winner of OSTAR 1980, would pull the lanyard. Applause.

Now for the problems. Most of the boats, their engines now sealed, could be towed out of the Hole only at high water, which occurred at 6 A.M. Once clear of the dock channel, competitors could raise sail, but they would then have to tack around Plymouth harbor until noon. The idea of nearly one hundred boats, all single-handed, trying to avoid each other in such a confined area for SIX HOURS caused muffled groans among the skippers. But this was only the beginning. The start had been moved from noon to 12:10 because the Royal Citadel overlooking the city would fire a twenty-one-gun salute at noon sharp in honor of the Queen's birthday.

"The OSTAR fleet," declared Commander Foster, poker-faced, "should have no difficulty distinguishing these guns from the starting guns." The groans among the British and American skippers became less muffled. In contrast, the French, so far as I could determine, absorbed this new information in stony silence. Kings, queens, birthdays . . . let's get on with the race!

"Competitors should also note," continued Foster, "that the Tall Ships Race will shortly start from Bermuda, and OSTAR boats may well find themselves sailing through the tail end of this fleet . . ." More groans.

Icebergs! Montagne de Glace!

The ballroom fell silent. The Ice Patrol's worst predictions were coming true. A most vigilant watch must be kept in the great slice of the North Atlantic laying 400 miles south and east of St. John's, Newfoundland. Skippers should also note that about a dozen oil and gas rigs, unmarked on any chart, lay on the banks of Newfoundland and Nova Scotia. Before leaving the States, I had acquired a list of these locations from the coast guard, and this was now presented to the skippers. Score another one for the diehard amateur. The discussion of ice continued. I sneaked a look across at Luis Tonizzo, the man who planned to take *City of Slidell* kamikazi fashion right down the rhumb-line. He was leaning back on his chair, left ankle hooked over his right knee, slowly tapping a pencil on his notepad—the picture of ultimate cool. The composure was unfeigned. Go for broke, baby. Devil take the hindmost.

Next on stage was Monsieur Argos, the big papa of satellite location equipment. He brought one of his dish-pan transmitters on to the podium with him. The device, powered by internal batteries, would not transmit properly if it were covered by wet ropes or a wet sail. If a skipper was in trouble he must activitate this red "panic button" and a search would begin. Important point: Even if the skipper subsequently solved his problem, he must leave the panic button depressed; if he did not, rescue craft would continue to search under the impression that the Argos had sunk. If the skipper was forced to abandon ship, a plastic latch could be broken and the Argos lifted off the deck into the life raft. Monsieur Argos then gave a dramatic demonstration of how to break the plastic latch. With quite a bit of perspiration and a mighty heave, he succeeded in snapping the plastic pin. The skippers clapped politely.

All in all, the conference left much to be desired. Radio frequencies, giving progress reports on who was where in the race, were jumbled. Some of the problem stemmed from the fact that France and England were on different time schedules. Or were they?

A chart showing the harbor at Newport flashed on to the screen. The finish line! Nothing could seem more remote. It lay on the far side of the universe, an Olympian peak pristine above the clouds of discomfort and hardship that lay ahead. How many will make it? The line itself ran from Brenton Reef Tower, at the mouth of Narragansett Bay, one mile northeast to red Whistle Buoy No. 2. It appeared to me to be surrounded by rocks. Would I cross the line, if I ever got that far, in fog, in darkness, or in storm? After making the finish, boats must sail a further five miles through three right-angle turns into Newport Bay and then through a final U-turn, into B Dock at the Goat Island Yacht Club. This must be old hat to the professionals. But several of us did not know the waters. I became increasingly uneasy. The boats' engines were sealed. According to the instructions, finishers must call up a chase boat on Channel 16 two or three hours before they crossed the line. This was fine for the speed machines. The crowds would be there. Everyone in the world would be watching. But how about the slowpokes arriving four, five, or even six weeks after the start? Who'd be watching for *them*? What if the chase boat didn't show, or couldn't find them in fog and darkness? The contestants would have to SAIL in, through three right-angle turns and hundreds of anchored boats in Newport Harbor. I heard my own voice asking a question.

"If there's a foul-up on the towing arrangements, are there any special hazards to watch for in a boat sailing in?" I was nervous but my voice sounded surprisingly brisk and authoritative. All in all, it wasn't a bad question.

"Oh, the chase boat will be there."

"Yeah, and goats have wings" growled an American voice, *sotto voce*, off to my right. The whole thing was too casual. The meeting broke up. Two Dutch skippers came over to say they shared my misgivings. A group photo was taken. Those about to go west, smile. Alan Wynne-Thomas, Jack Coffey, and I walked out into the sunshine and up the grassy hillside to the top of Plymouth Hoe. Coffey, the skipper of the 35-foot *Meg of Muglins*, was a retired businessman from Dublin. He was once a noted Rugby player but now, at sixty-four, he was the second oldest man in the race. I fumed on for a while about the slaphappy briefing. I was boring the others so I turned to Coffey with a change of subject.

"Did you hear the latest?"

"What can that be, Timothy?"

"The word's out that Mike Richey received the Last Rites."

"Then he must be awful close to the grave."

There was a hint of frost in Coffey's voice. I turned to perceive hostility in the Irishman's eyes. That's all we need! My thoughtless attempt to amuse had gone awry. I must watch what I said. Everyone around here, including myself, seemed to be uptight. Our trio strolled on up the hill. Perhaps this was each man's last chance to lean against the trunk of a tree, or behold a flower-bed, luminous with spring blooms. Then, just as we topped the rise we came upon a sight so fantastic that it blotted out all hint of contention. Right in the middle of a large swath of grass three uniformed technicians were feverishly—but unsuccessfully—attempting to inflate a hot-air balloon all done out in the colors of Paul Ricard apéritif. The company had opened a free bar down in the Courtesy Pavilion, but it was for the media, and the skippers had been shooed away. But even the media didn't want to drink Ricard's potion. In a change of heart the company decided to let the skippers have some after all. They opened a bar in a panel truck nearer the boats. But there were no takers, which was remarkable, given the hefty intake of most skippers. Now, in a final desperate move, the apéritif planned to float a massive balloon out over Plymouth Hoe. But the balloon clearly had other ideas. For a while, the skippers watched the antics, then they adjourned, laughing, to the bar of the Royal Western for a final lunch.

The place was packed tight to its oak-panelled walls. Many friends had come to bid the OSTAR skippers farewell and it was as much as four bartenders could do to keep abreast of the calls for Usher's best bitter. The French, soon to be driving their huge multihulls, were accompanied by a bevy of sulky teenage girls. They moved in a clump to the western end of the bar. Despite their disdain for warm English beer, they were knocking it back, forcing the bartenders to grapple with a continuous, and seemingly intractable, problem of changing French francs into British pounds. The other drinkers—Dutchmen, Finns, Americans—were becoming a mite impatient. Philip Weld, in top form, gleefully accepted membership in the Half Crown Club. A distinguished grey-bearded gentleman, clad in a clergyman's collar, sought to bless the competitors' boats. Then Margaret, Alan Wynne-Thomas's wife, drove us all to the biggest supermarket in town for a final purchase of fresh food. I awoke on my berth in *Johan* later that afternoon surrounded by sacks of English mackintosh apples. For the life of me I could not remember if the clergyman was coming, or not coming, to bless *Johan Lloyde*.

There were still a number of chores to be done. I had to seal my forehatch, help Lloyd Hircock shift the last of his personal belongings aboard *Moustache*, stick a number II on either side of my mainsail and have my last shower-bath for several weeks. The fleet sails at dawn. I must get all sail covers off, all ropes ready to run. An hour later Hircock came by and we off-loaded his gear from the cab. It was a chilly evening and we put on parkas and walked down West Hoe road to a fish-and-chips shop. By this time tomorrow we'd be at sea. As we emerged from the shop, we saw Warren Luhrs, his assistants, and several young ladies across the street. They waved, and we sunk deeper into our parkas.

"Now that's who I'd like to be," said Lloyd, holding the wrapper of warm chips under his arm. "Designing my own boats—rich, famous, fast."

I looked back over my shoulder. "He's got more at stake than we do. If he blows it, Hunter Marine won't sell a whole lot of boats next year."

We walked down the road and ate our fish and chips sitting on the seawall of the Royal Western. Off to the south, *Elf Aquitaine* zigged and zagged around her mooring. The achievements of Hircock and Hubbard, graduates of the same university back in Canada, had never been distinguished enough to merit entry into the alumni bulletin. Both of us were well into middle age and it was all too clear that neither of us was going to become president of a bank or chairman of a railroad. It was indeed a strange pass that brought us together now on this stone wall with our chips and our fish. We didn't talk much, but in all my imaginings I could not have asked for better company.

In a little while it was dark and we went into the club for a pint or two. The scene was boistrous. But we must all rise at five to meet the tide, and soon I tramped back to Mill Bay Dock. I saw figures in the darkness, moving from boat to boat. I went among them. Good luck, good luck. A shake. See you in Newport, God willing. Shades of the night before Agincourt, where King Henry's men were outnumbered six to one. He that hath no stomach for this fight, let him depart; his passport shall be made, and crowns for convoy put into his purse. We would not sail in that man's company, that fears his fellowship to sail with us. The figures moved across the decks in the darkness. Good luck, good luck. See you in Newport. Bon voyage, good luck.

5

The Expanding Universe

"Up to starboard."

"Arrr Gar?"

"Take me up to starboard," I yelled to the tow boat. "I'll make sail in the lee of Drake's Island."

"Arr Zor Gar?" The Devon words were torn to shreds by the brisk southeast wind. I gestured fiercely, and the tow at last moved in the right direction. *Johan* crashed forward into the sunlit waves. Mill Bay Dock gates were already half a mile astern. There was a fine nip in the air, and I was wearing two sweaters and a heavy parka jacket. Give her another fifty yards as a safety margin. I picked up the brass speaking trumpet.

"Okay. Let her go. Thanks." Brawny arms waved farewell; the tow boat turned and headed back for another customer. *Johan* rolled in the cross sea as I hauled in the dripping tow line. Then I stepped to the mast, and hauled down on the mainsail halyard. Up she goes, a white sail with one deep reef. I ran aft to the cockpit and sheeted it home. Johan gathered way. I let out eight rolls of yankee jib and streaked past the stone veranda of the Royal Western Yacht Club at six knots plus.

The alarm had gone off near my ear at 5 A.M. The condemned man ate warm porridge and drank several mugs of coffee laced with rum. I heard John Hunt stirring next door on *Crystal Catfish*. At 5:30, there was a hefty knock on my cabin roof. I went up to find Commodore Pierce and an oilskinned delegation from the Royal Western at the rail.

"Ready to go?"

"You said 6 A.M. There's still half an hour."

"Yes, but the gates are open. Got to get moving or we'll never get you all out of here."

Always *Johan*. They bounced me on the inspection. Now they were bouncing me on the departure. I looked around the deck. Ropes were everywhere. Hells bells.

"Okay. Give me two minutes." I went below, jammed the remains of breakfast into the sink, and quickly stuffed all my clothes and papers into five plastic garbage bags. Then I tied up the canvas bunk boards and reappeared on deck. Ready, Aye, Ready.

The tow boat took the line. I shook hands with Jack Hunt, Paul Porter, and Commodore Pierce.

"Hey, Paul, what frequency is the ham radio net on?" Porter dived below and jotted two sets of figures on a piece of paper and handed it over just as the two boats drifted apart. "Thanks, pal." Good luck, good luck. As *Johan* pulled away, I saw Susan Hunt standing on the pontoon.

"She looks great, Tim," she shouted.

"Not too fast, but seaworthy," I yelled back.

"She looks great."

In truth, she did. There was a wonderful sheer to *Johan*'s lines, from the tip of her bowsprit to the great rudder hanging stoutly upon her stern. She looked as if she could handle anything the North Atlantic had to offer. Here she goes. Last into the Race, first out of Mill Bay Dock! The launch turned her bow to port and they headed through the open lock gates. On one side stood a white-bearded figure huddled in an overcoat. I recognized Terence Shaw, the retired Royal Navy captain who preceded Lloyd Foster in the job as the Royal Western's sailing secretary. For the past two weeks, he and his wife had run the club's trailer at Mill Bay. Now, here's the old guy up at dawn to watch the fleet go out.

"Good-bye, Captain Shaw. Thanks for everything."

Shaw's face lit up. He did not attempt to compete with the engines of the launch. Instead, he just pointed his finger, pistol fashion, at *Johan* as if to say "She's Number One."

Soon I felt the first wave punch into the bow and tried to make the launch turn further into the wind. Half an hour later *Johan* was racing across Plymouth Sound toward Staddon Heights. Ahead lay the black shape of a nuclear sub. Such vessels generally ran a piquet boat to ward off unwelcome visitors. I intended to stay clear of any complications and went about on to the port tack. By now other sailboats were blossoming out of Mill Bay Dock to the north.

Already *Johan* was close to the start line. What on earth was she going to do for the next five hours? Rather than tack aimlessly about, I shaped a course for Cawsand Bay, outside the breakwater to the west.

The exhilaration of the morning, of sailing again, wiped away my apprehensions and my chagrin at being turfed out of Mill Bay before my time. Soon I doused sail and dropped anchor in three fathoms. Now to get the boat ready for sea. The first item of business was to take the life raft from its place decreed by safety regulations at the foot of the mast and stow it down below. I found a nice safe spot for it on the floor of the fo'c'sle.

This might be my last chance for a hot meal so I combined a can of beef stew with one of curried oxtail soup. I broke several chunks of fresh bread into this mess and ate it like an animal, straight out of the saucepan. Delicious.

On deck, the wind was backing to the east, and strengthening. *Crystal Catfish*, Confederate flag aloft, came roaring into Cawsand Bay. Jack Hunt brought her alongside to hang on *Johan*'s anchor, but the swell was so steep that the two boats ground together. No combination of fenders helped, so Hunt decided to drop astern on a warp. At the moment of casting off, a knotted rope jammed between the two hulls. Hunt reached down to clear it. The hulls slammed together and he pulled his hand clear just in time.

"For God's sake, Jack, it's not worth it. Cut the bugger."

"No, I've nearly got it." His hand dived in and out, and the two hulls crunched together again.

"If you get caught, forget OSTAR You'll be sitting in a Plymouth hospital."

"Nearly got it."

Finally Hunt pulled the rope clear and drifted astern. I took a bearing on a pub sign ashore in Cawsand. We seemed to be dragging. I picked up the brass trumpet.

"We're dragging."

"Shit," came back upwind faintly.

Lloyd Hircock, clad in immaculate white oilskins, appeared in *Moustache*.

"Can I come alongside?" Nobody wanted to drop anchor and have the trouble of hauling it back up.

"He's dragging," Hunt yelled back.

"What?"

"HE SAYS HE'S DRAGGING." Hircock waved and sheered

away deeper into the bay. The waves began to pound *Johan,* and she came up on her chain in short jerks. Hunt cast off and dropped his own anchor. White-haired Bob Menzies, aged sixty-four, circled by in *Dancing Dolphin.* He went close inshore before tacking; so close that I assumed he must know these waters well. He returned, with some ropes hanging over his bow.

"What's the weather, Bob?" Menzies was supposed to be an expert. Because of his wife's translating duties, he was the only English-speaking skipper to be invited to the briefing given by the French meteorological authorities for all French skippers. He had, it seemed, refused the invitation on a matter of principle. Such information, he and his wife believed, should be available to all.

By now the start line, three miles upwind to the southeast, was crowded with sails. Eleven o'clock. Better get the anchor up. I made my way forward to the windlass and inserted the three-foot long steel lever. I leant on it. Nothing moved. The windlass, it seemed, was frozen solid. I checked the latches. All were clear and I tried again, forcing the lever down, then up. Small shards of bronze appeared on the deck.

Now what?

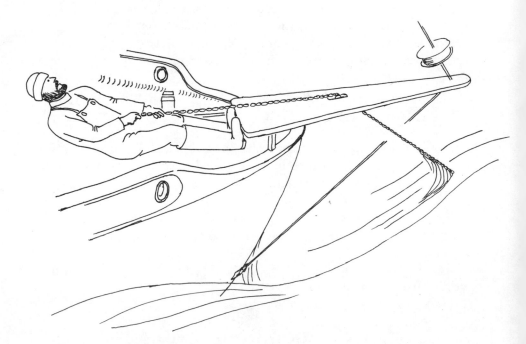

Brute strength and bloody ignorance.

Masterful contestant remains firmly anchored in Cawsand Bay as ninety-one boats speed across start-line! I hurled myself upon the windlass again. More bronze shards gathered on the foredeck. *Crystal Catfish* hauled in her own anchor and started to circle *Johan* slowly.

It was time for the idiot's last resort: Brute Strength and Bloody Ignorance. I would attempt to haul in the mother by hand. But what Brute Strength? I had spent the last nine months sitting in an office, grading student papers. I went below and put on a pair of heavy oilskin trousers. Then I sat down beside the windlass, braced my feet against the bow and grabbed the chain. Heave. Six inches came in, and then was grabbed back again with interest, as the next wave hit the boat. Try again. Heave. Nine inches came in, and I flipped it back on the frozen chain wheel. I repeated the move and got another nine inches. Then a foot. Eighteen fathoms of chain were still out there. Heave, heave, heave.

Sometimes I got more than a foot. Sometimes the boat lurched back and pulled the chain brutally through my clenched fingers. There was nothing the circling Hunt could do to help me. It was nearly noon.

"Head for the line," I yelled.

Hunt waved acknowledgment and faced away, shaking his head.

I resumed heaving, trying to judge the gap between waves. Occasionally I leaned back to rest, gasping on the deck. My hands were a mess. It was hard not to see the comical side of things. Yet I was worried. With two boats hanging on it, the anchor might have become so embedded that I would not be able to move it. Perhaps, I wondered—between heaves—perhaps I could sail it out; that is, get the mainsail up and zigzag the anchor out of the bottom? But that could get messy; if the anchor was really jammed in, I could knock the mast out of the boat. Now there's a headline: TRANSATLANTIC HOPEFUL DISMASTED AT ANCHOR IN CAWSAND BAY.

I kept heaving. Two feet in, one foot out. Now there was mud on the chain, and the boat was jolting hard on the top of each wave. That's it. Get her up so tight that the force of the waves jerks the anchor out. Two big bangs. Would the fairlead break? England was not releasing her sons too easily today. Another crash, then all went quiet, and *Johan* drifted sideways across the wind. Free! Free at last! I hauled the rest of the chain in as fast as I could. My hands were bleeding and I knew my legs were moving slowly as I approached the mast and grabbed the main halyard. Soon *Johan* was underway. I hitched up the steering gear, secured the anchor, and then—whole yankee unfurled—charged through the spectator fleet toward the line. The number on *Johan*'s side, and the red and white pennant at her crosstree, identified her as an OSTAR starter, and the boats scrambled to get out of her way. I trailed my hands to leeward to wash off the mud and the blood and got a sleeve-full of seawater for my troubles.

Five minutes to the warning gun. *Johan* was in among the contestants now, sailing parallel to the line on the starboard tack.

Johan, *all sail set, charges through the spectator fleet.*

Several boats, led by *Tyfoon VI*, approached from my port side. The 44-foot sloop was skippered by a Belgian shipbuilder named Gustav Versluys. *Johan* had right-of-way, but *Tyfoon*, closehauled at eight knots, was heading right at her. T-boned on the line! I estimated the distances carefully. Versluys, built like a butcher and rumored to be a count, was a very experienced racing skipper. He must be planning to go under *Johan*'s stern, missing her by about fifteen feet. I maintained course and speed. *Tyfoon* went charging by, but the stocky Versluys was not at the wheel—he was forward, wrestling with some piece of gear at the foot of the mast!

Boats were coming at *Johan* from all angles. The near miss with *Tyfoon* inspired me to sheer off and get away from the crowd. I sailed north up to the Plymouth breakwater and began to mark time. The only boat nearby was *Thursday's Child*. Warren Luhrs had gotten the same idea. He waved and sailed closer.

"Good luck," yelled Luhrs.

"Same to you." I wanted Luhrs, who'd had his share of bad luck in 1980, to make *Thursday's Child* the first monohull home. "Good luck, and remember, you're carrying the Flag." Luhrs waved acknowledgment. Both boats went about. My hands were hurting. When I looked up from the yankee sheet winch, I found *Johan*'s bowsprit gunning straight at *Thursday's Child*'s port side. Technically, *Johan* had right-of-way, but I was rapidly revising the rules of the road in this pre-start madhouse. I released all my sheets, and *Thursday's Child* slid by.

Johan jogged off to the south. There was a faint pop from somewhere. The five minute gun? Or the last of the salute from the citadel? I saw the multihulls weaving around off to port. Up above, a dozen helicopters hovered over the scene; their engines, I realized, were drowning out all other sound. It was hard to think.

The other boats seemed to be heading for the line. I waved to Bob Scott, chasing across my stern in *Land's End*. Now I was parallel to Alan Wynne-Thomas in *Jemima Nicholas*. The founders of the Half Crown Club gave each other a majestic salute across 100 yards of furiously churned water. They would not meet again for many months.

I had my eye on the Navy guardship. A rapier of smoke flicked up, without sound, from the fantail. That must be the gun, as fired by Phil Weld. Nothing could be heard through the helicopters' roar. The faster boats, led by *Thursday's Child*, moved quickly ahead. Nearly all were reefed. Eric Tabarly, it seemed, was making a late start right through the monohull line. A helicopter, all tricked out in Ricard colors, scampered ahead, marking the best route for the great man through the fleet. He was clad in pristine white oilskins and stood transfixed, like an Aztec god, at the helm of his speeding machine. I waved my arm cheerily but got no response. *Johan* must have been just another obstruction for Tabarly.

For the next hour or so, *Johan* was cornered in a clump of vessels that included *Nord, Gladys, Crystal Catfish, El Torero, Karpetz,* and, for a while, *Jester.* They were on a wet beam reach for the Lizard, on the southwestern tip of England. I ducked below to switch on my electronic log, and to find some ointment for my hands. I emerged on deck seconds later to find *El Torero* swerving hard to avoid me. The confusion was not helped by a number of spectator boats that, having gotten out five or six miles ahead of the line, were now sailing back through the fleet. *Karpetz,* a 32-foot cutter from Sweden, went sharply to port to avoid an incoming

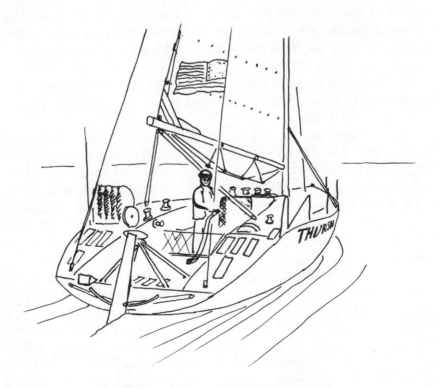

A symphony in high-tech, Thursday's Child, *slides by.*

multihull. Then she corrected her course too far to starboard and swerved right under *Johan*'s bowsprit. This was it, I thought, I'm going to run right up on to his deck. A strange fatalism overtook me. *Che sarà, sarà.* There goes the race. Probably sink both of us. *Johan*'s bow, on top of a wave, stood fifteen feet above *Karpetz*, beam on in the trough. Then it occurred to me that I could at least try to avoid him. I jerked the helm up. Hard astarboard! The boats hung there, five feet apart, and then grazed by. A red, outraged face stared out from *Karpetz*'s cockpit.

"I ham rrracing," yelled skipper Karl Peterzen angrily at *Johan*, whom he seemed to imagine was another tiresome spectator boat. For my part I was relieved at the near miss, and amused.

"So am I," I shouted back over my shoulder. Peterzen, still struggling to control his boat, saw the point and laughed.

"Zat makes two of us!"

"Right on."

Eddystone Lighthouse, sitting on a rock fifteen miles south of Plymouth, went by to port. In OSTAR 1980, with a different set of conditions, Phil Weld's *Moxie* was the only boat to weather Eddystone. *Johan* was now sailing at seven and one-half knots on a course that could take her past the Scillies to the edge of the continental shelf. This will be the longest night, traversing the world's busiest shipping lanes. Evening closed in. Only two other boats were still in sight, *Torero* and maybe *Land's End*, both on my port quarter. As dusk fell, a big white sloop passed me to the south. I checked the number. It was the French computer engineer Monique Brand in *Alliance Kaypro*. For the first time I came to appreciate the astrophysical theory of expanding galaxies; why should the furthest galaxies always be moving away at the fastest speeds? Now I knew. The explosion—or Big Bang—of the start had sent the 60-foot multihulls rocketing to the edge of the Atlantic shelf, while the smaller monohulls still struggled to get past the Lizard. Different speeds gave each boat its special, and often lonely, space. The last thing I was to see of any other competitor in the whole duration of the Observer Singlehanded was the starboard light of the speeding *Kaypro*. After that green glow passed ahead, the horizon of the expanding universe remained, for *Johan*, quite empty.

6

The Lords of La Mancha

"Sailboat *Johan* calling ship proceeding east at position approximately 49° 42′ north, 05°17′ west. Come in unidentified ship. We are on collision course, repeat collision course. Over."

There was no reply. My little VHF radio hissed quietly to itself for several more seconds.

"Sailboat *Johan* calling unidentified ship . . . " I repeated the message, then hauled myself up through the hatch into the darkness for another quick glance through the binoculars. Jesus. The huge freighter, lit up like a Christmas tree, was coming straight at me. The time was past 11 P.M. on the night of the start. The wind had moderated sharply and gone round to the south so that *Johan* was now loping along on a broad reach at three knots. The loom of the Lizard Light flicked across the horizon every three seconds twenty-five miles to the north.

The mouth of the English Channel constitutes one of the biggest mercantile bottlenecks in the world, and for many hours now I had been playing a game of cat and mouse with an unending stream of giant tankers and bulk carriers. They did not stay in the lanes designated for them on the charts, but came at me from all directions at such speeds that in the space of ten minutes they turned from dank glows on the horizon to illuminated cliffs of steel. Often they were so festooned with lights that even a close study through the binoculars did not reveal their precise direction until they were close enough for me to feel the thud of their engines through *Johan*'s hull. All Observer Singlehanded competitors were required to carry radar reflectors, but I had learned from

bitter experience that these hardly registered on the big ships'
radar plots. Thus the cats were blind and they moved so fast that
it was difficult for the little mice, moving by sail alone, to stay out
of their path.

I suspect it will be quite a while, however, before Parker Bros.
merchandise Cat-and-Mouse as a board game, ages eight and up.
First, players learn the rules only by playing the game. Second, for
full realism, they should be dog-tired. Third, losers should anticipate being churned up into catmeat by the big ships screws . . .

Once more, I tried to raise the unidentified ship on Channel 16,
but again there was no answer. It was time to send *Johan* to Panic
Stations.

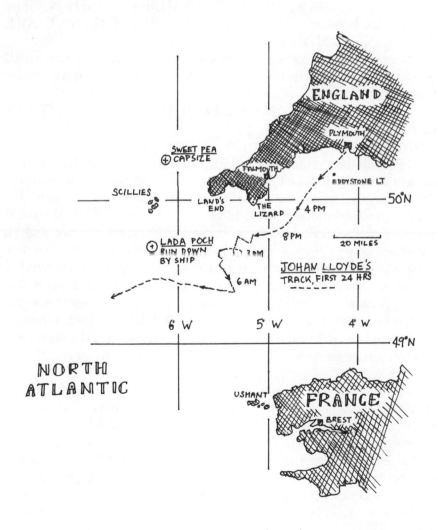

"Sailboat *Johan* to unidentified ship. You are coming right at me, range 600 meters. My masthead strobe goes on now. Come in, ship."

Hisssssss . . .

I reached up and threw the strobe switch, and, after a slight pause, a blessed streak of white light, one million candlepower strong, pulsed out from *Johan*'s masthead. Technically, this was a violation of international law; flashing strobes should be used only by ships in distress. But I was not standing on ceremony tonight. Now, with each flash of the strobe *Johan*'s shortwave radio began to emit an eerie "plink." Things were heating up. Beep, flash, plink. Beep, flash, plink.

"X-RAY YANKEE DELTA TO SAILBOAT JOHAN." The Scots voice boomed into the cabin. "WE SEE YOU AND ARE ALTERING COURSE TO PORT. OVER."

"*Johan* to X-Ray Yankee, thanks. Keep a look out for other small boats. Transatlantic sailboat race started from Plymouth today. Over."

"X-RAY YANKEE DELTA TO JOHAN. UNDERSTOOD. OUT."

"*Johan*, Out."

The big ship pounded by, Hilton on the hoof. In her wake I caught a smell of diesel fuel, rancid galley slops, and human ordure. Clearly, in such a crowded channel, they had no time for small talk. And neither did I. In my opinion this first night at sea was one of the most dangerous parts of the race for *Johan* and all the other competitors. I had prepared for it as carefully as I knew how. My boat did not have radar. I could not afford it financially, nor could I afford the heavy draw on the batteries. But *Johan* was equipped with an array of collision-avoidance equipment that was probably the most advanced in the OSTAR fleet. Indeed, when all systems were switched on, the navigator's station on the starboard quarter came to resemble the control room of a nuclear sub (see picture p. 73).

The centerpiece of *Johan*'s electronic defense system was undoubtedly a device called the Pernicka Radar Alert. This instrument, with its box-like aerial bolted to the cabin roof, was based on the High Frequency Direction Finders (or "Huff/Duff" in Royal Navy slang) used by U-boat chasers in the North Atlantic during World War II. When the submarine came to the surface, generally at night, to transmit its position and request new instructions from U-boat command, the convoy escort vessels would

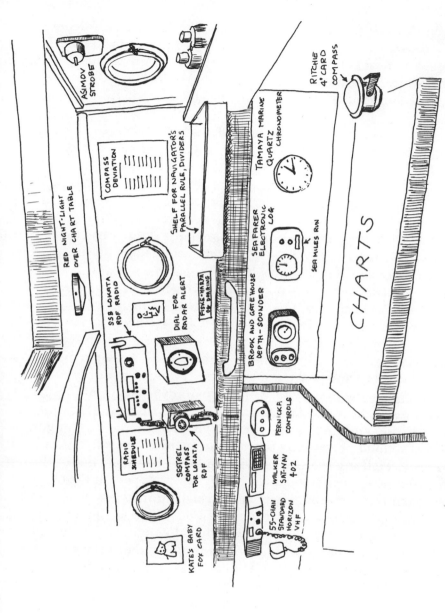

The navigator's station on Johan: what it takes to survive Cat-and-Mouse.

swing Huff/Duff to take a bearing on the radio transmissions. Then they would stalk down the bearing and attempt to nail the surfaced U-boat before it could sink any more ships. Some Huff/ Duff operators became so skilled they could tell when a U-boat had only just surfaced from the timbre of signals sent through wet aerials.

Now, on the night of June 2–3, 1984, it was the mice who had the equipment and we were striving mightily to stay out of the clutches of the big blind cats charging in from every angle. Most OSTAR boats possessed a form of radar alert that beeped if it detected incoming radar signals. The instruments, made by Loka-tor and about the size of a shoe brush, were very sensitive. But to discover the *bearing* of the incoming signal, the skipper had to scan the horizon with the device as if he were using a hand-bearing or an RDF compass. The big problem was that radar transmissions are intermittent and it was no easy trick to get a bearing, particularly from the deck of a boat that was itself bouncing.

Johan had the only Pernicka in the OSTAR fleet. It not only responded to incoming signals with a beep loud enough to awaken me; it also indicated, by means of lights on a circular dial, the approximate bearing of the transmission. Thus, on a murky night I could determine exactly in which quadrant to begin my visual search. More, the Pernicka had two ranges: these were short (one mile or less) and long (up to twenty-five miles). On a busy night like this I could be tracking three, four, or even five ships simultaneously. Half my time was spent standing, shoulders out of the hatch, scanning the horizon. The other half was spent at the chart table attempting to coordinate this visual information with the data coming in from the instruments. The whole navigating station was illuminated in a red night-light so I would not be blinded on returning to the deck. If I was unsure of the distance of a particularly menacing cat, I could flip the Pernicka to short range. If her transmission still came up on the dial, I'd know that she had penetrated *Johan*'s inner circle and that it was time for me to declare Panic Stations. So far, *X-Ray Yankee Delta* was the only ship to come that close, but I was carefully tracking two other vessels that seemed to be within the five-mile range.

Since these were busy waters, the only way *Johan* could elicit a response from a big ship on Channel 16 was by transmitting her precise location down to the nearest quarter mile. To do this, *Johan*, by Sat-Nav and other means, had to maintain an extremely accurate running plot of her position. But even presenting *Johan*'s position to within 100 yards did not always assure a prompt response, since the big ship itself—travelling at twenty knots plus—often did not know its own position at that precise instant. This may have explained X-Ray Yankee Delta's failure to respond to my earlier calls.

Perhaps I have already given too much detail about the deadly game that all the OSTAR boats were playing on their first night at sea. But readers who might one day find themselves in this same spot should know that Cat-and-Mouse has some important postgraduate refinements. First, watch out for warships. They are seldom well-lighted and their radar is so powerful that it can throw your detection equipment for a loop. The previous summer a new Royal Navy frigate, back from the Falklands, beeped my Pernicka even though the instrument was totally switched off. Second, appreciate the use of low-power one-watt transmission on your VHF. If a ship is coming close and is not answering your regular calls on twenty-five watts, switch to one watt and say, "I'm transmitting on one watt. If you can hear this signal, you're IT . . ." This approach had been surprisingly effective on *Johan*. Last, be prepared to apply the Principle of Penumbral Safety. It goes like this. The big cats are mortally scared of colliding with each other; they can see each other visually and on radar, and it behooves each big cat to give all the other big cats a wide berth. Therefore, the little mice can discover an element of safety by sailing close—but not too close!—to the big cats that are not heading straight for them.

It was past midnight, and I could feel the fatigue pulling like a woolen fog at the edges of my mind. I had been up since 5 A.M. and had spent most of the day sailing the boat hard in half a gale of wind. Perhaps I should use a stay-awake pill, but they'd given me bad aftereffects, including double vision, when I used them in the past. There was a pause in traffic and I went below to heat a can of thick pea soup. After a while I flipped on the radio and got light orchestral music from a station in Cornwall. I sipped the soup briefly; then, holding the mug in my right hand, clambered on to the engine box for another quick look around the horizon. As I did so, an announcer interrupted the music.

"OSTAR competitor June Clarke, the thirty-three-year-old British skipper of *Batchelor's Sweet Pea*, was rescued by the St. Mary's lifeboat last night when her trimaran capsized in gale-force

winds off the Scilly Islands. Another OSTAR competitor, believed
to be a large French multihull, has been struck and dismasted by
a cargo vessel. She is reported to be returning to Falmouth under
jury rig."

Bonk. Back to light music. I sat down for a moment, stunned.
I had been next to June in the skipper's conference. I thought
about her bandaged hand. *Johan* was moving along at only three
knots. How could they have "gale-force winds" only thirty miles
away in the Scillies? I climbed up the companionway and put my
head through the hatch again, still clasping my mug of soup. If
anything, the wind seemed to be moderating. Should it drop any
more, *Johan* would lose her ability to avoid an impending collision.
From midnight on, the tide would be flooding and it might even
push *Johan* back into the worst of the shipping. Who, I wondered,
was the French multihull? After the soup, I brewed a big mug of
black coffee and continued the task of working *Johan* through the
forest of moving Christmas trees. First light was at 5 A.M. or there-
abouts. Then the big ships would be able to see *Johan* and she
would be safe. Four more hours to go. Must stay awake.

Another bulletin come over the radio. Apparently June Clarke
had been in the water several hours before she was rescued. *Lada
Poch*, a 54-foot catamaran, had been rammed ten miles south of the
major shipping lane earlier in the evening. Loick Peyron, her
twenty-four-year-old professional skipper, suffered no serious injury in the accident. News of these early casualties helped push
back the mists of sleep for a while. At 1:30 A.M., the wind dropped
away altogether, leaving *Johan* slating about aimlessly in the flat
swells. Now the boat had no ability to maneuver, short of breaking
the seal on the engine and quitting the race. It began to rain. I put
on my oilskins and listened to the cold drops clicking down on my
sou'wester.

At about 2 A.M., a few puffs of wind came in from the west, and
I began to tack. The wind became flukey again. Half an hour later
I awoke to find myself sitting in the cockpit. It was raining hard
and the boat was heading due east back to Plymouth. What a fine
start it had been! Now *Johan* seemed keen to try it again. I looked
around, the rain smudging my spectacles. Astern, about half a mile
away, were the lights of a steamship. I grabbed the binoculars, but
they, too, were fogged up. I wiped them off with my thumb and
looked again. Red and green, straight up. The ship was heading
right for *Johan*. I felt as if I was gazing down the barrel of a large

cannon. Ready about, hard-a-lee. *Johan* began to turn. Then, in the faint wind, she lost momentum. I could hear the yankee flapping out on the bowsprit, but it was too dark to see precisely what it was doing. I decided *Johan* must be locked "in irons," unable to move either to the port or the starboard tack. I hooked up my safety line and clambered forward. I pulled the yankee out to port in an attempt to push *Johan*'s head round, but nothing happened. Then the sail jerked sharply against my hand and turned my thumbnail. I scrambled back to the cockpit and tried to raise the vessel on Channel 16. But I had been steering—and dozing—in the cockpit for too long and my plot of *Johan*'s position was not precise. I called again on one watt with the closing injunction, "If you can hear this, you're IT." Still no answer. The ship continued straight for me.

What now? The best move in the final stages of a run-down, I'd heard, was to place the boat end on. This increased the chances of a glancing blow or, better still, being thrown aside altogether by the ship's bow wave. But there was still the engine. Break the seal. By now I could see all the details of the ship's brightly illuminated superstructure rising up in a single column above me. I heard the engines pounding and the rustling skirts of the bow wave. Why can't they see me? *Johan*'s engine started with a whine and a thump. I fumbled in my oilskin pocket for the pliers to jerk off the seal. As I did so, the steamer turned imperceptibly to starboard, then swung away more sharply. Finally, someone on the bridge had woken up. The yankee was aback again. I dropped the pliers and ran forward to untangle it. As I did this, a searchlight snapped on and rivetted *Johan* in a beam of colorless light. I turned away, blinded, feeling as if I'd been thrust into another dimension. Before I could get back to the cockpit the searchlight snapped off and *Johan* was thrown on to her beam ends in the wake. I hung on the rail, cursing the freighter. The men on her bridge were doubtless cursing me in similar terms. The ship pounded off into the night and in a while her lights coalesced to resemble all the other Christmas trees. It was still raining hard.

Soon my anger at the ship began to turn back on itself. The near miss was, I realized, my own fault. I'd dozed off. I'd failed to keep a precise reckoning of my position. Moreover, I had simply FORGOTTEN that I had a strobe at the masthead waiting to be used. If my father had heard of such an episode, he would have made a wry face. And such fumbling would have earned me the mock-humorous contempt of Mr. Keeble, the last of the ancient mariners. In 1938, my father had acquired an old 44-foot yawl named *Melanie*, and took on a retired Thames bargeman as a paid hand. Nelson Keeble hailed from Pin Mill on the Orwell River and he became a second godfather to me. He taught me how to tie a Turk's head, sew in a bolt rope, and how to scull a dinghy with one oar. At age twelve I frequently made a hash of things. The lead-line mysteriously got wound around the forestay. *Melanie*'s spotless decks would somehow acquire a slathering of rich Suffolk river mud, and sailing dinghies would scrape chunks off her gleaming enamel topsides.

"I reckon you done a right fine job on my starboard rail," Keeble would remonstrate at the end of the day, as we sat in *Melanie*'s saloon.

"Sorry, Nelson."

The crinkled eyes would roll up to heaven and there would be a deadly silence, broken only by the sound of my father puffing his pipe in the corner. Not only had I caused Keeble a lot of extra work on *Melanie*'s topsides; my sloppy boatwork had shamed him in front of the professional hands on the other yachts. Now, nearly forty years later, I sucked my wretched thumb in *Johan*'s cockpit and felt the full weight of Keeble's censure upon me. My elaborate anticollision system clearly had some very human loopholes. Only luck had saved me from being rammed and ploughed under by the freighter. Luck was the antithesis of good seamanship. After

Nelson Keeble, formerly mate of the Thames Barge, Memory.

brooding for a while, I went below, worked an RDF bearing on the Lizard beacon, and tried to coax a new fix out of the Sat-Nav. It was now 3:05 A.M. Only two hours or so to daylight. Must stay awake. The old bargemen had a trick or two for that as well. I'd sing a song.

"Ten Green Bottles" echoed out, tunelessly, across the sullen black swells. Did my fellow competitors know the same trick? I thought of them all around me in the darkness—baritones, bases, tenors. What songs, I wondered, were they singing? Perhaps we could assemble a chorus—shades of Renfrew of the Royal Mounted—that could boom its way across the Atlantic.

Was that five green bottles last time around, or four? The wind seemed to be coming from every direction now. The pink rose of the compass was twirling around in its bowl and I was becoming disorientated. At 3:40 A.M. the Sat-Nav produced another fix that put *Johan* due south of Land's End. Either the machine was on the blink or the flood tide was shoving *Johan* backwards!

I continued to curse myself for the near miss with the freighter. But maybe it wasn't just my seamanship that was at fault. How could any one person be expected to keep a lookout, tend the sails, operate a radio, keep an immaculate navigational plot, steer a course, heat up soup, and avoid collision—all without any sleep? It was an impossible task. The simple truth was that no real seaman would be out here, alone, slatting around in one of the world's busiest ship lanes. Despite my fatigue, it did not take me long to move to a larger premise. Perhaps the whole enterprise of a single-handed race across the North Atlantic was cockeyed. The OSTAR, for all its regulations and inspections, was inherently unseamanlike. My worst move was not in mangling my navigation or in forgetting to use my strobe light; it was, quite simply, in signing up for this race in the first place.

I QUIT.

I quit, right here at 49°33.4'N, 05°29.6'W. And I want my money back. But that would not get me out of my present predicament. Unlike a tennis player, a singlehanded sailor could not just throw down his racket and go for a shower and a cold drink. Even if I had stepped out of the race, I was still on *Johan*, trying somehow to muddle my way through this unending night. I still had to stay awake and keep my boat away from the steamers. I continued to labor away at the chart table. The Sat-Nav was mute. I tried first to get an RDF bearing on the Scillies beacon, and then another from the station on Ushant in northern France. Every few minutes I'd pop up through the hatch to see how the Christmas trees were doing. My three RDF bearings—Lizard, Scillies, and Ushant—when drawn out in pencil across the chart made a triangle, or "cocked hat," about twelve miles across and twenty miles high! I started to shoot the bearings all over again . . . then I noticed, to my surprise, that I was chuckling. I snapped the RDF compass back into its bracket on the bulkhead. Trying to navigate like this was pointless. Indeed, this whole North Atlantic enterprise seemed kind of pointless. And now its very pointlessness began to appeal to me. I laughed some more. Perhaps, after all, it *was* my kind of caper. Wasn't there an element, in all OSTAR skippers, of Don Quixote charging his windmills? Why were we trying so hard to sail the Atlantic, when a hundred jumbo jets left Heathrow for New York every day?

We were, truly, the Lords of La Mancha. We had our faithful steeds, absurdly slow by jet-age standards, and come what may we'd ride them into the setting sun. Instead of complaining about the winds and the steamer traffic, I should welcome each new hardship as a chance to display even more knightly virtue. Soon, I struck up a new song.

> I am Don Quixote, the Lord of La Mancha,
> My destiny calls and I go,
> And the wild winds of fortune will carry me onward,
> Oh whither so ever they blow.

That was all I could remember, so I sang the words over and over. The rain rattled on my sou'wester. *Johan* tacked, and tacked again, and was pushed ever further backwards by the flooding tide. We floundered past several more Christmas trees. I went through several more mugs of hot coffee. Then the rain ceased and the sails flapped. A breeze from the west! But, of course, that was precisely the direction in which the gallant knights were trying to go. I could hear it coming across the surface of the water in the dark. Trim those sheets! I peered forward and could just make out the shape of the yankee. Soon *Johan* was making three knots on a course just a little west of south. At least that would take me away from the shipping. No rosy-fingered dawn ushered in this new day; instead sea, sky, and the flesh of my hands turned with exquisite stealth from black to dark grey and then to the hue of sallow oatmeal. The horizon was empty. The ships had gone, to yield up a scene of chilly desolation.

At last, I could eat and sleep. I set the Aries vane gear and went below. Too tired to cook, I broke a chunk of stale bread off the corner of the loaf and climbed into the lee berth. When I awoke two hours later, I was still clasping the bread in my right hand. I climbed slowly out of the bunk, smeared my bread with half an inch of English marmalade. Then I gulped it down and decided what to cook for breakfast. The longest night was over.

7

Going for the Gold

*I*t was the evening of June 6, four days after the start. A gale was blowing with mounting ferocity out of the northwest, and *Johan* was smashing her way, close-hauled on the starboard tack, through mountainous grey seas that must have come into this world somewhere near the coast of Greenland. On every fourth wave, for reasons known only to herself, she ploughed straight through the rising crest. In a magnificent explosion, the spray shot thirty or forty feet out from her bow. On the backstay behind my head the new ensign crackled like a shorted power line; already its corners were fraying out. I glanced up, in the fading light, at the double-reefed main and yankee. Perhaps I should reef some more. But this was *Johan*'s chance, her one slender shot at the gold, and while other craft might falter, she plunged on at six and one-half knots on a course of west-by-south—deadeye across the Grand Banks for Nantucket Lightvessel, now lying 2,532 nautical miles away round the globe.

Down below in the cabin the high-pitched howl of the wind seemed even more menacing than it did on deck. Everything—charts, bedding, clothes—was soggy with seawater. The big waves, when they came, struck the hull with the thud of eight-inch logs, end on. *Johan* would stagger, and endure a slight pause before five tons of water came crumping down on to the deck. As it did so, both hatches would shoot a showerbath of water into the cabin. Then *Johan* shook herself, climbed back on to her feet and—great heart—resumed her rush to the west.

Crash, stagger, pause . . . crump. The brutal litany had repeated itself without surcease for more than two days now. This might

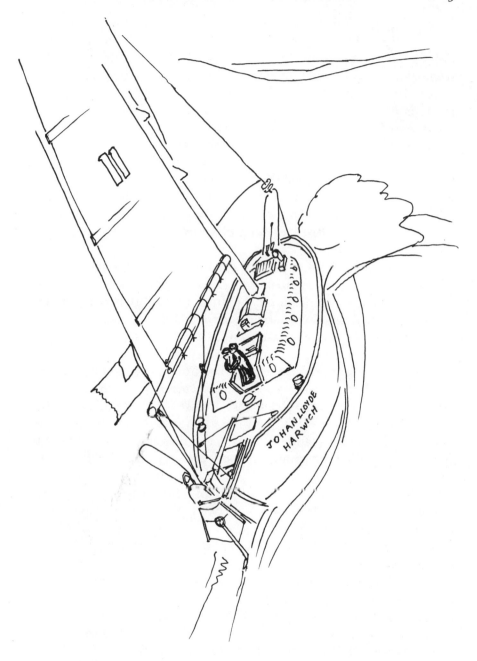

Crash, stagger, pause . . . crump: Johan *goes for the gold.*

be a competitive event but how much more of this pounding, I wondered, could even *Johan*'s stout hull take? Closer to home, how much more of this could her skipper take? Tonight, though feeling somewhat seasick, I was determined to pull in the 10:45 P.M. World Sports Roundup from the BBC.

This is London calling.

When the reedy-voiced announcer finally made his debut, it became clear that racing sailboats singlehanded across the Atlantic was hardly the most popular activity in the world. First up were the cricket scores. Yorkshire beat Warwickshire by six wickets declared. Then came a minor tennis tournament in Paris. A German soccer player was toying with the idea of switching teams. Then, finally, the Observer Singlehanded all in the last few seconds.

"Severe gales blowing in from the northwest have forced a total of fourteen boats to withdraw from the Observer Singlehanded Transatlantic Race," declared the announcer. "It is believed that more withdrawals may be expected shortly." Then came the details. *Alliance Kaypro*, the last competitor to be sighted by *Johan*, was dismasted and under tow to the Scilly Islands. McCoy's *Fury* had lost her rudder. *Refugee* had retired due to the skipper's injury. Dr. Christopher Smith's *Race Against Poverty* was damaged and returning to Plymouth. *Rizla* and *Marsden*, two trimarans, were both dismasted. The storm had knocked out the steering gear of the powerful *Tyfoon*, and she was returning slowly to Falmouth. *Quailo* had pulled a topmast shroud and returned to Plymouth. David White's mighty *Gladiator* was also under repair in Plymouth, but preparing to come out again. Bob Lengyel, the polar navigator, had also been driven back to Falmouth with steering problems.

As the casualty list lengthened, I began to wonder who was left in the race. Then I was struck by a disquieting thought. Perhaps the race had been cancelled, leaving me and *Johan* to struggle on against the North Atlantic alone, the single boat still doggedly attempting to reach Newport. I subsequently learned that many skippers, from time to time, experienced this feeling of betrayal, of having been left to continue the race alone. Some even felt that they had been the victims of a massive practical joke: We'll fake the inspection, the anxious "fellow skippers," the start. What a laugh! Just get him out there, then we'll mosey on back to the club bar.

I switched off the radio, and *Johan* plunged on into the night. There were worse things than a race against oneself. I could knock a few days off David White's time in *Catapha*. Then I began to think of the names that had *not* been on the casualty list. Warren Luhrs, Tonizzo, Tabarly . . . Peter Phillips. Where were they now? Doubtless somewhere in the murk up ahead and emphatically still racing. I began to think about the smaller boats. How was this weather affecting Bill Homewood in *British Airways II?* The little tri was one sixth the weight of *Johan*. Was she skittering across the waves like a bird or was she digging in? Was the canvas screen over the cabin door strong enough to repel these seas, or was Homewood up to his neck in water? I discovered this was no abstract concern, like the kind one might feel about the bond market. This was real anxiety. How *was* Bill Homewood? How was Mike Richey in little *Jester*, and how was Vasil Kurtev in his home-made *Nord?* Though *Johan* might be jumping all over the place, she was, by small-boat standards, very comfortable.

In one sense I was feeling feisty. This was *Johan*'s cue. But the storm was clearly taking its toll, both on me and on the boat. My first long night in the shipping lanes had acclimated me to a new plateau of danger. Yesterday's dire peril became today's routine. Now the continual pounding was acclimating me to a new level of violence. Primitive conditions, I noted, were reducing much of my existence to that of a brute. Gone were the loose muscles of the office. Haul that halyard, pull that winch, douse that sail, pump that bilge. The only answer to a quick violent event became a quick violent response. A fifty-pound sailbag popped out of the fo'c'sle like a mugger and was promptly hurled back from whence it came, with interest. A sheet jammed on a winch. Bam, bam, bam with the heavy heel of a seaboot, and it was free. Once, when I was reefing, the mainsail topping lift, carrying the full weight of the boom, broke with a twang. Without thought, I found myself lifting the spar, with its violently flapping sail, out of the sea and jamming it bodily into the boom gallows. Brute strength and bloody ignorance. Such a retrieval might have taken the combined strength of three persons on a normal cruise. Now, I did it alone promptly and without reflection.

Johan's violent motion had long since reduced the business of cooking—and eating—to the most rudimentary level. Just making a mug of coffee was as complicated as trying to tie a shoelace with one hand. I found the only way to get the ingredients—powdered coffee, powdered milk (liquid spills!), lump sugar, shot of Navy rum, and hot water—into the mug was to turn myself into a kind of human pendulum. Counteracting the movements of the boat necessitated jamming my hip against the galley bulkhead and swaying like a shadow boxer from the waist up. For days now I had gobbled all my food out of the same pan. Washing up was out (the water would be all over the cabin in five seconds); I'd wipe it out with a paper towel after each meal. The results were nourishing but what my five-year-old Kate would call "yucky." Canned fruit was poured on to the remains of canned spaghetti, which itself had ridden on a bed of oatmeal garnished with corned beef stew. This last was the great staple of life on *Johan*. It consisted of a can of corned beef, a can of stewed tomatoes, a can of boiled potatoes, and half a chopped onion, all thrown into a saucepan with a bit of curry powder and simmered for ten minutes. A dash of red wine will liven up the taste on the second day.

But I don't wish to mislead. Life at this minimalist level had, for me at any rate, a certain charm. My real worries concerned the boat. Steering gears, as the casualty list demonstrated, were vulnerable. This piece of equipment was the closest thing a single-hander had to a crew. Night and day, while he rested or performed chores about the boat, it adjusted the helm so the boat continued to point at the same angle to the wind. Some steering gears used electrical power, but most long distance gears used the force of the boat passing through the water to push her tiller—through a complex system of cogs and levers—to stay on course. *Johan*'s Aries vane gear was one of the simplest and strongest on the market. Yet under the continual battering of the storm, it had begun to emit a loud creaking noise, and I was concerned about what would happen if its rope guy lines broke under the strain.

Two other problems gnawed at my mind. The Sat-Nav, a radio computer that gave a very precise position fix by taking line-of-sight transmissions off circling U.S. Navy satellites, had been acting strangely since that first night in the English Channel. The satellites would pass over head every four hours or so, and each time, the Sat-Nav locked on to them. But then, after computing its data for ten or fifteen minutes, it spat out the words "No Fix, No Fix" on its little screen. After a careful study of the operating manual, I got the Sat-Nav to test itself and discovered that for most of the time its so-called byte rate was running too low. Simply put, it lacked the capacity to assimilate incoming data from the satellite at a fast enough rate. The byte rate should be 101.7, but my instrument generally displayed a rate in the low 90s.

I began to monitor the rate closely. It went up to over 101 after the Sat-Nav warmed up, for about thirty-five minutes. Then it began to sink away again. If I was lucky enough to snare a satellite in those thirty-five minutes, then I'd get a proper fix, accurate to within 200 yards of my actual position. If the satellite came up outside this thirty-five-minute window, then it'd give me another "No Fix." Opening the thirty-five-minutes window so that it would snare one of the circling satellites was a difficult, but not impossible, task. It did, however, become even more challenging when the window, perhaps due to the hammering it was getting in the storm, began to close, first to thirty-one minutes and then down to twenty-seven. It looked as if the rest of the trip would be made on Walter's Husun sextant; the only problem with that, though, was that I had not seen sun, moon, or star for several days now.

Johan's other big problem was also electrical in nature. I could not start the Volvo diesel to charge my batteries without opening the valve on the engine's exhaust pipe. Yet once this valve was open there was a strong chance that the heavy seas would strike the stern and force their way into the cylinders of the engine to produce a condition known as hydrolock. This was how Lloyd Hircock's engine on *Mustache* had come to be frozen solid during his voyage over from Canada. Repair, requiring total dismemberment of the engine, was impossible at sea. *Johan*'s instruments drew negligable power, but her traditional red/green/white night running light at the masthead flattened a Diehard after three nights; then it would have to be recharged on the Volvo alternator. One Diehard was already flat, and by now the second one was well drained. Which, I wondered, was the greater risk? Should I sail through the nights without lights, thereby sharply increasing the chances of a rundown? Or should I open the exhaust valve and attempt to recharge the batteries, thereby increasing the risk of hydrolock and the possibility of no electrical power at all for the rest of the voyage?

There seemed to be no easy solution. In many ways it was not unlike the quandary encountered by U-boats in this part of the Atlantic not long ago. When they ran submerged, they were relatively safe. But then they were also using electrical power, thereby hastening the hour when they must rise to the surface—with its perils—and recharge their batteries by running their diesels. Judging by the casualty rate, this was a dilemma that U-boat commanders had difficulty resolving. Now I had the same problem. Stay down and go flat, or come up and risk blowing my engine.

* * * * *

The storm was lowering my physical horizons. The cockpit and the deck were uninhabitable unless one had to perform an essential chore. Just to open the hatch for a shufty was an invitation to a soaking. After the first couple of days I spent most of my time in my bunk trying to keep my sleeping bag out of the worst drips. Sometimes, in sleep, I would escape the pounding. But sometimes sleep brought its own special fears. Once I dreamed that a big column of inch-long pink bugs was crawling up my left arm. I tried to brush them off but someone behind me said, "Careful, they're good to eat." I tried to be more gentle and save the little

Going through the bottleneck out of a bad dream into a real nightmare.

creatures. But the last bug in the line turned brown and sunk its teeth into the finger of my left hand. I flailed at it, but it hung on. Then I looked down and perceived a group of giant ants gnawing at the open wound. I slapped and pounded at them with my other hand, but to little avail. Then I concluded that this horror was too exotic to be credible; I must be dreaming. I called to Susan to help awaken me. "Help me! Susan, help me!" I heard the words from a long way off and I could only articulate them with the greatest difficulty. "Help me."

Susan was clad in a white nightgown and she tried to shake me awake. I struggled, too, but instead of surfacing in the big bed at home, I was pulled through some perceptual bottleneck into the cabin of a small boat fighting for her life in a North Atlantic storm. I had been hauled out of a bad dream and thrust into the middle of a real nightmare. Overall lay the high-pitched howl of the wind. A wave hit with a mighty crash, and the cutlery in the galley drawer banged upward. But it was knocked back down again by the crump of water on deck. I looked down at my left hand. There were no bugs gnawing it, but the salt damp had kept the abrasions open after my battle with the anchor chain in Cawsand Bay. Crash, stagger, pause . . . crump.

On the first night, while drifting around in the ship lanes, I had resolutely quit the Observer Singlehanded and signed my separate peace with the Atlantic. Now, here I was five days later racing my head off. But, as everyone asked so often in Plymouth, what was my strategy? I forced myself to think this through. The weather and my determination to keep on racing had somehow pushed me on to the Rhumb-Line or Heavy Duty route that would take *Johan* through the center of the ice, fog, trawlers, and the Grand Banks. The more I thought about it the more I realized that, frankly, the Banks scared the daylights out of me. It was not just the physical peril. It was the idea of the shoal water lumped up so close to the surface so far from the land; those shoals seemed like a sunken continent, an icy fog-flocked Atlantis of the north. That was the horror. Yet, for the last few days, as if I were in the grip of some outside force, I had found myself heading pell-mell right for them.

By first light of June 7 the wind was even stronger, and *Johan's* speed was up to seven and one-half knots, sometimes touching eight. I lay in my bunk. This was just too much wind. I was still trying to summon the will power to look out the hatch when *Johan's* movements suddenly became quieter, as if she were holding her breath. What had happened? Two possibilities passed in quick succession across my mind. *Johan* had suddenly passed into the lee of a big ship. But there had been no radar beep. It must be something else. *Johan* had been upwinded by a huge iceberg! In one movement I vaulted over the table and shoved back the main hatch, expecting the boat to strike momentarily. When I looked out I saw the mainsail still pulling nicely. I stared to windward. There was no ship and no iceberg. The yankee, instead of being reefed down to eighty square feet, had unrolled its full 300 square feet and was flapping furiously on a loosed sheet. The entry in *Johan*'s log explains what happened next: "5:15 A.M. The drum rope on yankee has parted and sail was totally unfurled in the blast. Went on bowsprit with Marlow heaving line and wound it circle by circle round drum. Then I hitched old anchor trip line to it and led it aft. Wonder of wonders, when I pulled, the sail furled. Sheeting in yankee was tough. This storm is blowing harder than ever and I am soaked to the bone."

This incident, with the seas breaking over me as I worked on the end of the bowsprit, combined with the shocking thought that I was about to hit an iceberg, brought about a major switch in *Johan*'s itinerary. No more Heavy Duty. I'd ease the sheets and run off to the south. I'd find some sunshine there for the Husun sextant, and maybe a few dolphins under the bow. And I'd be able to dry out and start the charging motor. This was, I suppose, yet another defection on my part. But it was not too serious a one. The scholars in our ranks—Jack Hunt, Alan Wynne-Thomas—had often noted that the Observer Singlehanded, with all its quirks, was a magnificent metaphor for life. I agreed. It was fine with me if Warren Luhrs and Luis Tonizzo went hell-for-leather down the rhumbline. But my metaphor was becoming more complicated. Yes, I was going for the gold. But my gold had to include just a little bit of sunshine.

8

Ghosts

The dolphins came every evening. Just when the dusk made it hard for me to read a book in my bunk below decks a sharp, high-pitched summons—eeek, eeek—resounded through the hull of the boat.

"They're here, they're here!" I shouted in wonder. Then I'd pull myself out of the berth and clamber through the hatch to behold five, ten, or maybe as many as two dozen streamlined bodies prancing through the waves around *Johan*'s bow. The dolphins were between five and seven feet long and they had green upper bodies and buff-colored bellies. They were of the commonest bottlenose variety, and they never failed to fill me with a sense of exhilaration. Was it, I wondered, just the sight of another living thing in this rather empty universe? Or was there a more profound connection between us? The stories were prolific and true. Dolphins had defended swimmers from sharks on numerous occasions. They had guided lifeboats safely to land and they had, by creating an immense fuss in the water, helped steer lone voyagers away from unmarked reefs.

I quickly hooked up my safety harness and went to the bow of the boat. Here I could count them—no easy task with such a spritely crew—and they could see me. Many zoomed, with a snort, from the side of one wave into the side of the next far too swiftly for a camera to be raised and clicked. Others skimmed along in the bow wave, rolling up an eye to examine me where I stood on the stemhead.

"Hi guys," I said softly, careful to make no sudden move. "How was *your* day?" I wondered if this could be the same crowd that visited me this morning and the previous evening. Hard to tell. Once I noticed a bottlenose with a large scratch down her left side. I looked carefully for her each succeeding evening, but so far I had not spotted her again. When I'd made my count I generally returned to the cockpit to watch the sport. I was lucky if it lasted ten minutes. On some undetected signal there would be a sudden SWISH and the sea became empty. The sense of loss was palpable. "See you tomorrow, guys," I said a little wistfully. Then I'd go below, pour myself a gin-and-lime gimlet and fill in my report card on the dolphins.

Cambridge University had commissioned all OSTAR skippers to help with a study of whales and dolphins by logging the time, navigational position, and the quantity of all sightings. The experts at the university had given each competitor a number of sighting forms and a big chart for identification purposes. I undertook the task with relish. The institution was—sort of—my alma mater. Thirty years before, I'd been a mechanical science student at Pembroke College. Then one morning, as I nursed a colossal hangover, I had been told my presence at the university was no longer desired. I had, in the classic phrase, been "sent down." Now the jolly old alma mater wanted me to track cetaceans out upon the Atlantic. And why not? If they hadn't broadened my horizons I'd probably have become by now a well-groomed demigod in the bowel of the BBC.

Johan had been heading due west in tropical sunshine for close to a week now. She was well below the 45th parallel, and a warm breeze from the south pushed her along under cloudless skies through waves of the clearest blue. On a typical day I'd awaken at the first hint of dawn. My initial move was to reach for the flashlight on the shelf above me and shine it up at the telltale compass bolted to the roof of the cabin overhead. Was *Johan* on course? If she was, I'd generally lean back for another five minutes before blowing out the kerosene nightlight over the saloon table and pulling on my old blue carpet slippers, now becoming slightly mildewed. I went to the navigator's table and switched off the masthead running lights and the radar alert system. Then I'd climb up on to the engine box, push back the main hatch, and check the horizon and then the sails.

Perhaps the boat had drifted five or ten degrees off her course in the night. Without leaving the warmth of the hatch I could twitch on two light lines and realign the Aries vane gear. Then I returned below, filled the coffee pot—no problem in these easy seas —and put it on the gimballed gas burner. Next, I read the electronic log. If I was feeling competitive, I compared it to the previous day's total. The figures for the last few days read 95, 115, 124, 116, 104—modest by multihull standards, but a source of pride to the monohull man.

After reading the log, I took my coffee, now laced with rum, back to my bunk and enjoyed the ritual of reading a page or two of the London *Telegraph* or Plymouth's *Western Morning News*. I had read everything in every paper three or four times by now, but the act of leafing through the pages over a cup of hot coffee helped me get a fix on the day.

Breakfast was generally served in the same big white mug that held the coffee. It consisted of a can of fruit cocktail, bought the previous year at *Johan*'s starting point in upstate New York, covered with a thin topping of Alpen breakfast food. The black cardboard package declared that its contents had been chosen "By Appointment" to several English kings and queens. Most mornings I relished the idea of royal jaws crunching down on the same nuts and brans that had come to grace my own table. This very box could have been their box, and their box could have been mine.

The imperial-pint white mug was then wiped out with a paper towel and placed upside down on the neck of the rum bottle in the bread locker; it used to go on a brass hook over the dishes, but the constant movement of the boat had caused the hook to wear a black groove in the mug's handle.

Mornings in these latitudes were generally reserved for chores. Though the sun shone I always donned an oilskin (for that stray wave) and a safety harness before going on deck to tinker with sheets and walk about checking *Johan*'s running and standing rigging for chafe or breakage. I routinely checked the lashings on Blagdon's Oar, lying along the starboard rail, and then started the Volvo for a two-hour charging session on Batteries 2 and 3. I calculated that I must charge one hour for every two hours' use of the masthead lights. The bilge pump in the cockpit had been making strange sucking noises over the last three days. I got my tools and tried to take it apart but the Avon rubber dinghy crammed into the lazaret made it very hard to reach. Today, I could not be bothered to haul the dinghy out and I restowed the tools down below. Then I took Walter's sextant out of its box and returned with it to the deck. The Sat-Nav had by now whittled its

time-window down to a space of about twenty minutes. To con-
serve whatever life might be left in it for emergencies, I had been
navigating exclusively by sextant.

As a young teenager taking sunsights with my father, I had
always approached the precious instrument with trepidation. The
measurements and the calculations, to my thirteen-year-old mind,
were numbing and prone to ghastly error. I had also been apprehensive that I might drop or somehow mishandle the instrument.
My father, however, seemed impervious to the danger. Sometimes
he would steady the Husan when I was vainly looking for the sun
by putting his hands over my own chubby paws. All too often,
even though *Melanie* was obviously off Gunfleet Sands or the Kent-
ish Knock, I'd end up locating her somewhere to the east of Ran-
goon.

On this voyage it was my custom to perch in *Johan*'s hatchway,
stopwatch on a string round my neck, and take four shots of the
morning sun. Later, in the afternoon, I'd take four more and do
the figuring for the day's fix then. Now that I was in the swing of
things, I had come to see that accurate, no-frills celestial navigation
was a whole lot simpler than most of the instruction books—and
my childish labors—led me to imagine. When the Walker Sat-Nav
was not sulking, it took up to thirty minutes from first locking onto
a satellite to produce a fix. I discovered, when my pencil was hot,
that I could shoot and compute a dead accurate line-of-position
with *H.O.249 Tables* in four minutes flat. Many of my fellow skippers, I was sure, could do it even faster.

The whole process was really just a question of timing. I liked
to imagine the globes that spin across the TV screen just before
the evening network news. I was particularly interested in the
sharp line that divides night from day. If I used a stopwatch to
record the exact moment the sun touched the horizon then I knew,
at that precise moment, I was somewhere on that line. *Johan* was
now travelling almost due west, day after day, along the 44th
parallel of latitude. If I snapped the precise moment, in Greenwich
Mean Time (called "Zulu time" by most OSTAR skippers), when
the sun touched the horizon I could check the almanac to find out
just how far I had moved toward Newport since the previous
sunset. The shadow of night spins across the globe, click goes the
stopwatch, and now it's time for Dan Rather.

Simple.

Most of the complexity of the navigation texts and instructional videocasettes arose from their concern for fine-tuning. They made a great fuss about such details, and seemed to write about them in the same weighty tones they'd used to explain the primary issue of when, exactly, that line-of-position passed overhead. One of their favorite topics was the sextant. All this elegant device did was enable the voyager to get a line-of-position while the sun was still high in the sky. Instead of waiting for nightfall, navigators could measure the height of the sun above the horizon, time the instant at which the measurement was made, and then compute— by means of special geometric tables—where the line of the elevated sunshot must fall on the surface of the globe. That's where we are now, somewhere on that pre-sunset line that stretches across the earth almost to the poles. *Johan* happened to be bouncing due west down the 44th parallel, so her precise position became 44° N and, with the help of the sunshot, 21° 19′ W. By tomorrow it would be 44° N and 23° 10′ W.

The fine-tuning generally took the form of small adjustments. There were, it seemed, four kinds of these:

1) Adjustments for the fact that the seasons came and went. As winter turned to spring, the sun climbed higher in the sky. Its slow ascent (and subsequent descent) was precisely recorded in the Declination Tables of the nautical almanac.

2) Adjustments for the height of the observer above the surface of the water—obviously the navigator on the bridge of a supertanker viewed a more distant horizon than the navigator in the cockpit of a small sailboat.

3) Adjustments of interpolation. Most actual sunshots produced data that fell between the conditions enumerated in the *Tables*; with some thin arithmetic slicing, the navigator's exact distance from the lines in the Tables could be figured. It was these paper-thin slicings that caused most beginners grief.

4) Adjustments for slight distortions in the sextant itself, generally of the order of one tenth of a degree of arc.

Most of these hassles over fine-tuning were eliminated when the navigator took sunshots once or twice a day, day after day. By putting markers in the relevant pages of the *Tables*, he could turn to more or less the same column of figures for each succeeding day.

In the old days, all that protected a ship's officers from the scourge of mutiny was their knowledge of celestial navigation. The men of the lower deck were well aware that even if they overthrew the afterguard they would not be able to navigate the vessel across an empty ocean. Thus, even the most enlightened captains had a vested interest in making the routine of "shooting the sun" as convoluted as a Druid religious rite.

For success, a mutiny had to include an officer in its ranks. Given the sharp stratification of shipboard society, this was a difficult condition to meet, but the *Bounty* mutineers found their man in Fletcher Christian. As I worked my way each day through the columns of figures in *H.O. 249*, it occurred to me that history was packed with instances of small priesthoods—both secular and spiritual—who used their power to withhold or obscure information to benefit themselves at the expense of the community in general. The Druids of Stonehenge made a fine case in point. Their massive rings of rock were originally erected to permit the priests to predict the summer and winter solstices and the seasons in between. Farmers, anxious to plant their crops, would give the priesthood a tithe of their harvest for such information. Like a ship's captain, the Archdruid knew it was not in his interest to reveal that any farmer could produce the same information by hammering a couple of strategically placed stakes into the ground.

If the farmers became restless under the burden of all that tithing, they could be brought to heel with a magnificent reversal of cause and effect: if you don't tithe, there will be no spring. Yea, verily, you'll be lucky if the sun comes up at all tomorrow. Nowadays, the secular descendants of the Druids had become well entrenched in the learned professions and in the worlds of defense, computer software, academe, welfare services, and—as I was later to learn to my cost—even the ranks of the United States Coast Guard. The chief characteristics of these modern day Druids were a certain *gravitas* of manner, a plausible address, and an uncanny ability to insert themselves between the benefit and those to be benefited. Then the tithing began . . .

Though there was scant chance of a mutiny these days, the Druids still had a pretty good hold on the infrastructure of navigation. Each year yachtsmen paid $20 to $25 for a nautical almanac that generally contained about 100 times more data than they could conceivably need. Esoterica on items as the Weir Azimuth Table, Versines, and Log Cosines jostle alongside the Declination Tables,

which contained the only information the average celestial navigator ever needed to get out of the almanac. And even the Declination Tables, though taken to microscopic tolerances, virtually repeated themselves every four years. Here's an example. The sun's
declination on June 2 at 14.00 hours GMT for 1980 and 1984 was
given as 22°15.1′ N and 22°15.5′N, respectively. Buy four successive
years of almanacs and navigate for life; present the four volumes
to your grandchildren and even they wouldn't be far off the mark.

It tickled my fancy to think that one day an enterprising publisher was going to put together an eighty-page pamphlet contain-
ing all the information an average navigator really needs. Even the
Tide Tables could be extrapolated from year to year. It would

Finding my place in the universe.

never go out of date. Sell it for $2 a copy and put the Archdruids of the Weir Azimuth and the Versine right out of business. Perhaps it could be called "The Passage Maker" or maybe "The Sheet Anchor."

*　*　*　*　*

On an average day aboard *Johan Lloyde*, with my navigating chores out of the way, I'd begin to think about lunch. Often I'd just have a snack of Ryvita crispbread and cheese, accompanied by a can of Whitbread's ale. I'd bought three cases of the stuff, cheap, at the Co-op store in Plymouth. Now I understood why I'd got such a good deal; the beer's sale date had expired many months before. The cans were going rusty in the locker but, despite the near-tropical climate, the beer still tasted pretty good.

In the afternoons I'd either nap, read, or unhitch the Aries vane gear and, for an hour or so, steer *Johan* myself through the valleys and over the crests of the great blue North Atlantic rollers. This —even more than figuring an astronomical fix or reading the morning newspaper—served to establish my position in the natural order of the universe.

On this leg of the race I was reading *The Secret Diary of Adrian Mole, Aged 13¾* by Sue Townsend. Lloyd Hircock and I both received copies as farewell gifts from Margaret Wynne-Thomas on our last evening in Plymouth. I was also reading *Lark Rise to Candleford*, Flora Thompson's trilogy about rural life in 19th-century England. Some lone voyagers attack a single book—like Gibbon's *Decline and Fall of the Roman Empire*—and plough straight through from beginning to end. Some puritanical whisper from my past told me to finish one book before I started another. But I followed a different approach when sailing alone. When one volume slowed, or my mood changed, I'd switch to another. Sometimes, on a long voyage like this, I'd had markers going in four or five books simultaneously, enjoying each in its special way.

On a couple of occasions now, the musky odor of rotting vegetation had come to me upon the wind; I must be smelling the land of the Azores, even though the islands lay, by my best calculations, more than 300 miles off to windward. The odor was so pungent that, had I not known better, I'd have said land lay just over the horizon. Such impressions, I suspect, caused many medieval maps to be littered with flyaway islands carrying names like Antilia, Hy

Brasil, and Ventura. Of course, some had a strong root in reality. The old name for the Azores, before they were lost in the European Dark Ages, was the "Insulle Fortunate Sact. Brandanu"—the Fortunate Isles of St. Brendon. And the mythical island of Avalon, generally located off to the northwest, was probably based on some ancient sighting of the island we now call Newfoundland. I had, in fact, been intrigued by such phenomena for many years. So much so that I had named my boat in honor of the old Bristol pilot Johan Lloyde, who, I was reasonably convinced, had discovered the coast of Newfoundland eleven years before the famous voyage of Columbus. (For a detailed account of Lloyde's voyages, see Appendix A.)

Once, in the summer of 1983, I'd "sighted" an Avalon of my own. One morning at about 43°N, 32°W—the precise location is confidential—I looked out the hatch and espied a line of steep cliffs about fifteen miles to the north. Behind the cliffs, gentle slopes of what seemed to be grass led up to several considerable mountain peaks, one of which was flecked with cloud. The image was even clearer through the binoculars. Though the chart put me in 1,700 fathoms of blue water, my eye flicked instinctively to the dial of the depth-sounder. Believe me, Avalon was no hallucination. A glorious photograph of this ocean hideaway now decorates our hearth in Syracuse. Susan and I plan to retire there one day.

My return voyage of 1984 produced some mysteries of its own. I was way out of the shipping lanes now and I had seen no other vessel for quite a while. But once, at night, I'd heard the thud of propellers, which the Log says I timed at two beats a second. My radar alert did not beep and I could see no lights, even after a careful scan through the night glasses. Who, I wondered, could these night-runners be? Were they warships? Dope smugglers? Gun runners? Perhaps it was a submarine, come up for air. Or maybe even the ghost of an old U-boat, charging its batteries or struggling to get ahead of tomorrow's prey. A shiver went down my spine. This was not so far from the spot where, only last summer, Robin Knox-Johnston had been run down by a mysterious, unlighted ship.

The airwaves began to produce some ghosts of their own. The BBC's transmissions from London, now nearly 1,000 miles away, were phantasmagoric. Some of this might be due to my radio. But it was also plain that the World News, that great beacon of light in Churchill's day, had become little more than a sputtering candle. Each evening, a government bureaucrat with a toothsome voice took all the events of the day and squeezed the juice out of them. Yes, Senator Gary Hart had defeated Vice-President Walter Mondale in another primary. But the critical information, the name of the state and the percentage spread between candidates, was omitted. Yes, the striking British miners had come up with new proposals, but the proposals themselves were not described. Why, I wondered, did the BBC spend millions for a global network of correspondents to produce such pablum? Wouldn't it be cheaper to just take it off the Reuters wire? Poor old England. Imagine that somewhere there must be a school that trains announcers to speak and think like this! Anyway, who on earth, apart from a few very damp OSTAR skippers, was listening any more?

On June 12, ten days after the start of the race, a couple of tidbits floated over the ether to *Johan*. I learned that the lead boat, the 60-foot catamaran *Jet Services* skippered by the saturnine Patrick Morvan, had collided with a log and sunk. This boat held the Atlantic speed record, set earlier in the summer, of eight days and seventeen hours from Sandy Hook to the Lizard. The lead now passed to *Travacrest Seaway*, skippered by the English policeman Peter Phillips.

"Hey, hey. Go, Peter, go!" I found myself shouting in the darkened cabin. But there was more. The 60-foot trimaran *Colt Cars GB*, the only other non-French Class I multihull still left in the race, had been dismasted and abandoned 700 miles to the west of *Johan*. "This leaves," said the plummy voice from afar, "seventy-one boats still competing in OSTAR 84. That is the end of World Sports Roundup."

"Wait a minute," I said impatiently, "tell us more." But now it was time for Big Ben, twanging down a very long drainpipe, and the World News. Seventy-one still in the race! That meant in the first ten days a total of twenty-one boats had been dismasted, capsized, sunk, or withdrawn. I put some water on for coffee. That's a quarter of the fleet down the chute. The Chief Inspector's predictions were coming true. What were the boats' names? I wondered idly if they still counted *Johan* in. By now she was way off the mark, perhaps 250 miles or even 300 miles south of the rhumb-line. There was no way for me to find out if the Argos was, in fact, still transmitting. Personally, I didn't care much either way. But it did have implications for my family. If Susan or my stepmother, Barbara, called Race Headquarters, and Argos was on the blink, they'd be told I was missing. I went up on deck and stared at the flat white incubus bolted to the cockpit floor. It knew all the answers but, like Tar Baby, it warn't saying nothin'. All it wanted was a free ride back to Monsieur Argos.

Susan had, I learned later, called Newport the previous day. They told her that *Johan Lloyde* was moving along at an average speed of five and a half knots on a course of 273 True (nearly due west) and lying fifty-sixth in the fleet. But of course I did not know she knew this. For the singlehander, isolated almost totally from civilization, such gaps in information can give rise to some very sudden fluctuations in mood.

9

Azores High

*J*ohan Lloyde's lunge south into the sunshine had, I began to
realize, important strategic implications. I had been unable,
or at any rate unwilling, to face the Grand Banks and therefore the Rhumb-Line Strategy and the Bump-and-Run Strategy
had gone by the board. For a while now I had been looking hard
at the Under-Waypoint-Weld Strategy. On June 12, the waypoint,
at 45°N 35°W, lay about 300 miles west of me. I studied the U.S.
Defense Mapping Agency's pilot chart closely. It was a remarkable
document. It contained a statistical portrait, for every month of the
year, of the weather conditions that could be expected in the
North Atlantic. Winds were marked in blue, currents in green,
and icebergs and storm paths in red.

In any particular month the entire ocean, all the way from
Iceland to the coast of Venezuela, was marked off in little rectan-
gles about 200 miles wide and 300 miles high. Inside each rectangle
was a blue wind-rose that showed, by means of a circle of feathered
arrows, the average strength and duration of the breezes in that
part of the ocean based on data accumulated over the last century.
Thin green arrows also laced through each square, indicating the
direction and speed of the prevailing ocean currents. The charts
also contained a wealth of information about barometric pressures,
magnetic variations, water and air temperatures, visibility, and the
paths of cyclones.

I now studied the chart for June with great care. The squares
next to Waypoint Weld claimed that winds blew at Force 4 (eleven
to sixteen knots) out of the southwest quadrant 60 percent of the

time. Fair enough. But before she could get to Waypoint Weld, *Johan* had to nip around the edge of the Azores High. This great nub of high pressure hung like a cloak over the islands and produced a greater number of flat calms than just about any other place in the ocean. I'd heard some grim tales about this hiatus. Jack Hunt had been becalmed in the High with *Crystal Catfish* for more than a week back in 1979. And a Canadian friend of mine, Michael Davies, had once rescued the crew of an engineless ketch that had been stuck in the Azores High so long it had exhausted its provisions.

I was racing and I had no intention of replicating *Crystal Catfish*'s fate. Yet each day, as *Johan* foamed along on the starboard tack, the winds gradually began to head her. The steadily backing wind combined with some green arrows on the pilot chart called the Azores Current to push *Johan* ever more south. Between June 12 and June 14, she ran 210 miles due west while at the same time being shoved 85 miles due south. It seemed as if the boat, despite my best efforts, was being slowly sucked into a meteorological black hole. I could not, of course, use my engine to escape. By the evening of June 14, *Johan* was fewer than 200 miles north of the islands of Corvo and Flores.

These remote pinnacles, with their cloak of high pressure, were more than a meteorological oddity. Separated from the main group of the Azores, they were nearly one thousand miles from the Portuguese mainland. They were, I knew, the westernmost land in all of Europe; indeed, they were further to the west than parts of Brazil. Identified on the ancient charts simply as Insulle Fortunate Sact. Brandanu, they had been jumped around all over the eastern Atlantic and doubtless served as the remote factual base for a host of flyaway islands through the centuries. I was aware that many of the stories about St. Brendan were fanciful. But some hard facts were known. The journey from the west coast of Ireland to Corvo and Flores was only about one hundred miles longer than the distance from mainland Portugal to those islands. And, judging by the data on the pilot charts, it was a much easier sail especially with the help of the Azores Current that was now pushing *Johan* steadily south. It was known that Brendan, after a lifetime of service in the abbeys of western Ireland, set sail with a few friends for his islands in about A.D. 550. He never returned. It is commonly assumed he devoted his remaining years to a life of tropical ease out in the Atlantic. But, as I was pushed deeper into the Azores High, I began to entertain another possibility. Perhaps old "Brandanu" had tried to return to the folks in Galway and Tralee. And perhaps, given the weird Azorean weather, he remained trapped for the rest of his mortal life in the middle of nowhere! The Azores were not precisely located again until 1432, when one of Henry the Navigator's captains came upon Santa Maria, the most easterly island of the chain. Flores and Corvo, 300 miles off to the northwest, were not rediscovered until 1452. The Portuguese king promptly gave Corvo to his uncle, the Duke of Braganca, and Flores, the larger island, to a young lady-in-waiting of the queen.

I was going for Waypoint Weld. I did not intend to get pulled into all this ancient romance, no matter how colorful it might be. On the evening of June 14, I went about and put *Johan* on the port tack. In the light westerly airs, however, the best she could point was due north—a course that not only took me away from the Azores High but also away from Newport. That night, more news drifted down the BBC's sonic drainpipe. Peter Phillips, in *Travacrest Seaway*, still held the lead, but with 600 miles still to go, his nearest rival (name not given) was only fifty miles behind. Eric Tabarly was lying third in *Paul Ricard* . . . while *Johan Lloyde* was plodding along almost a thousand miles to the rear. Correction. She was not "plodding along." She was, in fact, going backwards, *away* from the line.

I switched the radio off. For a moment, in the darkness of the cabin, I felt quite dizzy. I was, I think, experiencing a kind of horizontal vertigo. Almost exactly one thousand miles separate Berlin and Moscow, as the crow flies. I was already one thousand miles behind. That, strategically speaking, was quite a lot of space.

If I stayed on this present course I'd end up in Greenland— which was, incidently, quite a bit closer than Newport, Rhode Island. I opened the windward skylight to let the gentle breeze cool off the cabin. Then I lay down on the bunk and stared at the ceiling in the semidarkness. Like many singlehanders who have been at sea for a while, I was having difficulty making a clear distinction between thinking and deciding. Sometimes, I found, it helped keep things on track if I spoke out loud.

"*Johan*'s on a crummy course . . . I hate it," I said to the empty cabin. "I'll go about the moment I get to 45° North. That should get me away from the High. But 45°N is about ninety miles away. Let me see . . ." I pointed the flashlight at the electronic log. ". . . *Johan* is doing three knots. That'd take thirty hours. Or longer, if the wind keeps fading. Hmmm. Why bother going up there anyway. It's only a line on the map. Why not just go about now? Screw the Azores High. Go for the line."

After a little more cogitation along these lines, I pulled on a shirt and went on deck to put *Johan* about. It was past midnight. In a little while she was retracing her steps, sailing into a moonlit sea on a course of 220° True. Next morning I took some sunshots, and went back to the chart table.

If I kept going on this present course I should pass about forty miles to the west of Corvo. Maybe, with a little bit of luck, I'd catch a glimpse of the island. I dug around in my bookshelves and pulled out the British Admiralty *Africa Pilot*, Volume I, that used to belong to Walter. It was dated 1910 and the prose was stern.

Ilha do Corvo, the northernmost and smallest island of Ilhas dos Acores, consists of a single extinct volcanic mountain the crater of which occupies all the north-western portion of the island; at the bottom of the crater are two lagoons, lying at an elevation of about 1,300 feet, in which there are some islets.

Volcanos! Lagoons! Shades of Tahiti, William Bligh, and Fletcher Christian. The passage of each hour took *Johan* further into the High—and almost three miles closer to the Fortunate Isles of St. Brendan. Was the old wizard up on the cliffs now, I wondered, trying to cast spells on *Johan* and draw her ever closer to his ancient paradise? I read on. Flores lay just eight miles to the south-west of Corvo. Its peaks ran up almost to 3,000 feet, so perhaps I should sight it also.

Ilha das Flores, the westernmost of Ilhas dos Acores, is generally mountainous but is cultivated. In its north-western part Morro Grande, the summit, slopes gradually northward, in the southern part numerous cascades fall down the sides of the mountains to the sea.

I read through the passages again and again, entranced. Numerous cascades fall down the sides of the mountains to the sea! It would seem that old Brendanu had even bewitched the quills of the Admiralty surveyors. But at a range of forty miles I would barely see a mountain top, let alone glimpse a cascade. Perhaps I could run her off a bit more and close to twenty miles. The hook was baited. And now I bit. May be I'd put the Race Committee and Monsieur Argos on hold for a while to check out Brendan's lair. Perhaps they'd be so busy with the other boats they would not notice. I studied the chart for a while, then laid off a course for the Canto da Carneira lighthouse on the northern point of Corvo. It had an elevation of 779 feet and flashed white very ten seconds, and lay ninety-one miles away on a magnetic bearing of 208°. *Johan*'s helm went up, her sheets rans out and the Aries clicked on to a close reach. We'd be there by tomorrow . . .

But those who seek to enter paradise, I soon learned, should not take too much for granted. I'd failed to reckon with the Azores High, which now subjected me to an ordeal that bore an almost comical resemblance to that of Coleridge's Ancient Mariner. During the night the wind faded away, leaving *Johan* totally becalmed by noon of June 16 at a point that my sextant shots said was twenty-five miles north of Corvo. The island was only two miles across, but, according to the chart, it rose to a height of more than 2,000 feet above sea level. If my navigation was correct, I should

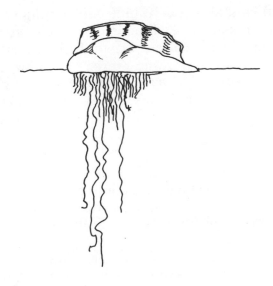

Portuguese man-o-war.

be able to see it easily from here. But the horizon was blank.

Perhaps *Johan* was in a wholly different part of the ocean than I imagined. One empty horizon, seen from the perspective of her cockpit, was exactly like every other empty horizon. Once more, I began to experience the dizziness of a vertigo set in the horizontal dimension; I knew where I was, but where the heck was the rest of the world? My feelings of unreality were further heightened by the scorching heat. Performing even the smallest chore left me gasping for breath. *Johan*, with no breeze to steady her, slammed around aimlessly in the greasy swell. By now a thick haze covered the surface of the water, limiting visibility to one or two miles, and I gave up my periodic searches for Corvo through the binoculars. I glanced overside and noted that half a dozen Portuguese men-of-war, jelly fish with a large pink bladder on their backs, were propelling themselves slowly toward the boat. I didn't even know these things could move! Could they somehow slither up *Johan*'s side, I wondered, and board me? The idea was preposterous, but I laid a winch handle beside my book, just in case.

When I tried to make a sandwich, I discovered that the remaining loaf of bread had, overnight, become a net of mildew. Then I attempted to cut a slice of cheese, but it had turned to a kind of curd inside its plastic package. Down in the cabin I toyed with the Walker Sat-Nav, but it continued to spit at me with "No Fix, No Fix." Later, I dragged out the Husun and tried some sunshots, but the heavy surface haze rendered them questionable. At about 5 P.M. local time—wherever Local was!—the sun still hung high in a hot and very coppery sky. I longed to take a plunge over *Johan*'s side, but cancelled the idea quickly. Portuguese men-of-war, bulbous gourds erect, seemed to be everywhere. Yea, slimy things did crawl with leg upon the slimy sea . . .

Once, when I was a soldier in the Middle East, I had watched the Scots Guards change their sentinels along the perimeter of our encampment. It occurred to me then that a couple of Highland bagpipes could, with their jaunty discordances, do more to raise morale than a whole armory of guns and bullets. I sifted through my tapes and pulled out the Pipes of the Queen's Own Scottish Borderers. Soon "The Bluebells of Scotland" and "The March of the Cameron Men" were skirling out at top volume over this hot and dismal scene. I doubt if the recital scared the jellyfish much, but, accompanied by a big tot of whisky, they provided a fine tonic for my own spirits.

Finally the sun dipped below the horizon. I poured another whisky, switched on my radar alert, and prepared to turn in. Though all *Johan*'s sails were down, and she was not underway, I flicked on her masthead navigation lights. On the off chance that I might be nearer to land than I thought, I set the depth sounder to its maximum depth and switched on. The needle bounced and kicked all over the scale: *Johan* was still out there in a thousand fathoms or more.

* * * * *

Beep!

I jerked awake. It was 3:15 A.M. I pulled myself out of the bunk and threw back the hatch. It was a beautiful moonlit night. Way off to port I saw the lights of the ship, probably a fishing vessel. The air was cool and a faint breeze was coming in from the east. Up went the mainsail, and the yankee was unrolled all the way. Soon *Johan* was going two knots right into the moonshine. Then the wind freshened. Three knots.

I took the high-power binoculars out of their box and looked patiently for the Corvo light, but could see nothing. The sun came up behind a bank of clouds, with the moon still high in the sky. Where was Corvo? The horizon, now much clearer, was blank. I opened a can of fruit cocktail for breakfast. The sun came out, and I took a couple of sextant shots on to a crystal-clear horizon. At least that should show if I am sailing down the right line for the Corvo. The line of position checked out, but it did not dispel the subconscious feeling that I might be in the wrong part of the ocean altogether.

Dead reckoning put me about seven miles due north of Corvo. Visibility seemed good, yet there was nothing but a low grey cloud on the horizon. Remorseless logic decreed that if the boat was where my navigation said it was, then the only place Corvo could be was behind that cloud. *Johan* altered course a few degrees to the east and drove on. After half an hour, even when viewed through the binoculars, the cloud still looked like a cloud. I poured another coffee and returned to the deck. A quick glance through the glasses and Wham! A sharp thin line was snaking down from the left side of the cloud like a bolt of black lightning.

Land Ho!

For a moment I suppressed my jubilation. Perhaps this was an illusion, another flyaway island. I took a quick bearing and got 191° Magnetic. The steep black line, its top concealed in clouds, had not moved. It had to be Corvo. I had found it! *Johan* had tacked her way across this vast empty ocean and found this little cloud-girt rock just where it was supposed to be. Old Brandanu had beckoned, and I had come. My navigation was right. And, hey, even the charts were accurate.

As I hopped around in *Johan*'s cockpit I was struck with another, more philosophical thought. For years I had listened to academic thinkers question the existence of an independent, free-standing physical reality. Their arguments had been subtle, and like most subtle arguments, close to irrefutable. But now I knew they were wrong. Nothing they could say would convince me otherwise. It was not all in our heads. There *was* a free-standing reality. I had travelled the empty spaces, my father's magical sextant had reached across the solar system, and, lo, I had found Corvo!

Soon *Johan* was reaching along Corvo's eastern shore. Cliffs rose vertically for more than 1,000 feet, at which point they became lost in mist. Seagulls, which I had not seen since coming off the shelf, wheeled about the rocks. Such a lonely fortress must, through the centuries, have been a natural hideout for hermits and for mutineers, bent on avoiding the noose. Perhaps it had served as a penal colony. Just the place, I thought, to imprison the Count of Monte Cristo . . .

The morning sun swept some of the mist off the grassy slopes above the cliffs, but there was no sign of humanity save for a patchwork of low stone walls that enclosed a latticework of minute

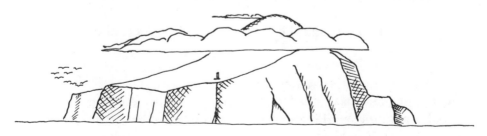

The free-standing reality of Corvo.

fields, each yielding nothing but grass. Then I saw her, the first landborne creature I had glimpsed in weeks. I stared through the binoculars, hypnotised, as a single Guernsey cow picked her way gingerly through the rocks high up on the island's shoulder.

Johan swung round the southern tip of Corvo, where the little community of Vila Nova crouched, seemingly exposed to the full force of the Atlantic's gales. The village, according to my ancient *Africa Pilot*, subsisted upon dairy products and the export of grapes for the Portuguese wine trade. It had, at least in 1910, a single church and 600 inhabitants.

Soon the morning haze lifted and nine miles off to the southwest I caught a glimpse of Flores. The volcanic peaks were significantly higher than those of Corvo. As Johan coasted along I leafed through my paperback copy of Hakluyt's *Voyages* for any early mentions of the Azores. I discovered that the bay just south of Santa Cruz, on the eastern side of Flores, was the scene of a great naval battle in 1591. Here a single English ship, the *Revenge*, under Sir Richard Grenville, had fought a fleet of fifty-three Spanish ships to a standstill.

Flores's harbor for fishing boats was too shallow for *Johan*, and the chart suggested visiting boats anchor in eighteen fathoms, in Revenge Bay. This, however, presented serious problems for my cutter with her frozen windlass. After my experience in Cawsand Bay, I doubted if I had the strength to raise a chain and heavy anchor from such a depth. I decided to try my luck on Channel 16.

"Sailboat *Johan Lloyde* for harbormaster Santa Cruz, over."

I repeated the call.

" 'Arbormaster to *Johan Lloyde*, over."

"This is *Johan*. May I speak English?"

"Go right ahead." It was the voice of a young man.

"I draw six feet—two meters—is there a place to moor near the town?"

"Yes, just go through the rocks on the markers to the Maiden's Pool."

"The Maiden's Pool?"

"The young girls have swum there for many generations, in the shelter of the rocks. Just look where the yellow crane is."

"I am singlehanded and I have no engine. Can I get a tow?"

"Oh yes. Where are you now?"

"Seven miles north, east of Corvo."

"Wait . . . I see you."

"You have sharp eyes."

"I have binoculars, and I am halfway up the hill, in my father's house. My name is Umberto. My uncle is 'arbormaster, and I will call you in one hour."

"Roger, and thank you. My name is Tim, Tim Hubbard."

" 'Allo Tim 'Ubbard."

"Hallo." I had just been privileged to meet my first member of the extensive Augusto family which, I soon learned, had a finger or two in just about every piece of business on Flores and Corvo.

For the next hour *Johan* glided on down the coast. I could make out colonies of neat stone houses, perched in the hills back from the cliffs. This island had a population of 6,000 souls and boasted several villages, twelve churches, a cathedral, a post office, and a hotel. The town of Santa Cruz, so far as I could make out, appeared to be no more than a gaggle of buff stone houses at the foot of a small mountain. At the top of the mountain stood a large il- luminated cross.

"Umberto to yacht *Johan,* over."

"*Johan,* come in, Umberto."

"I cannot find my uncle, who will tow you. He works now with the freighter in the bay. Ask him for a tow."

"How will I find him?"

"He will come to you, okay?"

"Thank you, Umberto."

"Goodbye. See you tonight."

The arrangements seemed sketchy, but then the Azoreans were supposed to be born seaman. They ought, by now, to know what they were doing. I looked up to see a big steamer anchored in Revenge Bay, just to the south of Santa Cruz. Every now and then a fleet of three or four launches hauled a couple of wooden lighters full of cattle and oil drums off to the freighter. I was also slightly mystified by Umberto's final words—see you tonight. Was he, as a representative of the harbormaster, coming aboard *Johan?* Would I have to grapple with papers and have dues to pay? Or was this some kind of social invitation?

I spotted a launch returning from the freighter. I steered to- ward it and waved. It was piloted by a short and immensely mus- cular man with white hair.

"Umberto said you will give me a tow," I shouted.

"No speeek Engleesh."

"Tow?" I held up the end of a rope. "I have no engine. *En tenho nao motor.*" I had learnt the words carefully from my Berlitz. The old man laughed and signalled, by a casual flap of his hand, for *Johan* to drop her sails. There was a deep swell running. One moment the launch was six feet below *Johan*'s rail, then it was two feet above her. When the sails were stowed I took a rope from the launch and put it over the samson posts. It was hardly in place before we were off. The launch was far more powerful than the one that towed me out of Mill Bay Dock in Plymouth. Five, six, seven knots. I grabbed *Johan*'s tiller. We seemed to be heading for a gap twenty feet wide between two saw-toothed rocks. Behind them I could see half a dozen sailboat masts beside a stone dock. This might be Azorean panache, but it was far too fast for me. Again, I reminded myself that these folks had centuries of practice running boats through steep surf on to the beach. He who hesitates was lost. Now *Johan* was close to hull speed. Even if she got through the gap in the rocks, the boat would not be able to avoid smashing into the jetty or the other boats. I picked up the speaking trumpet and yelled at the harbor master to slow down. No speeek Engleesh. Vrrooom.

Maybe I could break the seal and stop *Johan* on her own engine. I fired up the Volvo and grabbed a pair of pliers. The launch, with *Johan* on her tail, scythed through the rocks. Fifty feet away, straight ahead, stood the jetty. Without warning, the launch stopped dead in her tracks and began to go astern. Now what? I pulled hard on the helm and *Johan* went flying by to starboard, still doing six knots. There was no way I could avoid smashing into the yachts ahead. But all was not lost. The launch was behind me and the towrope came taut with a twang. *Johan*'s speed dropped as the launch went full astern. Locked in this reverse tow, the two vessels slid slowly past the jetty. As they did so, a young man in uniform leapt four feet through the air on to *Johan*'s foredeck, picked up my boathook, and, standing on the bow, fished up a heavy rope floating on the surface of the Maiden's Pool; this quickly came taut, acting like an arrester wire under *Johan*'s bow. The sailboat slowed, and stopped. Then she was muscled into a berth alongside a 40-foot ketch flying the Austrian flag. I was still shaking. Centuries of experience, I concluded, seemed to have conditioned the Azoreans

to cut absolutely all margin out of everything. Yet miraculously
OSTAR competitor No. 11 lay, after several weeks of hard racing,
safely at rest in the Fortunate Isles.

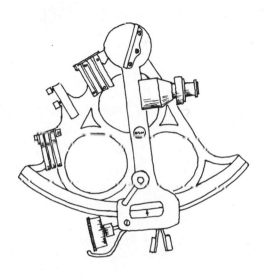

10

St. Brendan's Beacon

This was a snug harbor. *Johan* was moored fore-and-aft on a web of heavy red ropes strung out across the Maiden's Pool. A makeshift breakwater of volcanic rock and great square concrete blocks gave her fine protection to seaward. Also in the Pool were a dozen or so other yachts, including a 55-foot steel ketch from Bermuda and an antique 59-foot bowsprit schooner from Maine. No boat could have reached this little rock sanctuary in the middle of nowhere without putting at least a thousand miles of open sea under her keel. The nearest cape of Portugal lay a cosy 994 sea miles to the east, and the nearest cape of Newfoundland lay some 1,090 sea miles off to the northwest. Each year scores of yachts left the shores of Europe and North America to savor the romance of Flores. But each year most turned back. Those that did finally arrive off Santa Cruz had proven—each in its own stalwart way—that they could handle almost anything the Atlantic chose to hurl into their path. Once, however, they had safely threaded their way past the dragon's teeth at the entrance of the Maiden's Pool, there was nothing the wind or waves could do to imperil the safety of even the smallest craft. For the first time in weeks, crews could roll up their charts, unhook their safety belts, and, if they chose, drink more than their share of wine.

Tides were only one foot in old St. Brendan's haven. But, I noted, there was another, larger movement in the level of the water: over the period of a minute or so the deep sea swell caused a steady two or three feet rise and fall against the jetty. Moored off like this, the boats need not grind their rails against the stone dock. I restowed my sails and then looked down into the water below;

I could see every detail of the sandy bottom two fathoms down. In the days before universal pollution I had sailed in the Bahamas and in the Red Sea, but I had never seen coastal water as clear as this. In a little while I went below, tidied the cabin, and wrote up the Log. As I did so, I heard a low creaking hiss from outside the hull. It sounded as if *Johan* was floating in a large bowl of soda water. I checked the gas cylinder behind the stove. It was tight shut and I went on writing for a while. Then I dropped the pen, and climbed on deck. My neighbor the Austrian was sitting with a young blond lady under an awning in his cockpit. They were, judging by the bottles, drinking vodka and tonic with a slice of blue-looking lime in each glass. We introduced ourselves, and the Austrian expressed curiosity about the big "II" on *Johan*'s deck and sides. I explained and then asked, "What is that strange hissing noise in the water?"

"That noise?" The Austrian laughed. "That is the sound the little shrimp make when they move. I have come here many years now, and you can always hear them, except on stormy days."

There was a commotion on the dock behind me. The Austrian nodded.

"They are calling for you."

Turning, I saw a man, dressed in police uniform, beckoning me over. I held up five fingers to indicate I'd be there in as many minutes. Then I carefully pulled the Avon dinghy out of the lazaret and inflated it. I tossed it into the water and rowed to the jetty.

"Passaporte?"

"Yes sir. Right here." I stepped on to the dock but the gendarme, armed with a night stick and a revolver, shook his head.

"No, no. Not 'ere. See Capitan in office." He pointed off toward the town behind him. A few minutes later I set off through the streets of Santa Cruz with my passport, *Johan*'s documents and— for want of a guidebook—my paperback copy of Hakluyt's *Voyages*, first published in 1600. Most of the town's dwellings were but one story high. Generally the walls were of whitewashed stone and the roofs of curled orange tile set in the Spanish fashion. The street I walked up was barely broad enough to take a single horsecart. The side walk was not more than a foot wide. On the steeper parts of the hill above the harbor the road turned to cobbles. I passed the cathedral, built of black volcanic rock and white plaster and set back from the road in an elegant piazza. Its three stories made it the tallest building in town. Quite a bit of grass, I noted, grew in the cracks of the stone steps up to its gaily painted doors, now flung wide to receive the Sunday worshippers.

I continued on up the little street. Inadvertantly I found myself looking through open windows, right into the living rooms of many houses. I nodded to the occupants within, who seemed untroubled by the intrusion. *Bom dia, bom dia.* Good day, good day. Smiles all round. At the top of the hill I came upon a small triangular courtyard shaded from the afternoon sun by the foliage of several low, thick-trunked sycamore trees. On the far side I saw an office with an iron grill across the windows. Customs and Immigration. Surprisingly, the two men behind the counter spoke neither French nor English, and we conferred in pidgin German. All was in order. More big smiles. Welcome to Flores, welcome. When

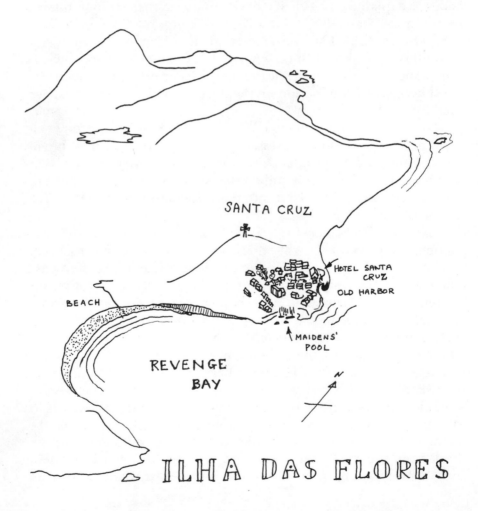

SANTA CRUZ

HOTEL SANTA CRUZ

OLD HARBOR

BEACH

MAIDENS' POOL

REVENGE BAY

N

ILHA DAS FLORES

the official came to mark my passport he didn't simply press the
seal on to the paper. Instead, the stamp was raised high over his
head and brought down with a resounding thump. This overhand
smash, I soon discovered, was a basic stroke in the armory of all
Azorean officials. Perhaps they sensed that bureaucracy was
becoming irrelevant here in paradise; the big thumps might somehow bridge the gap to Lisbon.

I collected my papers and strolled back through the streets of
the town. Flores is the Portuguese word for flowers, and here they
were. Every garden, no matter how small, was blooming. Blue and
white hydrangeas seemed particularly popular. Occasionally I
would pass a doorway strung with beads that led into a darkened
bar where men played cards and dominoes. But there seemed to
be no stores. Similar streets in English ports like Falmouth or
Fowey would have produced half a dozen little bakeries and
butcher shops.

Halfway down the hill the ground seemed to rise and buckle
beneath me. For a second I imagined that I was in the middle of
an earthquake. Then I realized that it must all be in my legs, and
that my sense of balance was still attuned to the motion of *Johan*.
I moved on carefully and eventually found myself standing on a
small promontory that overlooked both the Maiden's Pool and, off
to the south, Revenge Bay, now empty even of the anchored
freighter. Weary from the hot sun and my night of searching for
Corvo, I sat down on a white bench and opened up my Hakluyt
for "a Report of the Fight about the Isle of Acores, the last of
August, 1591," written by Sir Walter Raleigh. This was a battle that
had changed world history. Yet, perhaps because it had been
fought in such a remote setting, it escaped the notice of many
historians, including myself.

Three years after the defeat of the first Armada in 1588, a small
English squadron of six warships and half a dozen cargo vessels
came to anchor in this bay—about one mile across—now lying
below me. For these sixteenth-century crews, it was the last stage
of a long voyage to the Caribbean, and many of the sailors, plagued
with scurvy, were brought ashore to a makeshift hospital. I looked
around. It was easy to imagine the infirmary housed under a few
old sails beside a stream that came out of the forest and coursed
down across the beach about 300 yards off to my right (see picture
p. O). On August 31, 1591, wrote Raleigh, the commander of the
British squadron received word that a Spanish fleet of fifty-three

warships was approaching. This was, it seemed, King Philip of Spain's second great Armada against England. Knowing that he was badly out-gunned, the British commander, Lord Howard, slipped his cables and sailed off to the north. Sir Richard Grenville, in command of the *Revenge*, delayed his departure to pick up ninety men from the hospital on the beach. Then the *Revenge*, now on her own, attempted to sail out of the bay by cutting between two parts of the Spanish fleet. She almost made it. Several Spanish ships approached, but sheered off when the *Revenge* ran out her guns. Just as Grenville was reaching open water he came under the lee of one of the Spanish flagships, the colossal three-decker *San Philip*, which "becalmed his Sails in such sort, as the Shippe could neither make way or feel the Helme." The *San Philip* swung round and opened fire, and the *Revenge* replied with a broadside of bar-shot that came close to sinking the Spaniard. The spell had been broken. Now the rest of the Spanish fleet closed in. The ensuing cannonade quickly carried away the *Revenge*'s masts, thereby denying her all power of motion. For the next fifteen hours, the Spanish fired broadsides into the stationary hulk, while the crew of the English ship continued to work their guns against the entire Armada. The *Revenge*, though the battle was clearly lost, just would not surrender. In exasperation, the Spanish admiral ordered four of his biggest galleons to attack simultaneously, run alongside, and board her. But, reported Raleigh, the Spanish multitudes "were still Repulsed againe and againe, and at all times beaten backe into their owne Ships, or into the Seas."

Sir Richard Grenville, always in the thick of the fighting, was wounded three times—once so severely that for a time he could not speak. By the next morning five Spanish galleons had been sent to the bottom and many more were badly damaged. By then the *Revenge* had received more than 800 cannon shots through her hull, but still she floated. More than half her crew were dead or incapacitated. Grenville, now mortally wounded, commanded that the ship be scuttled to avoid capture. But his subordinates disobeyed him and opened surrender negotiations with the Spanish admiral. Eventually the hulk of the *Revenge*, her gun-ports running with blood, was towed back into this bay and anchored while the Spaniards tried to treat their wounded and patch up what was left of their fleet. If this was the damage that could be inflicted by one English ship, they must have wondered, then what would twenty such ships do? They limped home to Spain. Grenville's quixotic feat of arms had a disquieting impact upon the Spanish navy's morale, and Philip was subsequently compelled to abandon his idea of a second Armada against England.

As I sat on my bench in the sun, I realized that Raleigh's account, for all its eloquence, left many questions in the air. What, exactly, had Grenville been trying to do? Did he have a strategy? Or was he just a Devon brawler with no discernible plan? Why had he lingered to pick up the men in the hospital? Wouldn't it have been quicker to send the third officer ashore with half a dozen men to lead the invalids into the hills until the danger passed or until they could be picked off the far side of the island? Was it possible that Grenville, with icy logic, had decided that a stout-hearted stand by a single ship in Flores might save England from another invasion? Even so, such an action ran directly against Howard's orders. Perhaps the English admiral was in a state of funk. On seeing the *Revenge* surrounded, why had he not returned to the fray, or at least attempted some diversion?

One of the most intriguing sentences in Raleigh's narrative, however, had almost nothing to do with the battle. It concerned the initial appearance of the English squadron in this idyllic bay. He wrote of the sailors "refreshing themselves from the land with such things as they could either for money or by force recover." This indicated that some kind of community already existed on this shore more than four centuries ago. Who were these people? Were they castaways, awaiting the first friendly ship out? Were they part of a penal colony? Or perhaps luckless colonists dispatched—and probably forgotten—decades ago by some great lord back in Lisbon? Raleigh's remarks suggest they knew the meaning of money, i.e., they were not in a state of total barbarism. And they implied that the residents of Flores had something worth stealing —presumbly vegetables and livestock and, maybe, womenfolk.

Had these early settlers, I wondered, come across any relics of Brendan and his monks? Did they, too, have the Faith? Or were they—in their huge isolation—condemned like the *Bounty* mutineers on Pitcairn to live out a terrible saga of incest, betrayal, and murder?

I closed Hakluyt with a snap and looked out once more across the bay. The story of the battle with its inexplicable—and even pointless?—gallantries left me in a somber mood. The tranquility of the scene, with its rustling surf and the distant chirp of birds, made the one-sided struggle of the *Revenge* almost as remote and as unreal as the ode that Lord Tennyson composed on the 300th anniversary of the battle:

> At Flores in the Azores Sir Richard Grenville lay,
> And a pinnace, like a fluttered bird, came flying from far away:
> "Spanish ships of war at sea! we have sighted fifty-three!"

I wandered slowly back to the Maiden's Pool. Most of the visitors on the other yachts had awoken from their siestas and were now taking their later afternoon dip. Though many flags flew—Swedish, Austrian, French, Australian, American, Spanish—the crews seemed very much alike. Most were in their thirties and forties and were tanned a deeper hue of brown than the native Azoreans. I saw no children. While the men had powerful shoulders, many also displayed the first hint of a spare tire around the midriff. The women were uniformly slender and bronzed of limb. All seemed to exude a kind of catlike satisfaction with themselves and the world in general. This was it, their smiles seemed to say, this was Nirvana. These polyglots splashed and dived in the azure waters of the Maiden's Pool in the growing shadows of the great mountain peaks to the west. Few had troubled to put on a swimsuit. As I paddled back to *Johan*, one sylph from a German cutter dived right under the Avon dinghy and came up smiling. I was anxious to join the fun. But after so long a time alone at sea, I was shy and pulled on a fig leaf of plaid before plunging over *Johan's* side.

After a while, I swam out to the rocks with some saltwater soap and had my first real wash in weeks. Back on board *Johan*, I dried off vigorously and pulled on my white slacks with a clean blue workshirt. Then I poured a gin and tonic and went up to sit in the cockpit. Though my swim was most refreshing, the story of the *Revenge*'s lonely struggle out beyond the point remained with me. I looked around the Maiden's Pool. Three or four dinghies were now slowly making the rounds of the bigger boats. A French couple paddled past *Johan* in a small wooden boat. With them was a large brown and white cat. *Bon soir*, good evening. Each of us spoke the other's language, lifting our glasses as we did so. Then the lady gently raised up the cat's paw, too, in greeting. This little gesture combined with the gin to brighten my disposition. I waved back. No longer was I witnessing the frolics of a few zonked-out hedonists. These people had all sailed 1,000 miles across an open ocean to be here; they deserved every bit of pleasure that came their way. I mixed myself another gin. I could break my ironclad limit now I was in port. In a little while it was not too difficult to view the occupants of these bronzed bodies as a Homeric band of adventurers bewitched, as Odysseus might have been, by the beauteous spell of the Fortunate Isles.

The skipper from the steel Bermuda ketch rowed over. The word, apparently, had gone out that *Johan Lloyde* was in the Observer Singlehanded. Mike was a big, cheery man and asked after several of the skippers he knew in the race. In turn, I got to know a little more about the other yachts in the harbor. Most, it seemed, were "sea gypsies," who spent a greater part of their lives drifting around the Atlantic with the seasons. They headed for the Madeiras or the Antilles when we had three feet of snow on the ground in upstate New York. Then they moved north to the Azores or Bermuda in the spring and up to Maine, or to Scotland's Hebrides in August. These, then, were the modern lotus-eaters and for them it was almost always afternoon. They had to endure no winters, no mortgages, no tax, no cops, no corporate ambitions, and no irksome bosses. They had escaped, in short, most of the burdens of contemporary society.

If a skipper should become bored with too much easy living, all he or she had to do was persuade a few fellow adventurers that Cape Breton, the Baltic, or the Faeroes looked good, pass the hat for a few provisions, and haul up the anchor. Many Sea Gypsies, I learned, had hardly touched the mainland in years. Though by now hundreds had been drawn into this nomadic life along the outer skirts of the North Atlantic, almost all knew of each other, or at least of each other's boats. No one, unless by choice, need be lonely. Love and companionship came and went with the wind, floating between ships in the same easy fashion accorded to the exchange of paperbacks and a roll or two of tattered charts. No soreheads need apply. Most Sea Gypsies had, over the years, picked up some basic shipboard skills—be it seacook, wire splicer, or diesel mechanic—that enabled them to turn a dollar or two in the bigger ports. Some, like Mike in the steel ketch, had acquired a small patch of backwater land at a very favorable price.

"We've got a little farmhouse here," he said, gesturing to the peaks behind us, "and a few acres of vines. The wine isn't of commercial quality yet, but we like it." He began to paddle on to the next boat. "Come up and have a taste some day."

"I'd be delighted to," I replied, by now hardly aware that *Johan* was supposed to be racing her way across the Atlantic. After so long alone at sea, tensed, even in sleep, waiting for gear to break or some freighter to strike, there was an overpowering temptation to relax once more into the carefree routines of life ashore.

The only restaurant in town, I learned, was that of the Hotel Santa Cruz, just off the Old Harbor. After another cocktail, I pulled on my dark green jacket and rowed ashore. Then I made my way back up the hill, across the cathedral piazza and into the oldest part of the town. The hotel, two and a half stories high, had been built of stone sometime late in the last century. In the years before the first world war it had, I was told, been a noted watering spot for adventurous European socialites. Though clearly still an establishment of substance, it carried a strong hint of better days. Elaborate wrought-iron verandas jutted out from the bedrooms on every floor. After the strong sunlight of the street, the lobby was cool. *Boa noite*, good evening, *boa noite*. I pushed open a door with ornate curlicues cut into its frosted glass panel and entered the bar. Two heavy fans, bolted to the ceiling, revolved slowly over the scrubbed white stone floor. I pulled a stool toward me and set my foot on the brass rail. I had no escudos, of course, but this was not a time to stand on ceremony.

"Una cerveja, por favor."

The bartender, wearing a less than clean white jacket, placed a bottle of Sagres Best Export Ale on top of the bar and then hung a small glass over the neck. It was my first cold beer in more than a month and I filled the glass and took a long swig before placing an English five-pound note on the bar top. The waiter raised his eyebrows and turned away, without comment. I looked around. One half of the tables were occupied, generally by dark-complected men in Sunday suits. Over by the windows, with their view of the terrace and the sea, sat a group of women and several small children. Opposite them were three very tanned American couples from the green schooner, speaking quietly among themselves. The only other non-islanders in the hotel bar were two men, both unshaven, sitting near the wall. They wore T-shirts and cut-off jeans.

Soon a major debate was underway behind the bar about the precise exchange rate for the English pound. Yes, it was more than a dollar, but how much more. Would it be possible, I asked, for me to also dine in the restaurant? The proprietor, a slim bald man, appeared. He listened to his subordinates and then walked down the bar toward me.

"It iss Sunday," he said in English. "We cannot talk to the bank on exchange, but why do you not dine here, and pay us tomorrow in escudos?"

"That is most generous of you. Muito obrigado."

"Our pleasure, Senhor."

By now some fast Azorean repartee, accompanied by much laughter, was bouncing back and forth across the room. I hoped that my monetary problems were not the cause of all this merriment. Then an old man, his eyes twinkling, looked straight at me and said in English. "My friend 'ere"—he pointed to the leather-faced gent sitting next to him—"My friend 'ere say dat on dos terms 'e will eat 'ere effry day. Pay always tomorrow!"

The laughter echoed round the bar. I laughed, too, and, with a dramatic gesture, ordered another beer for myself and the two old guys. The natives, it seemed, were well disposed toward the sailor who looked in at their windows. And now the proprietor of this grand hotel offered to stake me to the price of drinks and a dinner. Could this pleasant reception, I wondered, have anything to do with the fact that no tourist jumbos had yet managed to get their wheels down on the grass airstrip of Flores? If you were prepared to make the long sea voyage from the mainland, then, it seemed, the people of Flores would greet you with consideration. In their eyes, I was not a tourist, but a bona fide traveller with news of distant parts. I was just burnishing my nice theory of island hospitality when the two men in cut-off jeans fell to arguing with a waiter.

The unshaven ones, it seemed, had been trying to make a meal off the bar favors and had already received a second platter of cheese and salt pork tidbits. Now they were protesting—in heavily accented English—the exchange rate on their American dollars. The proprietor appeared. I could not hear the conversation but at the end of it the owner shrugged his shoulders and the visitors looked disgruntled. Later they were joined by a tall, bearded man who appeared to be called Olaf.

I ordered another beer and wished that Susan could join me at this bar. She would be wearing a white suit and brimmed hat and her hair would be swept back behind her ears. We would perch on these high bar stools and drink dry martinis and smoke Russian cigarettes and imagine that Peter Lore and Bogart were plotting in the corner somewhere behind us . . . but she was not here and I picked up my bottle and pushed my way through a second set of cut-glass doors into the hotel dining room. Here the view of the ocean was obscured by lace curtains. Stuffed leather couches lined the walls, and several potted plants were posted about the room on ornate brass stands. But the air was fresh and cool and the tables were spread with newly laundered linen. A few couples, dressed in their Sunday best, were halfway through their dinner.

I pushed my way past a plant and sat down at an empty table for four. For a while I fought the temptation to switch seats so that the plant stood between me and the other diners. This was absurd. I had been alone too long. I forced myself to look around the room. Off to my left sat a tall blond young man with rimless spectacles. He was sitting entirely on his own, at a table for eight! I pushed back my chair and walked over.

"Are you American?" As I uttered the words, I realized how sappy they must have sounded. My attempts to recoup were no better. "What I mean is, do you speak English?" The young man came right back.

"You make this sound like darkest Africa," was his disdainful

"You make this sound like darkest Africa!"

reply. "For your information I am *not* American. I am Swedish. But, as you see"—here I received a withering smile—"I do speak passable English."

"Yes. Very passable English." This was precisely the kind of smart aleck response I had dreaded. For a moment I stood by the table and said nothing. The silence grew longer and longer. Then the Swede coughed politely, and began to toy with his napkin. Finally, I summoned my courage.

"Look," I said. "I am here alone. May I join you for dinner?" There was another moment's silence.

"Please do," said this self-possessed Swede. "Have this chair."

"Thank you. My name is Tim Hubbard."

"Pleased to meet you. My name is Kurt Eriksen."

My new companion, it seemed, was a graduate student at the University of Stockholm and was here in the Azores to perfect his Portuguese for the exam into the Swedish diplomatic corps. I could make little sense of the menu, written as it was in scrawling long-hand, and asked Eriksen to order for me whatever he was having.

"Which boat are you off?" I asked, when the waiter left.

"Oh, I did not come by boat."

"How, then?"

Eriksen grinned at my puzzlement. "I flew in by plane."

"You flew your own plane, from Portugal?"

"No. First to Horta, then to Flores."

"You are an adventurer."

"Perhaps. And how did you arrive here?"

"I came in the cutter *Johan Lloyde,* from England, today." Eriksen looked surprised.

"Then you must be the captain of boat No. 11. You are racing across the Atlantic, alone?"

"Yes. But how did you come to know this?"

"My landlady told me." Eriksen chuckled. "The whole island seems to know of your arrival. But tell me, if you are racing, how is it you come to be here dining in such archaic splendor at the Hotel Santa Cruz?"

"The wind blew me south. And I like islands." Soon the dinners arrived. An entire chicken, charbroiled black and resting on a bed of onions, olives and rice, was placed before each of us. In addition, we each received a big lettuce salad and a sizable loaf of bread. The waiter returned and opened two bottles of cool white wine.

"Good health."

"To you, too."

We ate steadily for a while. The fresh food was a delight after two weeks of cans. The wine went fast, and I ordered another bottle.

"Isn't there a distinctive pronunciation to Azorean Portuguese?" I asked. "Won't that disconcert your professors in the diplomatic exam?"

Eriksen laughed. "Yes, there is. But I also happen to be writing my doctoral dissertation on islands. Or, to be more specific, I am writing about the influence of island geography on the structure of society."

"Which societies are you studying?"

"Any I can find. I am intrigued by the fact that even from the beginning—take the first Peloponnesian war between Athens and Sparta—island cultures seemed to have nurtured democratic societies and the inland polities have tended to produce authoritarian societies. It has happened again and again, and I am trying to discover why this should be so. For instance, can you really tell me that it is just chance that Iceland and England, homes of the world's two oldest parliaments, are both islands?"

"A good part of the reason might be military," I said. "Islanders have natural boundaries to defend, and they're not so worried about outsiders being pulled in to settle local disputes . . ." I told him about the *Revenge*'s singlehanded struggle with the second Spanish Armada.

"A fine example of my thesis," said Kurt, a gleam in his eye. "England versus Spain, a struggle between islanders and mainlanders, between the demand for freedom and the demand for order. Take these islands here . . ."—he gestured around the dining room with his wine glass—". . . what king back in Lisbon could ever impose a harsh regime on the Azores? The people, if they found it unacceptable, would not suffer in silence. They'd just jump into their boats and sail away to somewhere less oppressive."

"Like the Sea Gypsies! The yachts in the harbor are a good example of that. They don't like taxes or drug laws, so they sail over the horizon."

"To Flores? Yes." Kurt smiled wryly. "I don't know how many books they have perused on political economy, but their instinct leads them in the right direction."

"They vote with their sails."

"Precisely, as of old."

"I have another footnote for you," I said. "Could it be that the business of simply sailing a boat is itself a primer for democracy?"

"How so?"

"Well . . . people who go to sea and grapple with the elements as fishermen or traders undergo a levelling experience. They are forced to see how insignificant mankind is for Nature and how dependent they are for survival upon even the most 'unpopular' member of the crew."

Kurt seemed intrigued with the thought. And for my part, I was delighted to be having a discussion that was not, for the first time in ages, somehow associated with the Observer Singlehanded.

"It works," decided Eriksen, "until the boat becomes so big that the crew—like the sailors on a battleship—has to be placed in a hierarchy. Then you are well on your way to having another authoritarian regime."

"Hierarchies seem to be inherently undemocratic," I said, thinking of some of the tussles I'd had with the bureaucrats in my own university.

"Of course," agreed Kurt, taking another swig of wine. "It is interesting to note that it was the reptiles who invented the 'pecking order' millions of years ago." His words were articulated with scholarly precision. "And it is interesting to note that the *soi-disant* R-complex part of the human brain—that which we hold in common with the reptiles—is the prime mover in the establishment of human hierarchies."

"That is a disquieting thought."

"Yes and no," said Kurt. "There is comfort in it, too. Next time you are confronted with a bureaucrat or a snob—we have our share of both in Sweden—just tell yourself 'This man is a reptile, this man is a lizard,' and it will make all troubles much easier to bear."

Though I was intrigued with Eriksen's theories and I longed to hear more, the beer and the wine were beginning to render my brain somewhat fuzzy. Kurt, though merry, seemed unaffected. If he passed his language exam—and how could he fail!—then the Swedish diplomatic service was about to acquire a most formidable new recruit. We called for the bill. As we waited, I asked him if his theory of islands had any bearing on modern power politics.

"But of course," he said, spectacles gleaming in the restaurant lights. Though Russia and the United States were of continental geography, they had become so big that they were often led to think of themselves as islands—Fortress America, etc. Modern weapons—nuclear bombs, missiles, satellites—had presented them with the traumatic realization in recent years that they were, after all, not islands of security but traditional inland states with a pushy neighbor just a few minutes away across the border. "The growing sense of insecurity has made both regimes markedly more authoritarian, both at home and in their buffer states, like Poland and the banana republics of Central America."

The bill arrived, and I signed for my portion of it—about $6 with the two bottles of wine—and we stood up. Kurt started back to the hotel bar. I told him I'd meet him there in a few moments and stepped outside for a breath of air. How many other revellers through the centuries, I wondered, had rolled back to their ships down these same cobbled streets? Perhaps some of my own ancestors, at least two of whom served under Nelson at Trafalgar, had stumbled down this very hill. I moved further out into the street and looked upward. Never before had I seen the stars shine so brightly in the firmament. Though my feet were planted on the cobbles of this little rock in the middle of the Atlantic, it was so beautiful that for a moment I thought I must've died and gone to heaven. This island sanctuary, one thousand miles from anywhere, was seldom marked in schoolroom atlases. For most people, it didn't even exist.

My thoughts turned somber again. When the querulous potentates of Washington and Moscow had pressed all their red buttons, launched their missiles, and annihilated most of civilization, this little rock with its unfashionable hotel and its feckless castaways might still be here. Perhaps, with a few additions to the municipal library, it might become the Iona or Lindisfarne of the postnuclear world, the one small beam of light on a very battered and very savage globe.

St. Brendan's Beacon.

No one would be able to locate it on the charts, for all the charts would have been incinerated. But every evening, whispering over the ether into their improvised junk-box radios, might come a few words of solace and encouragement for the survivors of Europe and America. This is St. Brendan's Beacon calling, from somewhere in the North Atlantic. Give us this day our daily bread . . .

11

Trouble in Paradise

Nights were long here in the Azores. When I eventually pushed my way back into the bar I found that all the children had been taken home and that what seemed to be a major booze-up was now under way. To add to the festive air, a man with an immense black moustache had begun to play an accordian on the far side of the room. After pushing slowly through several clumps of patrons, I found Kurt at the distant end of the bar, and he ordered two more Best Export Sagres Ales. Just as I reached for my bottle, I felt a hand tug at my sleeve.

"'Allo, I am Umberto. We spoke on the radio this morning. You are Tim 'Ubbard, No. 11."

"I'm delighted to meet you." Umberto, in his late twenties, was short and dark haired. He had a ready smile and was holding a bottle of Sagres Ale in his right hand. He asked about the Observer Singlehanded. It turned out that Flores had succored several damaged boats in the 1976 and 1980 races, "But you are the first Observer boat we see that 'as nothing wrong with it." Umberto clapped me on the back and did a fast translation into Portuguese. Once more, there was laughter in the bar.

"The hospitality of Flores is legendary," I replied, realizing I was speaking to a wider audience. "I decided that no race would be complete without a visit." Mumbled translations were going on all around me, accompanied by cries of Bravo, Bravo. "I also understand why you said on the radio 'See you tonight'. I thought I might have to search many waterfront tavernas to meet you. But now I realize there is only one place to come in Santa Cruz—here!" There was more applause, and many beer bottles and glasses were raised in recognition of such eloquence.

"Yes, this is it," said Umberto looking across the sea of dark faces with a certain pride. "I trust you will stay for our Summer Festival. We have not one, but two bands and much dancing. Many other yachts will come up from Horta for the occasion."

I was fast falling in love with this place—the mountains reaching to the clouds, the laid-back polyglots in the Maiden's Pool, its grand old hotel, and its seminars on world affairs. And now there was to be a festival with cheap wine and dancing in the streets.

"I'd love to stay," I said to Umberto. Soon another Sagres was thrust into my hand, and the party began to gather momentum. But it also became increasingly clear that not quite everyone was enjoying their sojourn in paradise. Kurt Eriksen was now deep in conversation with the men in cut-off jeans and their bearded captain, Olaf, who was from Norway. It seemed they had a new complaint. They had sailed their 27-foot sloop *Daphne* from Bermuda with a fourth man, a German named Bruno. Now Bruno, the only one who knew anything about sailing or navigation, had jumped ship, taking with him $100 in cash from Olaf's wallet.

"When I find that shit I'll cut his goddam fucking throat," said Olaf in passable English. "He's a dead man." According to the Norwegian, who was 6′ 2″ and a former bosun in the merchant marine, the sloop had a rough voyage. They also had experienced the gales that had dismasted and damaged so many OSTAR boats. The *Daphne* had split her mainsail and for much of the time had lain ahull with no sail up at all. Once a following sea smashed into the cockpit and left the cabin knee-deep in water. All were miserably seasick. Olaf was particularly exercised because Bruno, the crew member who knew most about sailing, refused to obey his orders.

"He says he is a Kung Fu expert," said Olaf. "But once I got so fed up I challenged him to a fight and his face go white and he back down."

"A fight in the cabin?" asked Kurt.

"Yah. He's chickenshit. When they don't take my orders, I just go to my bunk and say the hell with all of you—let the goddam boat sink." For a while Kurt talked to Olaf in Norwegian. It seemed that Olaf was sailing from Florida to Europe to meet his girlfriend in Spain. But now she was leaving him. Also, the banks were after him in Miami for not making payments on the boat. After cursing out Bruno some more, Olaf turned to me.

"Kurt say you are professor?"

"Yes."

"How old are you?"

"Forty-nine." Where, I wondered, was this interrogation leading?

"Will the Miami banks have me arrested in Spain?"

"I doubt it, not unless you've managed to commit a felony along the way."

"What is a felony?"

"Killing Bruno would be a felony."

Clearly, this was food for thought. Olaf talked to Eriksen some more in Norwegian. The diplomat-to-be led the ex-bosun off to a table in the corner, and soon Olaf was sobbing into his hands. I attempted to strike up a conversation with Olaf's crewmates, a heavyset Belgian and a tall, thin fellow who seemed to be French. But it was not easy. In a while, Eriksen returned and someone ordered another round of Sagres Ale. I invited him aboard *Johan Lloyde* for cocktails at five the following day. Perhaps we could return to the hotel for dinner.

"I'd be delighted. I would like to see your yacht very much. How long do you plan to stay? Perhaps you could rent a bicycle and come see the volcanic lakes and the village of Faja Grande on the west side of the island. It is completely exposed to the Atlantic."

"I must telephone my wife tomorrow," I said. "I don't want her —or the OSTAR officials—to think I'm in trouble."

"Of course not. There is a phone in the Post Office. Five o'-clock, then, down at the Pool?"

A little later I said goodnight. I went out of the side door and strode through the starlight down the cobble street to the docks. With some difficulty I launched my Avon dinghy and paddled back to *Johan.* For the last few weeks I had slept in my clothes. But now I carefully put on my pajamas and settled down in my blankets for the first full night's rest in quite a while. The last sound I heard was the gentle fizz of the little crustacea an inch or two away outside *Johan's* hull.

* * * * *

Bang. Clatter. Thump.

I awoke with a start. Where was I? *Johan* must be on the rocks! I struggled up and out through the hatch. After a moment I per-

ceived two shadows crouching down by *Johan's* starboard rail. So
far as I could make out they were attempting to shove Blagdon's
Oar overside into the water. The visitors seemed surprised at my
emergence from below.

"What in hell is going on?"

The shadows jumped back.

"We jus' borrowin' your oar." The voice was slurred. It was the
Belgian and the thin Frenchman from the hotel. "Olaf took the
fuckin' dinghy back to the fuckin' boat and left us ashore."

So much for my night of rest. I pondered for a moment. These
characters made me nervous. Perhaps a little compromise was in
order. "You can borrow the oar, but get it back immediately."

"Okay. We get it back."

"Tonight."

"Okay, okay." Now the tone was querulous.

I returned below. On deck there were some angry whisperings,
then giggling that ended abruptly with what sounded like a blow.
Two minutes later I heard the sound of a struggle and returned
to the deck. What now? I climbed into the cockpit. The two men
stood forty feet away, waist deep in the surf. So far as I could make
out, they were fighting over *Johan's* dinghy. Blagdon's Oar was
nowhere to be seen. I had lent them the oar but these midnight
Calibans had taken the dinghy. The shadow that must have been
that of the Belgian delivered a soggy smack of a punch to the face
of the Frenchman, who slowly keeled over into the surf. If I butted
in again, these fellows might turn on me. Perhaps this scene was
just a piece of drunken horseplay. But perhaps, also, I was becoming a witness to murder.

The body of the Frenchman was lying horizontal in the water,
but it was too dark to see if he was face down. The Belgian made
no attempt to assist. My principal concern at that moment, I'm
ashamed to say, was not so much for the man as for my Avon
dinghy. I took a deep breath. I was not, I reminded myself, rising
to a point of order in the University Senate.

"Look, you motherfuckers," I bellowed out across the roar of
the surf, "I said you could borrow the oar. Not the boat." The
Belgian's face turned toward me in the gloom, but he made no
other movement and I heard no reply. "Get that man out of the
water," I shouted with as much authority as I could muster. "And
get that bloody boat back here, immediately. On the double. The
oar, too."

The Belgian must have encountered this tone many times before in his sorry life. Slowly he waded round the Avon and began to tug at the body of his friend. Soon the Frenchman lay across the dinghy in a posture that suggested he was either gasping for air or being very sick.

After a while, the two men, heads down, paddled the Avon back to *Johan*. Somewhere among the ropes of the Maiden's Pool the Belgian located Blagdon's Oar and pushed it, with difficulty, back aboard. The Frenchman's nose was bleeding badly. Though I was apprehensive, I realized that I must speak with the voice of authority for a while longer.

"Don't get any blood on my decks," I said firmly. Mumble, mumble. The stocky Belgian climbed across *Johan*'s foredeck as if this was all in the night's work. I decided I didn't like him one bit. "Why did you hit him?" I asked. Mumble, mumble. I saw the Calibans safely on to the deck of the unfortunate Austrian, who was now awake and full of Germanic oaths of his own. After much tugging of ropes the pair eventually clambered off the ketch on to their own little sloop where Olaf—who seemed to have a girlfriend aboard—greeted them with yet more shouts and curses.

* * * * *

Next morning after breakfast I tramped up the hill to the bank building in the square. My neat theory that only meritorious individuals ever made it to an out-of-the-way place like Flores had, clearly, gone belly up. I recognized the bank manager, a young man dressed in an open shirt, as one of Umberto's friends in the hotel.

"Tell me, do you party like that every evening here in Santa Cruz?"

"Yes and no." The manager smiled. "We have a beer or two, but it is also a chance to practice our English."

"You must be acquiring a very colloquial version of the language."

"That is true." He grinned and I had the strong impression that Azoreans—the young at least—look less to mother Portugal and more to northern Europe and America as a bridge out of their economic isolation. The Spring Festival began in two days' time, so I cashed £50 of English currency, and a $50 traveller's check. The transaction involved a surprising number of forms; each one eventually got stamped with a mighty overhand smash. As I collected my passport and escudos, a short blond man entered the bank and cashed $50 worth of U.S. bills into local currency. He spoke English with a heavy German accent. As I walked by he glanced up.

"You are No. 11, the lone voyager?"

"Correct. And you?"

"I am off the *Daphne.*" So this was the great Bruno—mutineer, martial artist, and scourge of Norwegian manhood. His manner was urbane (he pronounced "voyager" the French way) and he was half a head shorter than I. This meant that Olaf the Bosun must be a foot taller and all of sixty pounds heavier than this troublemaker. The great confrontation in *Daphne*'s storm-wracked

The Cathedral of Santa Cruz.

cabin, Kung Fu or no Kung Fu, was moving from high drama to low farce.

"I hear you had a memorable trip from Bermuda."

"It was two weeks of raging paranoia. That Olaf knows nothing about either boats or sailing. He does not even know what reefing is! When we refused to take his orders he tried to cut his wrists with a broken bottle."

"He thinks you owe him money."

"It is the reverse. I paid $400 in Miami for my supplies. He bought nothing but soup—imagine, one thousand cans of soup in the bilge! Now I have arranged for passage off the island."

"Take care. They are looking for you."

"I am not afraid of those punks."

"Well, good luck."

"And you also."

I was still chuckling when I reached the Post Office. I informed the postmistress of my desire to call Susan in Syracuse, N.Y., and was invited to fill in a form. When duly completed, it received two hefty stamps. Then I joined the line outside Flores's single phone booth. After a quarter of an hour, I entered the cubicle and tried to call upstate New York. "I am sorry," said the voice of a woman who seemed to be in Horta, "but all channels to the United States are busy. Try again soon, please." I drifted away to write postcards to my older daughter Stephanie, my stepmother, and Rufus. The required postages were carefully computed, then each card got a desk-demolishing smash from the postmistress. I joined the phone line again. Some of the people ahead of me seemed vaguely familiar. Fifteen minutes later I learned the channels were still busy. I must call back "in a little while."

By now I knew the ropes and walked straight to the end of the queue. At least half of the people ahead of me had been here when I started. My lengthening sojourn in the phone lines gave me a chance to think. Ought I to be abandoning the race like this? Perhaps, after all, I did not have the temperament to be a true lotus-eater, even for a few days. Yes, I relished the prospect of some more high-powered chats with Kurt Eriksen. And the genial sea-nymphs of the Maiden's Pool undoubtedly had their allure. But I recalled the fate of Odysseus's companions who, on eating the fruit, forgot their families and home and lost all desire to return to their native Ithaka. Would I remain here forever? Or would I be lured into joining the Sea Gypsies and drift, unremembering, from island to island with the seasons?

I was tempted. But my adventures with the low-life types on the *Daphne* had shown me that there was another side to paradise. I suspected I could drift with the lotus-eaters of the Maiden's Pool for only so long. Then I'd be drawn by boredom and sloth into becoming a Caliban, a boozy malcontent provoking fistfights and stealing dinghies in the moonlight. For many years after my dismissal from Cambridge my father had, perhaps rightly, feared that such a fate awaited me. "This is my hooligan son from America," was Walter's affectionate way of introducing me to his neighbors on my rare visits to England.

I stepped out of the phone line.

"Quero enviar um telegrama," I said to the postmistress. "Pode dar-me um impresso, faz favor?" A minute later I was filling in the new forms. Message Reads: HEAD WINDS PUSHED JOHAN TO FLORES STOP NO DAMAGE STOP TELL COMMITTEE STILL IN RACE STOP. LOVE YOU JAKE. The forms, filled in triplicate, received their authenticating smashes. I paid $6.12 in American currency and ran out the Post Office door. Wasn't the hooligan son supposed to be racing? And didn't the faithful *Johan* still have a fine chance of beating her sister *Catapha*'s record of thirty-nine days, seventeen hours, and fifteen minutes to Newport? I jogged back to the Maiden's Pool. On the way I purchased five loaves of coarse Azorean bread, two bottles of red wine, and a can of frankfurters made in Germany. In the little shop they spoke neither English, nor French, nor German. Yet when my purchases were totalled on the cash register, the words at the top of the bill came out in plain English. THANK YOU, they said, PLEASE COME AGAIN.

12

Into the Void

It was supper time. *Johan* was breezing along at three-and-a-half knots on the starboard tack, wind out of the northeast. A tape of the Penguin Café Orchestra was on the player, and Corvo and Flores were a dozen miles astern, just beginning to release me from their wind-shadow. Both had acquired, in the last few minutes, a tinge of grey about their higher peaks. My meal, now heating up in the saucepan, consisted of canned peas and frankfurters with hot mustard and fresh bread on the side.

I had returned to the Maiden's Pool, breathless, a few minutes before noon. José Augusto—Umberto's uncle—was, it seemed, just leaving the dock for his midday meal. I persuaded him, in sign language, to give *Johan* a tow out. He agreed, but indicated that it must be immediate or he would be in trouble back at the house; the white-haired patriarch made sharp chopping movements against the back of his neck. *Johan*'s departure was thus almost as precipitate as her arrival, and I had no time to leave Kurt Eriksen a note to say I'd miss cocktails and dinner. Later, as *Johan* sauntered past the rocky promontories of northern Flores, I raised Umberto on Channel 16 and asked him to convey my apologies to Kurt at the hotel that night. Umberto tried to take some of the sting out of my departure by saying "a race is a race, you got to keep going . . ."

"*Johan* to Umberto. I feel like the Flying Dutchman, over."

"Non, non. Remember, you are the boat from Flores."

"I shall not forget. I will leave the Portuguese ensign on the mast. It will remind me of Flores all the way to Newport."

"Thank you. We at the Hotel Santa Cruz will remember the flag, too."

"Flores and Corvo are the most beautiful islands in the world, and one day I shall return with many friends and celebrate your Summer Festival in the proper fashion."

"Yes, I know you will come back. Goodbye, Tim 'Ubbard."

"Goodbye, Umberto."

Things were getting emotional. And radio procedure had gone to the winds. But this was my final communiqué with St. Brendan's Beacon. I could not bring myself to utter the deadly word "Out." I left the channel open on receive. A few more garbled sounds came over, but I did not reply. The radio hissed to itself for another ten minutes, and then I switched off.

I looked around. In many ways it was good to be back at sea again. For one, it was a darn sight cooler than the land and, except

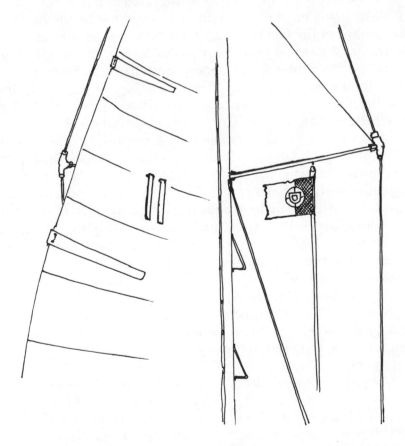

My passport to reality.

for the few strays I had brought with me, there were no flies out here. No dolphins had come by this evening (perhaps they were searching for me up ahead), but half an hour ago *Johan* had surprised a large turtle swimming resolutely toward Flores. She must have been in 1,000 fathoms of water. From whence did she come? How did she navigate? Or was this a mere chance encounter with the island? Somewhere I had read that the only creature with a palate tough enough to eat the peppery Portuguese man-of-war jellyfish was the sea turtle. Bon appetit, Madam!

Now my own supper was ready. I ate it out of a china bowl, sitting in the cockpit. After a few mouthfuls I took a sip from a bottle of red Azorean wine and looked astern. The tinges of grey on the mountaintops of both island had, in the last few minutes, been transformed into long plumes of mist. *Johan* pushed the water away from her bow in gentle, rolling swoops, and every now and then the electronic log emitted a soft click as yet another sea mile passed under her keel. I glanced down at the big compass in the cockpit. We were sailing due west, straight into the sunset.

As dusk fell, I went on a purge, swatting the last of the flies that had free-loaded their way on to the ocean with *Johan*. Later, I tuned into the long drainpipe of the BBC's World Sports Roundup. The leading Observer Singlehanded contestants, it seemed, were now approaching Newport. Peter Phillips had torn a jib and fallen back to fourth place. Eric Tabarly and Marc Pajot, former master and pupil, were grappling for the lead with a third, unnamed boat. Who was the mystery skipper?

The report continued ... *Crédit Agricole II*, under the command of BOC winner Philippe Jeantot, had capsized and *Umupro Jardin V* had stopped to help. Florence Arthauld's *Biotherm II* was in Horta, Azores, with structural damage. *Double Brown*, a 35-foot catamaran from New Zealand, had broken up close to the Grand Banks. "Her skipper, Mr. John Mansell," said the metal-voiced announcer, "has been located and safely rescued by Mr. Alan Wynne-Thomas, another OSTAR contender, sailing the monohull *Jemima Nicholas*." End of broadcast.

It took several seconds for the news to sink in. Well done, Alan! The Half Crown Club to the rescue! I switched off the set and realized I had been holding my breath to catch every word. What had happened to Mansell's boat? How had the rescue gone? Half a dozen possibilities swept through my mind. Both skippers, it seemed, had opted to go right through the ice. Had Mansell struck a berg? For me, the most impressive aspect of the rescue came from the announcer's word "locate." I'd had enough trouble just finding a great lump like Corvo. How, I wondered, had Alan managed to find *Double Brown* in all those miles of ocean?

The BBC transmission made me feel that *Johan* was part of the race again. No doubt Big Brother Argos had tracked my brief defection to Santa Cruz. But with all the excitement at Newport and the drama of Mansell's rescue, perhaps the Race Committee would hardly notice. In a little while I switched on the radar alert and—after a final scan around the horizon—turned in to my bunk.

I did not awaken until first light. *Johan* had held impeccably to her course in the night and was still pointing due west. But her speed had increased to four knots. I lit a flame under the kettle, pushed back the hatch, and looked astern. The horizon was empty. There was not even a fleck of cloud to show where the islands might have been. I took the binoculars out of the rack just inside the hatch and focused them. Nothing. The Fortunate Isles, where saints immortal reign and everlasting spring abides, had sunk into the limbo from which they had so mysteriously arisen. Already, it was as if they had never existed and I had never been there. So I awoke, and behold it was a dream.

But this dream was different. It had really happened. I looked up at the starboard cross-tree. No matter how addled my single-hander's mind might become in the weeks ahead, the little Portuguese ensign snapping at its halyard above would be my passport to reality; this, it would declare, was the boat that found Corvo.

After another cup of coffee, I checked the log and hauled out the Husun sextant for a sequence of shots. The data agreed, putting *Johan* at 32° 22′ W, or about forty-eight miles due west of Flores. Then I pulled out the big charts. The time had come, I knew, for some serious thinking. I turned to a new page of the Log and wrote at the top the words "Strategic Planning."

This was the tough part. It was logical to assume that the contrary winds that had wafted me down to Corvo had also afflicted the OSTAR competitors immediately ahead and immediately astern of *Johan Lloyde*. By now, I calculated, my opponents would probably be strung out in a great arc under Waypoint Weld, about 300 miles to the north. Perhaps, I thought, I could use my extra southing to competitive advantage. Or, at any rate, I could play an outsider's game that might—given the vagaries of the North Atlantic weather—get me over the line ahead of them.

I studied the charts carefully. The little green arrows on the pilot maps for June and July showed that the Gulf Stream was now pushing east in the squares above 40° N at ascending rates of five-, six-, eight-, and nine-tenths of a knot respectively. Below this latitude, the currents curled back on themselves in great whorls that occasionally ran in the opposite direction to the west. Perhaps I could jog north a bit to escape the Azores High, and then cut down and bounce along old Jormungand's soft underbelly to a point about 37°N and 68°W. This new waypoint was level with Norfolk, Virginia, and on the same longitude as Bar Harbor, Maine. I decided to call it Waypoint Virginia.

By coming in low like this, *Johan* might well harness the Stream's back eddies. While my opponents were tacking back and forth around Georges Bank against the prevailing southwesterlies and the Stream (now running at one and a half knots plus), *Johan Lloyde* would be prancing down on a quarter run from Waypoint Virginia and slicing across the Stream straight into Newport Harbor. Such a plan was, in short, a modified form of the Left Hook strategy. I might come in last. But at least I had a chance of beating a good number of other boats to the post.

There were two drawbacks to such a plan. The first, and the lesser of them, was that like it or not I was choosing to play Jack Hunt's game, a game in which he was the expert and I the rank amateur. As a veteran Atlantic navigator and as the architect of the Deep South strategy, he had slept for years with the pilot charts under his pillow. *Crystal Catfish*, though a traditional long-keeled cutter like *Johan*, had a surprising turn of speed in certain winds. Also, Hunt had a powerful ship-to-shore radio that enabled him to play the local weather patterns like a violin.

The other problem was that this strategy led me right through the middle of what many skippers called the Great Void, that gigantic spread of emptiness that lay under 40°N between the longitudes of 30° and 60°W. This was one of the remotest parts of the North Atlantic. The water, due to its proximity to the near stagnant Sargasso Sea, was unduly saline. Almost no birds flew here and few ship lanes ran across the area's invisible boundaries. My little shortwave radio, even now, could obtain the BBC only with great difficulty, and for technical reasons no American stations could be expected to come in for at least a thousand miles (see map, p. 142).

While the eastern Atlantic was comparatively shallow, the floor

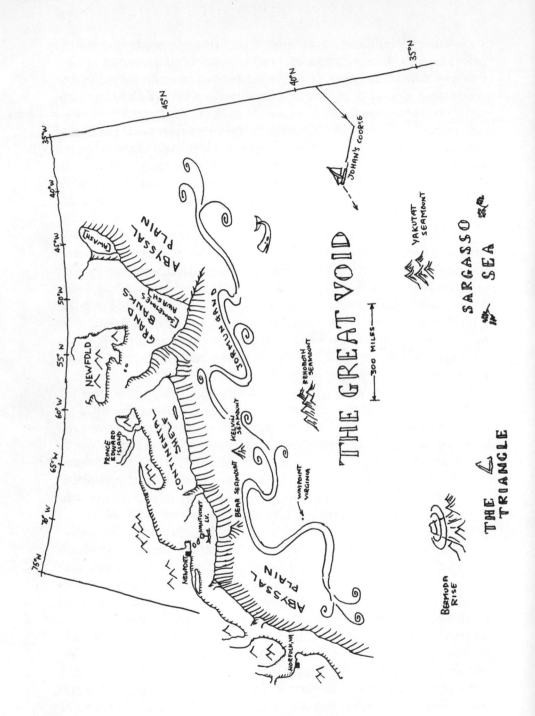

of the Great Void sank to 3,700 fathoms—far deeper than Mount Kilimanjaro was high. An American penny flipped over the side, after twinkling for a few seconds in the ship's wake, would take more than six hours to settle on the bottom. The Void also had its own underwater peaks, or seamounts as they were called. A few had friendly names like Bear and Kelvin seamounts. But others were more sinister. My keel would pass well north of Yakutat. But the submarine range named Rehoboth rose up more than two miles from the ocean floor and lay, only a few hundred feet below the surface, right across *Johan*'s path.

Of one thing I was confident. My boat, though the varnish on her bulwarks was peeling and long streaks of rust now ran down from her chain plates, was as sound as ever. Her sails retained their stiff, dynamic curves, her bottom was clean, and the water in her Monel tanks was still fresh as a mountain spring. Susan had written out several lists of supplies. But I had mislaid them. Due in part to boredom and in part to business with other chores, I had not brought myself to resurrect her menus for three meals a day for forty days. When stocking up on supplies, I had just bought a case of corned beef, a case of canned spaghetti, a case of unsweetened orange juice . . . until it looked as if I had a big enough pile to keep me going. Though I'd been at sea for quite a while, the lockers under the saloon berths still seemed quite full of cans, many of them purchases before the voyage began in upstate New York. Despite the warnings of the Old Salts, I'd left all the paper labels on and they were still quite legible and none seemed to have floated off into the bilge. Some cans however, after one and a half Atlantic crossings, were beginning to rust a bit at the edges.

The case of long-life milk that Alan Wynne-Thomas had persuaded me to buy in Plymouth was still almost intact. Bottles of Iceberg Gin ($4.88 from my hometown liquor store) and cans of Whitbread and Utica Light beer were still piled knee-deep in their assigned lockers. The only blot on the culinary horizon was the declining supply of Rose's lime juice. Recently I'd taken to mixing my Iceberg with canned orange juice on alternate evenings. I still had more coffee, tea, Bovril, Bournvita, Cacao, Horlicks, and other strange English hot drinks than I knew what to do with.

Since marine insurance companies would not give untested singlehanders anything but outrageous rates, I had not been able to afford any kind of coverage for my transatlantic crossings. For this reason I had prepared *Johan* to be as self-sufficient as possible and to be able to go where few other boats could go. Her lonely and very chilly voyage down the St. Lawrence and across the Gulf had been a great test of that. For these reasons, she'd always carried much more equipment than the Chief Inspector had required on his checklist in Mill Bay Dock.

The circumstance I feared most was dismasting, either by lightning (no doubt there'd be plenty of that in the Great Void) or by being knocked down in a tropical storm. To handle this possibility, *Johan* carried a set of extra large cutting and filing tools, a big vise that could be bolted to a workbench, spare stays, and a set of special winches and ratchet pulleys. While these might not permit me to restep my 43-foot mast—as one OSTAR competitor had managed to do in 1980—they would at least make it possible for me to erect a plausible jury rig with one of *Johan*'s booms, on the stump of her present spar.

My second great apprehension was an attack by whales. This was not an abstract threat. Numerous boats in previous OSTARs had been attacked and even sunk by them. Though I did not know this immediately, two boats in 1984—*Go Kart* and *Tjisje*—were to be sunk in similar assaults. And Luis Tonizzo's *Slidell* was to survive an attack that lifted the entire boat bodily out of the water. On two occasions on my way over from Canada, schools of whales —which I tentatively identified as Minkes whales—had sported around *Johan* for an hour or so. Though the incidents were 1,500 miles apart, the final phases of the encounter were identical. After the whales had snorted and played ponderously at a distance of 150 yards, there was a sudden silence. Then a single creature surfaced like a black nuclear sub twenty feet from *Johan*'s port side and cruised alongside for several seconds. In both cases I was paralyzed with awe and apprehension. Then the whale sounded, and the visit was over.

If a pod of such monsters intended to destroy *Johan*, there was not a whole lot I could do about it. But at least I could minimize the risk. Whales, I'd heard, were more likely to attack a boat whose bottom was painted red or brown, so I made sure *Johan* was painted with blue anti-fouling. I made sure that all my through-hull instruments (including the log) had no external appendages that could get ripped off in an affectionate brush. Though I am no hunter and tend to dislike guns, *Johan* also carried a great blunderbuss that fired balls of lead about one inch in diameter. This was the last resort. My son, then a strapping sixteen, had tested this monstrous weapon and nearly knocked his shoulder off. Perhaps as a result I had not yet brought myself to fire it. I realized that its use in anything less than a mortal show down could only serve to put my assailants into an even meaner mood. I, too, wanted to save the whales. But I also wanted to survive them, since they clearly had a lot of old scores to settle.

Strategic Planning. When set beside such disasters as dismasting and whale attacks, the problems of navigation seemed minor. Yet I was worried. If I lost track of the calendar, and could no longer identify the days of the month, then the columns of figures in the almanac would become useless and neither the sextant nor a revitalized Sat-Nav could help me locate *Johan*'s position on the face of the globe. To keep my mind on track, I would customarily make an emphatic note of the new date when I first put the kettle on the stove each morning, and then I would enter the distance travelled since the previous morning. But in the heat of the Azores High I realized that I was having increasing difficulty distinguishing thought from action. Sometimes I did not remember making certain entries in the Log, but when I looked, there they were. On other occasions, I was confident I'd entered some sunsights or other important data. Yet when I checked the page, I found it was blank. A good portion of my time, I was dismayed to discover, seemed to be spent in a kind of waking dream. My eyes were open. I could see things. But it was as if the part of my mind that initiated action had become disconnected. I would get out of my bunk to check the distance run, or the wind speed. Some time later I would "awaken" to find myself staring at the instruments over the chart table. What had I come over here for? Which instrument was I supposed to read? Sometimes it took the strongest act of will, exercised over a period of several seconds, to reestablish the mental link between thought and action.

Now, in a determined effort to keep at least one foot planted firmly in reality—and the endless columned figures of the navigational tables—I took to writing the date each dawn in black marker numerals one inch high on the bulkhead over the chart table. Then I restowed the marker on a different shelf to indicate it had done its work for the day. At night, just before turning in, I would ritualistically transfer the marker back to the shelf over the chart table, ready for use at first light.

Strategic Planning. I studied once more the big Atlantic charts in *Johan*'s saloon and wondered what kind of life existed in the submerged canyons of the Rehoboth range of seamounts. Some whales, for sure. But it was also easy to imagine the presence in those midnight deeps of far more hideous creatures, their bodies squashed flat into an evolutionary *cul de sac* by 10,000 tons of oceanic pressure. When hauled to the surface, they would undoubtedly explode. I shuddered. Clearly the Great Void had—for me, at least—a nongeographic dimension. It was in these waters that Donald Crowhurst had thrown himself over the side of the speeding *Teignmouth Electron.* This was where singlehanders became disorientated. Even a tough nut like Chay Blyth, on the last leg of his nonstop circumnavigation in *British Steel,* confessed to seeing strange men covered in barnacles swarming onto the deck at night. On *Johan*'s voyage over to Plymouth in 1983, I had made an informal study of hallucinations. So far as I could determine, the phenomena generally had their beginnings more in sound than in sight. All the gurglings that occur as a boat moved through the water often resembled the sounds emitted by the human throat. On several occasions I had heard "voices" in *Johan*'s engine room, clear as a bell. On another occasion, a voice like that of a subhuman creature being slowly strangled came out of a locker full of damp sweaters. At the time my mind correctly interpreted these as the sounds of water against the hull or in the cockpit drains. I was able to say firmly to myself, "I'm not going to have a hallucination" and make it stick. Obviously, if a singlehanded skipper is close to exhaustion or spaced out with loneliness it becomes increasingly difficult for him to make that resolve. At the same time, it also occurred to me that voyagers on boats with large crews might also experience hallucinations and yet not know it. For example, if a crew member was down below and heard voices, it would be easy for her to say "Oh, that's Pete on the foredeck" and go on unconcernedly about her business. Only the singlehander was in a position to know that the voices could not emerge from human mouths.

People might consider my solution to the problem of hallucinations on *Johan Lloyde* as somewhat stark. But it worked. About ten days out of Nova Scotia on my way over I had laid it down in Standing Orders that There Will Be No Hallucinations On This Ship. Hallucinations were simply unprofessional and unseamanlike. And Nelson Keeble, my old bargeman from the Thames Estuary, would have spat a wad of tobacco over the side and grinned if I'd even mentioned the topic to him. When I perceived strange sounds and saw strange movements in the corner of my eye, I pronounced them chimera and got on with the job of sailing and navigating the boat.

This worked pretty well while I was awake. But I discovered that no regulation in the world, no matter how ironfisted, could control a singlehander's dreams. Indeed, as my Log attests, I had experienced some of the most vivid dreams of my life while single-handing the previous summer across to Europe. Perhaps they were a reflection of my psychic condition at the time. But I suspect that, as much as anything, the isolation and the blankness of the horizon may have been responsible; it was as if the uninterrupted empti-ness was pushing my mind on an inward voyage of its own.

The most powerful of these dreams took a remarkably similar form. They generally involved lifelike and usually friendly en-counters with relatives and friends who had died years before. Why were they, I had wondered, returning to me now? Perhaps I was conducting an elaborate *pas-de-deux* with something called my Death Wish. But that did not seem right. The vivid singularity of these meetings, with the dream *personae* so subtly in character, could not be explained for me in such categorical terms. Also, these were not mere flashbacks to the happy times when we were all alive together; in my dreams I was aware that they had died. Often these spirits displayed some embarrassment at their changed con-dition, occasionally flashing archetypal images of decay. One in-sisted on always keeping the right side of his face turned away from me, while another had daubed his features with a heavy layer of makeup. But the eyes sparkled. And I heard jokes that, even when recalled on awakening, made me laugh out loud.

Over the winter I mentioned the dreams to a colleague at the university. He chuckled and, with a kind of take-it-or-leave-it smile, handed me a book. It was a collection of medical accounts of experiences that had occurred, technically, after the death of the patient. In these accounts, the victims of heart attacks and strokes had—after dying in the traditional sense—been revived by the powers of modern emergency medicine.

The survivors reported a remarkable commonality of experi-ence that was usually the same for believers and nonbelievers alike. As a rule, the patient had the impression of passing down a long dark tunnel into an open, lighted space. Here he or she was greeted by a so-called Guide, usually a relative or close acquaintance who had already passed on. Then the newcomer was led forward to meet a being described as the Figure of Light, who welcomed the voyager with a warm and complete acceptance. Home at last! For Christians, the figure would assuredly be that of Jesus. Other religions would identify it with one or other figure of special holiness, and agnostics often saw it as the embodiment of the Anthropos, the collective spirit of all humankind. After reading the book, I could not help wondering if the phantoms of my mid-ocean dreams were staging a friendly warm-up for future service as my Guide across the Styx. Perhaps I had, without knowing it, come very close to death on my voyage toward Europe. So far, on my return across the ocean, my dead acquaintance had left me alone. But now I strongly suspected that if *Johan* laid her course across the Great Void—with its heat, its dearth of shipping, and its absence, even, of seabirds—then my friends would return to my dreams accompanied, perhaps, by specters of a less sympathetic nature.

I comforted myself with the thought that such spooks and other midnight visions must have sailed into the dreams of the early Norse explorers and of the Pilgrim Fathers. Perhaps they'd even disturbed the sleep of such fire-eaters as Drake, Hawkins, and Grenville. All these men, however, had sailed in company. No singlehander, by contrast, could restore his equilibrium on awakening with a chat and a few shared grumbles about the food.

Strategic Planning. I seemed to have pondered these issues for the better part of a day. But though I was on the brink of the Void, there seemed precious little to show for it. I climbed on deck and checked the sails and the course. Still due west. Then I retired below again and poured myself a stiff gin and lime. After a few swigs, I pulled the Log book toward me once more. The top part of the page was filled with jottings about the weather, currents, and likely movements of my fellow competitors. Then came a blank space of three or four inches. Below the space now appeared four lines of doggerel written in a bold hand that did not wholly resemble my own.

> I dream'd a dream last night
> Beyond the Isles of Skye;
> I dream'd a dead man won a fight,
> And that dead man was I.

13

Down the Up Staircase

P assing through the various mid-Atlantic weather systems was like climbing up a staircase for five or six days and then stepping off into space. The wind speeds on the Beaufort scale went from 0 to 2 to 4 to 6 and then blew a full gale for a couple of days before suddenly falling away to a flat calm in which *Johan* thumped around in a massive swell without a drop of wind to steady her. Then the cycle would begin again: 2–4–6–8 gale-calm. As *Johan* moved up the staircase, she began to divest herself of her raiment until she was pounding along at seven or eight knots and was almost naked of canvas (see diagram, p. 151).

Unlike those of a great courtesan, however, *Johan*'s garments—particularly on the uppermost steps—came off only with a lot of low-life struggle. Her mainsail had but two seven-foot-deep reefs, and getting in that second slab of canvas, singlehanded, came to be a chore I dreaded. With experience, however, I had devised a system that enabled me to reef without reducing *Johan*'s speed, close-hauled, through the water. Many of the more expensively equipped boats like *Thursday's Child* had a spider web of lines that enabled their mainsail to be reefed from the cockpit. But *Johan*'s more primitive system still required a crewman—me—to go forward to the foot of the mast, which generally meant a thorough soaking.

A second and final reef in the mainsail generally took me about twenty minutes, and longer if I was feeling seasick. My first move would be to change out of my dry clothes into jeans and T-shirt that were already clammy with saltwater. That was the part I disliked most. Then I'd clip on the harness straps that met in a stout metal plate that lay on my chest. The center of this plate had a hole through which the hook of my lifeline was clipped. Then I'd don the thigh-length seaboots I'd bought at the trawler fleet store in Canso, Nova Scotia, and pull on my yellow vulcanized rubber oilskin coat that came well below my knees. As a final touch I'd wind the *Observer*'s daintily monogrammed little spray towel around my neck. Feeling somewhat like a samurai, I'd then clump my way aft and stand under the mainhatch. In the next lull between waves I'd push it back, hook up my lifeline to the heavy plastic-coated cable that ran down the center of the ship, step out into the cockpit, and then slam the hatch shut before the next wave could hit.

Old Salts generally have decided opinions about which side of the ship you should move forward on—windward? leeward?—but so far as I could determine, both had their advantages and disadvantages and I usually gave myself a choice. The trek to the foot of the mast was only twelve feet long, but it was a universe away from the cockpit. The motion was always much sharper up there, and often it was all I could do to hold onto the stanchions that stood up from the deck forty inches on either side of me. The force of the wind running past the sail was also much greater, and when a sea came aboard there was no shelter into which I could duck. All I could do was turn my back, take a deep breath and hang on tight. On my earlier expeditions to the mast I had worn a woolen watchcap, but after the second was whisked away and washed overboard in the welter of wind and spray, I now generally went bareheaded.

My first move was to slacken off the main halyard a few inches, just enough to let the far end of the boom slip into its lee side notch on the gallows. Next—and this is where I sorely missed a crew—I'd haul myself back to the cockpit to tighten the mainsheet, thereby ensuring the boom would remain firmly in place. So far, the mainsail was still pulling *Johan* forward, closehauled, with almost undiminished power. Back at the foot of the mast I'd now slacken the main halyard a couple of feet and then use the winch on the side of the boom to haul the clew-line on the reef cringle down to the reefing sheave on the outboard end of the boom. As the line came up taut I'd slacken off some more halyard until the cringle on both sides lay tight against the boom. Then I'd work my way back down the boom, bundling the loose parts of the sail together and tying them very tightly with the reef points that were

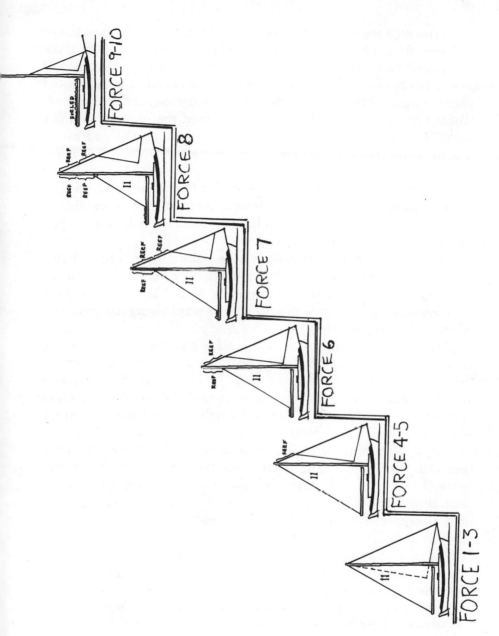

The weather staircase.

laced through the mainsail every eighteen inches. Some boats used roller-reefing, which wound the sail abound the boom, though the more modern approach was "slab" reefing that only pinned the sail to the boom once every five or six feet. Robert Clark, the noted yacht designer, once told me that the best way to retain the productive curve on a sail was to use old-fashioned reef points, so that's what *Johan* got. Tying them up one-by-one along the boom was undoubtedly the most tiresome part of reefing *Johan;* I had made life a little bit easier for myself by using white rope for the lower points and bright red rope for the upper reef points. When they were all snugged down I then released the mainsheet a few inches and hauled back up on the main halyard so that the boom popped up out of its notch on the gallows.

Reefing the yankee, of course, was quite a bit simpler. I just released the sheet and hauled in on the furling-drum line until the size of the sail balanced that of the main. Then I'd winch the sheet back again, and the boat would be on her way, losing hardly a foot of forward motion.

After a brief jog up to 40°N to escape the Azores High, *Johan Lloyde* climbed through a major weather staircase that left her, by the evening of June 23, at about 37°53′N and 42°20′W. She was now about 480 miles west of Flores and deep into the Great Void. I was concerned, however, that the wind might be pushing me too far south too soon. We were already almost on the same latitude as Waypoint Virginia, with still 1,500 miles to go. With the wind over the starboard bow, I now tried to nudge us a bit further north again. To judge by the entries in *Johan*'s log, the Void was already beginning to take its toll, if not on the boat, then upon the mind of her skipper. An entry for June 24 read:

> Haven't seen a ship since I left the Azores. I can hardly tell one day from another. No birds. Just NOTHING out here. Blue waves, eternal northwesterlies. The prop spins. The log clicks. I reef. I unreef. The dolphins come. They go. It's as if *Johan* is just stuck in one place— transfixed, day after day—same sea, same light, same wind.

Though I tried to be imaginative in the galley, all the meals seemed alike, and after a while I just opened the nearest can and threw it on the stove. Then, through laziness, I began to skip meals altogether. Apart from the changing digits on the electronic log, the only way to measure any progress at all was to note the chafe on the yankee sheet against the lower shrouds and the location of my page marker in John L. Motley's magisterial three-volume work *The History of the Rise of the Dutch Republic*, first published in 1856. On previous sailing trips, my reading had generally begun with the classic works of literature and philosophy and then, after a couple of days' hard labor, descended to adventure yarns and whodunits. Now, it seemed, I had come full circle to this fulsomely documented and elegantly presented account of how King Philip of Spain sought to impose his divine will and his Inquisition upon the people of sixteenth-century Holland. I was reminded on a number of occasions of my discussion with Kurt Eriksen in the Hotel Santa Cruz. At one point the Spanish king became so chagrined with the people of the Netherlands that he condemned the entire population—three million men, women, and children—to death by burning. According to Motley, when the Pope and the other Catholic monarchs of Europe remonstrated with him, King Philip relented. Instead of decreeing death by fire, Philip's highest juridical body—its official title was the Council of Blood—solemnly ruled that the Dutch people should have their sentence commuted to the less painful death by strangulation. O Merciful Monarch! When the Dutch people finally took up arms against this royal monk, they were greatly helped in their struggle for freedom by the network of islands and waterways lying in the Scheldt Estuary below Antwerp. This long-fought struggle did much to mold the character of the Dutch people. Was it mere chance, I wondered, that no fewer than ten skippers now racing in OSTAR 1984 came from the Netherlands? This gave the Dutch, expressed as a proportion of national population, far and away the heaviest representation in the race.

In the last few days I had received two important but barely intelligible transmissions from the BBC. On my second evening out from Flores, the long drainpipe had declared that the initial batch of Observer Singlehanded boats had crossed the line in Newport. The first boat over was *Fleury Michon*, skippered by Philippe Poupon, the twenty-nine-year-old professional navigator who was also once a protégé of Tabarly. This was the dark horse that had stalked Pajot and the Master right up to the line, the mysterious third boat that the BBC had not managed to identify. *Fleury* had, it seemed, covered the distance from Plymouth to Brenton Reef in just sixteen days, twelve hours, and twenty-five minutes. She had reached newport at 7:05 P.M. local time, just as it was getting dark.

With hardly any sponsorship, she had pipped such multimillion-franc ventures as *Elf Aquitaine* and *Paul Richard* at the post. But it was a close-run thing. Just twenty-three minutes after *Fleury* crossed the line, Marc Pajot brought *Elf* storming in out of the darkness, followed by Tabarly in *Ricard* just two hours later. Peter Phillips, who'd held the lead for so long, crossed the line three hours behind Tabarly. Never had so many front-runners been so tightly bunched. "No less than thirteen boats," said the BBC announcer, "have beaten Mr. Philip Weld's record, set in the trimaran *Moxie* in the 1980 Observer Singlehanded."

I had never been introduced to Philippe Poupon. Our closest encounter had been in the soup section of the Co-op food store in Plymouth, where we had nodded hello. For quite a while, Poupon had stood among the bustling English housewives laboriously reading labels and occasionally tossing a can or two into his shopping cart. He was tall, with hair in Byronic dishabille, the romantic hero setting forth to hammer the elements down to size. Perhaps I should have gone over and offered my services with the soups, but I suspected that my French was as halting as his English seemed to be. Now he'd taken his old crimson tri and beaten the hi-tech *Elf* by twenty-three minutes.

But the BBC was not yet finished. Indeed, the announcer was for once loosening his waistcoat to give some real coverage. Perhaps the most striking news of all was that Warren Luhrs had somehow pushed *Thursday's Child*—the 60-foot sloop with the pendulum rudder—into tenth place, crossing the line a mere ten hours behind the flying *Fleury*. Luhrs's time, I learned much later, would have been even better if he had not blown out his best jib 1,000 miles from Newport and if he had not broken a steering cable early in the race. After sailing back to Plymouth for three hours (and thus losing a total of six hours), he'd repaired the cable with a spare halyard and got back on course. Without these setbacks, *Thursday's Child* might have swept the field. As it was, she sailed the shortest route of any boat in Class I. Many of the French skippers, with their huge sponsorships, were profoundly disturbed by the idea of a lowly monohull getting up so close; a small mob of them stood on the Goat Island dock for hours, anxiously quizzing Luhrs about the magical capabilities of his sloop.

One night later the BBC came back on the air to say—surprise! —it was all a frightful mistake. Philippe Poupon and *Fleury Michon* were not, after all, the winners. Instead, the accolade must go to the good-humored Breton, Yvon Fauconnier, forty, and his 53-foot trimaran *Umupro Jardin V*. Though Fauconnier had come across the line ninth—exactly ten hours behind *Fleury*— the Race Committee, after another stormy session, had ruled that he must be credited with the sixteen hours he'd lost standing by Jeantot's capsized *Crédit Agricole*. All the other boats previously ahead of Fauconnier must also go back one place. Of course I did not hear the details until much later. But the supporters of Poupon and the initial lineup argued that Fauconnier's delay had put *Umupro Jardin* into a different series of weather patterns. For this reason, they maintained, the boats were really competing in two quite distinct races. "I won an Observer race," Poupon subsequently told the press, "and he won an Observer race." The issue was further clouded by the ambiguous circumstances of Fauconnier's delay. He had offered to pick up Jeantot, but the BOC winner had refused to be rescued. Instead, he insisted on remaining with the capsized *Crédit* until a French naval vessel arrived from the Azores to salvage her. At that point should Fauconnier have left him to his fate, or should he have continued to stand by?

Fauconnier's subsequent observations to the press rationalized but did not clarify this dilemma. "I couldn't leave Philippe on his boat," he later told Barbara Lloyd of *SAIL* magazine. "His only purpose was to salvage it, and I was the only person around to help him. It is not a pleasure to lose your boat at sea." Thus, on hard-headed analysis, it would seem that *Umupro Jardin* dallied not to save life but to save a boat. Was that a valid reason for crediting Fauconnier with time lost? Putting it another way, was Jeantot's determination to willfully risk his own neck by staying at the scene dissolve Fauconnier's obligation to stick around?

The Race Committee's decision raised other problems. Was Fauconnier's corrected time of 16:6:25 the new record that competitors in subsequent OSTAR must strive to top? No boat had, in fact, ever sailed the Atlantic that fast. *Fleury's* 16:12:25 clearly stood as the time to beat. How, then, could Poupon set the new record and yet still be only second in the race? For quite a while after the race Poupon sought to put a good face on his disappointment, but under sustained needling by the press (How do you feel, how do you feel?) the erstwhile champion finally broke down and wept. At that moment his arch-rival, Marc Pajot, climbed to his feet and went forward to comfort him. A few moments later Philip Weld, the man who'd set the record in 1980, stood up and proposed that the Race Committee announce a double victory. "This year," he declared, "so far as I am concerned there are two winners." The statement was one of the few pronouncements that received the applause of all those present.

At the time, however, *Johan Lloyde* and the fifty boats still competing in their various classes knew only the barest outline of events. The BBC announcer signed off with a final bulletin on Dr. Ian Radford's sloop *Ntombifuti*. He had, it seemed, awoken one morning to discover his bilge full of water and immediately activated the panic button on his Argos. This, within minutes, led the Race Committee to initiate an international search and rescue operation by all ships in the area.

Jemima Nicholas, which had just picked up John Mansell from *Double Brown*, was directed by radio to join the hunt for *Ntombifuti*. Just as Alan Wynne-Thomas began his search, however, Radford tasted the water in his bilge and found it to be coming from a ruptured water tank. He then switched off his Argos emergency signal and resumed the race.

Such a decision would have been fine except for the fact that it was contrary to race regulations and that Wynne-Thomas and several other OSTAR skippers continued their search for Radford, unaware that *Ntombifuti* was romping on ahead of them to Newport.

I did not know Radford too well. But I recalled there had been a similar mix-up in Plymouth over the matter of a Half Crown Club T-shirt. Radford's name had somehow gotten on to a list of people who wanted a club shirt. However, when I took the shirt to him he refused it.

"What would I want with a thing like that?" he asked me, with an expression of disdain.

"You told Alan you wanted one."

"Well, I don't."

"Okay, okay."

Radford stumped off down the pontoon without another word. Now, it seemed, the black-bearded medico had left a few more people standing in his wake. I felt sad for *Jemima Nicholas*. She'd had such a fine chance of winning Class III and now, it seemed, she'd become the mid-Atlantic rescue boat. Like *Umupro Jardin* she would be credited with the time spent picking up John Mansell. But the added weight of Mansell and his salvaged gear could only slow her down. Under the unwritten rules of long-distance singlehanded racing, Wynne-Thomas must continue to perform absolutely all navigational and sailing duties. John Mansell, however, was permitted to go to work as hard and as dramatically as he chose in the galley and at any other domestic chore where his presence had increased the burden on the skipper.

*   *   *   *

I switched off the radio. The big boats were in. The crowds and the camera crews could go home, and the Argos system could shut down—for financial reasons—to just one fix a day. The BBC, except for a couple of breathless bulletins, would lapse into silence. Though I was by now 1,500 miles behind the leaders, there was on this occasion no feeling of horizontal vertigo for me. Yes, the speed queens and the big-buck sponsors were off the tracks. But several dozen boats, minute pools of light spread for hundreds of miles across the face of the ocean, continued to slide on through the night. They could not see each other, and, no matter how high the plane flew, no camera crew could film this scattered throng. These skippers back in the pack were not casualties; they simply had less financing and less equipment than the front-runners. Like the contenders in the original Observer Singlehanded race, they were still pushing forward and they continued reefing, tacking, and swinging their hearts out upon the winches just as they'd begun, alone. Yet, in its special way, each unseen pool of light was connected with every other pool of light, just as each rose-lit chart table was connected to every other rose-lit chart table, and each competitor wearily scribbling calculations at that table was connected to every other weary scribbler. Far from the public eye, and even further from Plymouth and the magnificent Courtesy Pavilion that had housed the media in Mill Bay Dock, the real Observer Singlehanded Transatlantic Race was just beginning.

14

The Newport Profile

*T*he mapping bureaucrats were to blame, as much as anyone, for warping the minds of transatlantic sailors. These quiet, precise homebodies sat at their great hydrographic desks in the U.S. Defense Mapping Agency and the British Admiralty sucking their pencils and trying to figure out how the world should be divided up. In another age they'd have been assistant deputy Druids or perhaps medieval clerks charged with illuminating cosmologies that sent the sun whizzing round the Garden of Eden. But today, in the present hierarchical setup, they had the power to decree that the North Atlantic ocean must be chopped up into Zones One, Three, and Five. Or, if you prefer the British system, Zones H, A, J, and D.

Before *Johan*'s trip to Europe in 1983, I ordered all her charts from a catalog so labyrinthine that even the librarian in my university's map room had trouble understanding it. But halfway through the delivery process I was told that—lo!—the whole system had been changed. Not only would all charts henceforth have different numbers; they would also slice up the face of the earth into different areas and be laid out on substantially different scales. We started to make our way through a second labyrinthine catalog (obtained with the greatest of difficulty), only to discover that some of the most useful charts of all, like the elegant U.S. 126 (North Atlantic Ocean—Northeastern Part), had been stamped obsolete and abolished. The new zones meshed well with the block-aesthetics of officialdom. But, so far as I could see, they had almost no bearing at all on how a long voyage under sail was actually put together. Though the charts covered the area within each new zone quite effectively, there was often only the skimpiest coverage of how a boat might get from, say, Zone A to the adjoining Zone B. The Orwellian message seemed, to me at least, quite clear. Stay in Zone. Those who change Zones do so at their peril.

This principle, writ large, applied right across the North Atlantic. Charts of Plymouth and the English Channel were on the largest scales, giving about two miles to the inch. These charts sat, like Russian matryshka dolls, inside other charts, covering larger and larger areas in smaller and smaller scales until finally, for the Great Void in the middle of the Atlantic, the only chart left available was U.S. 121. This biggest, grandma matryshka doll stretched its sides all the way from Cape Hatteras and Tangier, Morocco, in the south, to Jan Mayen Land, nearly 300 miles inside the Artic Circle. As the voyager came out of the Void and approached the

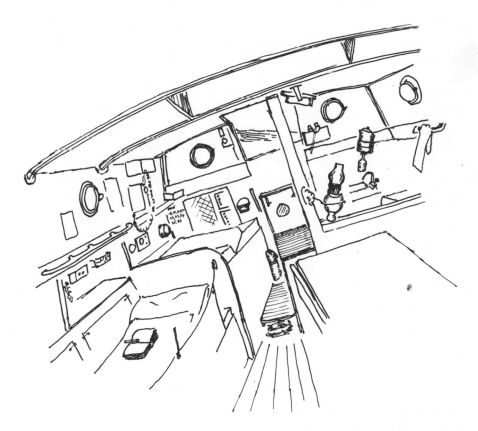

Johan, *now on port tack, claws her way toward Waypoint Virginia. The location of my book mark became the best measure of time passed.*

American shoreline, the chart scales expanded again, step by step, until the final scale was large enough to take a walking tour of the Newport docks.

This new desk-forged policy had the effect of sticking an invisible arrester wire on to the psyche of most transatlantic sailors. Even the veterans' morale was warped out of shape by the feeling that their speed was somehow inversely proportional to their distance from land. The further they went, the slower they went. Once on U.S. 121, a boat could sail her heart out all day—as *Johan Lloyde* was now doing—and make only an inch. Perched on the capstone of the great Atlantic arch, I lost all sense of forward motion. Here the ocean, and the race across it, seemed about 1,000 miles longer than I had bargained for.

To dispel the feeling of running in place, I pulled out all my charts of the U.S. East Coast and then penned in the areas covered by each chart with squares on Chart 121. When *Johan* gets to 41°W, I told myself, she'll be hanging in under U.S. 109 (Eastern Seaboard), and when she gets to 51°W, she will nip neatly on to the southeast corner of U.S. 14003 (Cape Race, Newfoundland, to Cape Henry) and will increase her speed from one inch a day to three inches a day. Then, only a little further ahead, stands the border of U.S. 13006 (West Quoddy Head to New York), where she will really open up and zoom along at ten inches a day.

Out in the middle of U.S. 121, *Johan* continued to climb through succeeding staircases of weather. Often the southwesterlies would attempt to push her away from her intended rendezvous with Waypoint Virginia, and when she had the chance she'd fight her way back down to 38°N or 37°N. For a while now, I had given up on the complexities of trying to make the Walker Sat-Nav cough up or spit out a fix. But I found I could use my sextant position to program the instrument to give me data on the relative position of Nantucket Shoals Lightvessel. On the evening of June 22, it showed Nantucket to be lying at a distance of 1,413 nautical miles on a true bearing of 275°. In the next twenty-four hours *Johan* clocked up 141 miles on the log, and Nantucket now lay 1,283 NM away on the rhumbline, at 277°True. I attributed the disparity between the 130 miles of progress on the Sat-Nav and the 141 miles on the log to the growing effects of the Gulf Stream and the fact that *Johan* was on course not for Nantucket but for Waypoint Virginia. The figures for subsequent days read as follows:

Date	NM to Nantucket Lightvessel	Day's run toward Nantucket
June 24	1158	125 (from previous day)
25	1125	33
26	1054	71
27	957	97

On June 27, the log contained the jubilant entry, written in letters one inch high: INSIDE THE 1,000-MILE CIRCLE! Then, in a significantly smaller typeface, I congratulated myself with the words: "The Plan is working. Watch out, *Catapha*, and all you other slowpokes. *JOHAN* is on the war path."

* * * * *

Beep.

I was dreaming. I dreamed I was visiting New York City, and I wanted to talk to an old friend of mine who, before he'd died five years ago, used to work for *Time* magazine.

Beep.

In the dream I called the magazine from a pay phone, and a woman researcher told me in a concerned voice that James Grant did not work there any more. I stood in the booth and checked the phone directory. Though a bright light was shining on the page, and made it hard to read, I found an entry for James G. Grant and dialled the number.

Beep.

Jimmy answered. He seemed very busy, but agreed to meet for a short while. What was the address again? I tried to check the book, but the light made the page unreadable. I knew I was wanted elsewhere. I felt myself being pulled away. I would not leave until I got the address. Or maybe I could just settle for the phone number and call again later . . .

Beep.

I got the first three digits. I cudgelled my brain 472. . . .? What was the rest of it? I was surfacing. Now I knew I was asleep

somewhere, but I didn't want to wake up. I forced my way back
into the phone booth, and scrabbled around for the number. I was
aware, in the back of my mind, that I was tampering with the dead.
But I did not care. Jimmy had said come on over and I was going
over . . .

Beep.

I awoke with a start. It was 3:44 A.M. I groped for the flashlight
and shone it up at the telltale compass on the ceiling of the cabin.
The course was 260°, just a little south of west. *Johan* was one reef
down, and closehauled on the port tack. I tried to move, but my
body was gripped with an immense lassitude.

Beep.

Jesus. With a great effort I dragged myself out of the lee bunk
and pulled an oilskin over my shoulders. I was irked at being
awoken from my dream and I dreaded the thought of going out
into the wet night. I shuffled aft and with a mighty effort pulled
back the hatch—normally I could do it with one hand. A slosh of
water came down and soaked my chest. I stared off in the darkness.
The Pernicka said the radar was dead ahead, but I could see nothing.

Beep.

Another shower of water came down the hatch. A small gale
was blowing and waves seemed to crumble down on *Johan* from
all directions. Still, I could see no ship. *Johan* rose twenty feet to
the top of a wave. There it was, right ahead, a single masthead
light. Must be a freighter, but it was hard to see which direction
she was moving in. I attempted to get a clearer look through the
low-power binoculars, but all I could see was ragged hillsides of
water. The radar warning beeped again down by my right foot. I
held the glasses steady and glimpsed the superstructure of a
freighter just as another dollop of spray sluiced down the hatch.
She was heading straight for *Johan*.

Shades of my first night in the English Channel. But now there
was more than enough wind, which seemed intent on pushing
Johan right under the bow of the freighter. I was still groggy,
suspended between the dream world and this wet reality, and I
was in no mood to put *Johan* about and wrestle, twice in ten
minutes, with a very angry set of yankee sheets. I tried to raise the
ship on Channel 16 several times but there was no answer. I
changed into my already soaked deck clothes and then pulled on

my safety harness and oilskins. I flicked on the strobe and pulled myself through the hatch.

"S.S. *Delta Ganges* to sailboat. What are you wanting, over?"

I ducked down below again.

"*Delta Ganges*, we're on a collision course. I am very fine on your starboard bow, range 400 meters. Can you see me, over?"

"Seeing nothing, over." The voice was querulous, almost as if its owner had, like me, just been awoken from deep slumber.

"I have masthead strobe going, over."

"Seeing nothing, over."

I cursed and clambered back through the hatch into the cockpit, disconnected the tiller from the Aries and, in a thunderous shaking of sails, put *Johan* about. The yankee sheet came in very slowly. There was no strength in my arms. Perhaps I had a fever. I found myself wondering why someone had not invented a clockwork winch that would harness all the power of the released sheet to help haul in the new lee sheet? The rope I was so laboriously hauling in right now would soon fly off into the darkness as I went about again in a little while. It was a cool night but I could feel the sweat pouring off my face. The *Delta Ganges*, her green starboard bridge light reflecting strange shapes off the lumpy sea, went pounding by. Then I put *Johan* about and fought the yankee sheet again. By the time I had finished, the *Delta Ganges* had vanished into the murk. I switched off the strobe, went below and pulled off my oilskins and clothes. The sweater and jeans I climbed into were only a shade less clammy than the ones I'd taken off. Then I made a cup of strong coffee and laced it with rum.

If the Pernicka radar alert had not awoken me, I would have been talking to Jimmy Grant at about the time the freighter hit. Was Grant's statement that he was very busy a warning for me to stay clear? Or maybe it had been an open situation. Certainly the sleepwalker on the bridge of the *Ganges*, who could not spot a million candlepower strobe under his nose, had been incapable of affecting the equation either way; if I had not heeded the call of the beeper, the freighter would have just ploughed on in . . .

*　*　*　*　*

One night later, *Johan* picked up her last transmission from the BBC. Though it was almost unintelligible in parts, the words on

OSTAR were clear. Just four days after the first 60-foot multihull crossed the line, the *City of Slidell*— the 35-foot sloop in Class IV with Luis Tonizzo at the helm—came skimming into Newport. Luis had zipped *Slidell* straight through the fogs and bergs of the Grand Banks and, two whale attacks notwithstanding, somehow hurled her across the line in the unbelievable time of twenty days and twenty-three hours. This unprecedented feat of seamanship and endurance had brought the Nelson/Marek Class IV sloop in ahead of all the monohulls in Class II (length 40′ to 45′) and all the monohulls in Class III (35′ to 40″). *Slidell* had travelled a total of only 2,986 miles, a shorter distance even than that sailed by *Thursday's Child*. Despite the sparseness of these statistics, it was clear that if OSTAR 1984 had been handicapped like any other sailing contest then Tonizzo's massive square paw would now be held aloft in Newport as the winner of the entire race.

With the news of *Slidell's* feat came some additions to the casualty list. Bob Menzies's 37-foot wooden sloop *Dancing Dolphin* had sprung a leak and sunk. Menzies himself had been rescued by a Greek freighter. Assisting in the rescue was Bertus Buys, skipper of the 35-foot Dutch sloop *Sea-Beryl*, who had risked his own ship to run alongside *Dolphin* with a heavy-duty bilge pump. The 31-foot cutter *Karpetz*, which *Johan* had nearly run down just after the start, had struck a drifting buoy and sunk. Her Swedish skipper, Karl Peterzen, had been picked up by a passing freighter after pressing his panic button. Later, I learned that *Tjisje*, the 29-foot Dutch sloop, had been attacked and sunk by whales. And I learned that Bill Wallace's 30-foot *Novia* had been capsized and dismasted.

Of the ninety-two boats that started the Observer Single-handed, only sixty-six were now—by my calculations—still valid contestants in the race. The hard-eyed prediction of the Royal Western's Chief Inspector seemed to be coming true: one third of the boats in Mill Bay Dock were not managing to get anywhere near to Newport. In the days ahead I found myself wondering if all these casualties could really be attributed to simple "bad luck." Or did the dropouts have some quality in common? Putting it another way, was there a Newport Profile and a Loser Profile? If I had taken a stroll around the pontoons in Mill Bay with a canny and experienced expert like the Chief Inspector, would we have been able to point to each boat and with fair accuracy predict ... Newport ... Washout ... Washout ... Newport, etc., on down the line? This, of course, would not be so much a judgment of the boat (which would, by then, have passed inspection) as a psychological judgment of the skipper. I reviewed the long list of the fallen once more and, disquieting though it might seem, I came to the conclusion that there was a clearly discernible Newport Profile. And I was prepared to bet a clean $100 bill that the Chief Inspector had, over years of scrutinizing entrants to the Observer Singlehanded, come to the same conclusion.

What, then, was the magic ingredient?

In my opinion, it added up to a combination of a special kind of outlook on the world, a special kind of anger and a special kind of laughter. They might be described like this:

1) *Outlook.* The skipper with a Newport Profile was, philosophically, a skeptic. The world, he believed, was a dangerous place; it was not created for man. Nature, even at her most amiable, was an anarchistic trickster who must be closely watched. This skepticism often seemed to extend to human institutions. The Newport skipper disliked the idea of life in a world of *position,* where a form of safety and self-esteem might be enjoyed in predictable man-made hierarchies. Instead, he preferred to inhabit a world of *process* in which quick judgment and shrewd timing were necessary for survival. For this reason, every kind of hierarchical authority—be it that of a headwaiter, a yacht club commodore, or an Archdruid in the government chart office—was immediately and irrevocably suspect.

    The Newport skipper's chief defense against Nature the Trickster was an unquenchable penchant for asking "What if . . . ?" What if my bilge pump clogs? What if my battery goes dead? What if my main halyard breaks? What if whales attack? Should the skipper not push the catechism to the very end of the line, then he might be rated a very nice fellow. But he had unwittingly conceded that Nature was not a total Trickster and maybe that the world was made for humanity after all. Result: one more OSTAR statistic.

2) *Anger.* The psychic energy, or determination, to keep going in the face of profound hardship or discouragement often seemed akin to a kind of controlled anger. This was not the rage of someone who had lost his temper, but the

unflinching resolve to keep on fighting even when the odds seemed hopeless, to keep on sailing out into the Atlantic when the rational part of the mind was convinced that the race had been cancelled, or that OSTAR was all part of a gigantic hoax.

Harnessing such anger was playing with high explosives. If it got even a little out of control it would quickly become a kind of blundering fury, or it could backfire into a petulance too haughty to spot the telltale signs of trouble up ahead. Chalk up two more types of OSTAR statistic.

3) *Laughter.* Bad luck, in Nature's mischievous regime, often ran in chains. Sometimes not one or two but half a dozen or more things, for no apparent reason, suddenly went wrong. At first the Newport skipper's response was analytical. Then it was one of controlled and carefully directed determination not to panic or be dismayed. But as the chain of disasters extended beyond the implausible to the outrageous, the skipper could either go berserk or throw back his head in a great bellow of laughter. This chuckle was not forced out, miser-fashion between clenched teeth. It was, in truth, a great gust of delight at the sheer cussedness of the universe.

Like fire itself, this special kind of cosmic laughter was a gift from the gods. By no means all human beings were blessed with its unconquerable logic: the greater the outrage, the greater the mirth. An assured procedure for becoming a statistic was to embrace the contrary proposition: the greater the outrage, the greater the rage.

Judging by the sound of their laughter alone, I knew that men like Luis Tonizzo, Bill Homewood, Alan Wynne-Thomas, Lloyd Hircock, Jack Hunt, David White, and the Dutch skipper Goos Terschegget would be sure to arrive in Newport. They had the delighted roar of men who were already in Valhalla.

Unfortunately, I could not include myself in this select group. But, then, neither could I be placed with the dropouts. These, as a group, seemed to believe that the universe was an orderly place. They themselves were neat. They got on quite well with headwaiters and with a certain kind of woman. As lads, they went home early. But the real problem, I suspect, was that their hearts were cold. They had no real laughter in them and no appreciation of Nature's perverse ability to disrupt the best laid plans of human-kind. Perhaps they were just Zone sailors. It was of them that the men in the Pentagon and the Admiralty were thinking when they sliced up the world into manageable blocks. Stay in Zone and all would be well. They were not exactly imposters in the starting lineup of the Observer Singlehanded. But then again, neither did they belong in Valhalla. As I said, they went home early.

15

Sabbath at Sea

The evening of Thursday, June 28, found me hanging over *Johan*'s chart table, sucking my yellow pencil. It just didn't make sense. Either my navigation was falling apart or *Johan* was locked in a major geophysical anomaly. However you sliced it, the Left Hook strategy seemed to be in tatters. Since the evening of the previous day, when I had coaxed the Walker Sat-Nav into confirming that *Johan* had broken through the 1,000-mile circle, I had sailed on a course of true west, or 290°Magnetic. My progress in longitude, as stated by Sat-Nav and my sunshots, was confirmed by the electronic log: I had, it said, sailed 102 miles west in the space of just over twenty-four hours. Yet *Johan*'s new latitude did not make sense. Instead of remaining more or less constant it had, in the last day, jumped from 37°58′N to 38°54′N. Thus, it seemed, that besides travelling 102 sea miles due west, *Johan* had also contrived to move no fewer than fifty-six miles due north. I could make no sense of it. Then it struck me.

"Ahhaaa," I said out loud. "Jormungand!"

I had not expected him so soon.

The little green arrows on the pilot chart showed the Gulf Stream moving due east here at 0.8 knots. But the old serpent must have caught *Johan* in an eddy that pushed her due north at a speed of more than two knots for an entire day. That was almost fast enough to create a wind for *Johan* to sail by!

My estimates, sketchy at best, put most of my fellow competitors in Class IV in a clump about 240 miles to the northwest of *Johan*'s present position. If I let the Stream push me any further north, then I'd just become a Johnny-come-lately bumping along in their wake. If *Johan* was to have any chance of beating them over the line then she must struggle south again in the hope of hooking into a whole new weather system around Waypoint Virginia.

On this, my first evening in the grip of old Jormungand, I was presented with a spectacular sunset. Fluffy clouds in many shades of pink seemed to sit on the water all around *Johan*. As darkness came the wind dropped. I stowed sail and tried to jam all *Johan*'s little rolling things tightly into their corners. Later that night I came on deck to see violent lightning flashes far off to the south-west, but I heard no thunder.

Next morning was flat calm. The serpent, I realized, could now shove me anywhere he chose; without wind or the use of an engine there was no way *Johan* could resist. After a breakfast of fruit cocktail and coffee, I took advantage of the calm to make a leisurely tour of the deck. I hadn't liked the look of that lightning in the night. If *Johan* was in for a pasting, I'd better make sure everything was shipshape. I came to the yankee sheets. Whichever way I rigged them they somehow managed to chafe against the shrouds. I bound up their latest wounds with grey duct tape. I was also increasingly concerned about the thin lines that ran forward from the Aries vane gear to control *Johan*'s rudder. The two lines, made of durable Marlow braid, came forward through small plastic blocks and crossed quite far back under *Johan*'s long tiller. At this crossover point they chafed against each other and often against the under side of the tiller itself—so much so that they were beginning to gouge grooves for themselves in the hard laminated wood. When I sheathed them in duct tape like the yankee sheets, it didn't work; in the space of a few hours, everything, including the underside of the tiller, became a sticky mess. My next move was to raise the inboard end of the tiller a few inches by means of a short truss suspended from the boom gallows. This kept it clear of the cross-over point but also caused the gear to emit an ominous creaking in any kind of wind, and it clearly hampered the Aries's ability to keep *Johan* on course. I pondered the solution to this problem of steering for many hours. I could not replace the lines without going over the stern in the dinghy. Nor could I replace the merely chafed part because the ensuing knots would not be able to pass through the little blocks.

Some slight swell seemed to be coming in from the southwest. Such waves, it was said, told the becalmed mariner where his next wind was coming from. Frankly, I could not understand the rea-

son for this. How could waves travel faster than wind? Perhaps
their momentum just carried them further. But what, in the mean-
time, had happened to the wind that created them? I had never
known this old telltale to fail. Until today. The waves kept coming
up from the south, but no wind followed in their wake.

With my chores done, I turned to my place in Volume III of
Motley's *History of the Rise of the Dutch Republic*. The masterful King
Philip of Spain now arranged for the assassination of the great
Dutch leader, William of Orange. Bad move. The people got really
mad. After a while I pushed the book aside and thought about the
Dutch skippers I had met in Plymouth—Bertus Buys, Dr. Dick
Huges, Henk Jukkema, Goos Terschegget. Stout fellows. There
was, of course, no such thing as a national character. But surely
there were national traits. How was it, I wondered, that there were
nearly a dozen entries in the Observer Singlehanded from Holland
and not a single one from Germany, which had a strong yachting
tradition and a far longer coastline on the North Sea?

Maybe it was just my fancy. But was there a more profound
dimension to this business of sailing across a huge ocean alone?
The challenge certainly called forth extraordinary abilities. If I
were an arbitrary despot like King Philip of Spain (or one of his
twentieth-century counterparts), from which group of citizens
would I have most to fear? Forget Baader Meinhoff and its ilk. My
despotic head would lie at its uneasiest, I decided, if I knew that
the likes of Tonizzo, White, Tabarly, and Terschegget—grinning
like maniacs—were planning to climb, tunnel, or blast their way
into my palace. Of the entire population, this was the segment I
would fear most. Men and women who manifested the Newport
Profile were, in a sense, the outriders of modern democracy. They
were harmless enough now, bashing their way across the Atlantic.
Their political potential was untapped; they were, if you like,
village Hampdens, the bridesmaids who—pray to God—would
never be brides. Such obscure talent would only become important
if our present liberal democracies were pushed aside by an authoritarian hand. That was unlikely to happen in the near future. But
perhaps it was good for society to know that the outriders were
there, a light-stepping insurance against totalitarianism. Perhaps
it was not, after all, a complete coincidence that Prince Philip,
Duke of Edinburgh, had agreed to serve as the chief patron of the
Observer Singlehanded. Such alliances, no matter how tenuous,
were always a smart move for a constitutional monarch. They

helped assure that he or she could not be too easily replaced by an *unconstitutional* monarch.

A faint breeze came in from the southwest. The waves had been right after all. By nightfall *Johan*, all sails set, had gone about nineteen miles on the log but only eleven miles over the ground. Her latitude remained virtually unchanged. Jormungand, it seemed, had now switched his tail to run due east. I had recently read up on the Gulf Stream in my book of sailing directions and had been amused to learn that even toward the end of the eighteenth century, many merchant captains had refused to acknowledge its existence. How, I wondered, had the old buffers managed to explain the somewhat jerky progress of their ships to the passengers? Finally an exasperated Benjamin Franklin, who knew all about the Stream from the New Bedford whalers, ordered that the current be charted to speed up the passage of the European mails.

Such unpredictable currents were causing havoc with my dead reckoning and I now sought to extract at least one confirming fix each day from the Sat-Nav. The instrument's effective byte period seemed to be down to twenty minutes after warm-up. If it did not snare a satellite in that time, I had to switch off, let the instrument cool down, and then switch on again in the hope that something would come by. Once I'd received a complete fix I was able to press a button labelled ALT (Alert), which would then accurately predict the precise time that satellite would come overhead. In this, my first encounter with the vagaries of Jormungand, Satellite No. 11 (*Johan's* lucky number!) had come by on both June 27 and June 28 to save my bacon. Now I plotted out its arrival time for as many future passes as I could muster. All I'd have to do then was switch on the Walker fifteen minutes before the satellite was due and hope for the best.

More lightning, like the signs of distant battle, was visible off to the southwest. The breeze freshened. By midnight the moon had not yet risen, but the sky was illuminated by millions of preternaturally bright stars, and *Johan*, on the port tack, was going like a train. On every third or fourth wave she dipped down her bow and two-foot deep waves of solid water came racing aft between the starboard bulwark and the side of the cabin. Each wave was laced with little flecks of phosphorescence. I was exuberant at the return of the wind. I reached out to tighten the yankee sheet on its cleat. The water brushed across my hand. It was bathtub warm. Why not have a swim? I had made it to the Gulf Stream.

Some part of me, deep inside, had heeded Bill Homewood's advice to the nervous back in Plymouth: imagine you'll drown three weeks from today. But the three weeks had passed. It seemed that I might survive after all. *Johan* and I were coming home. Soon I would see Susan and the kids again. Let's celebrate a little. Within seconds I'd tossed all my clothes down into the cabin and was walking forward, stone cold sober and totally naked, without even a safety harness. I grabbed the taut yankee sheet in both hands and lay down feet forward in *Johan*'s starboard scuppers. Wave after wave of blinking phosphorescent dots washed right over me. I looked up and could just detect the glow of the green masthead light among the stars above. The sky seemed to mirror all the little luminous dots flashing past my skin. For a while it was as if I were connected by some mystical bond to the entire universe. Then the hubris set in. I, J.T.W. Hubbard, was capable of doing just about anything. Why should I be confined to this little cabin and these narrow decks? Was not the strength of my arms and shoulders such that I could roll in the sea beside *Johan* as she sped through the darkness? I would hold the stanchion in a single hand as I lay in the foaming water six inches beyond the rail. It was easy. Then, after a while, I'd simply haul myself back on board.

I had my hands on the rope rail and began to step outward. My expectations were too enchanting to be dangerous. But it crossed my mind that climbing over the rail, even on such a beautiful night, was rather an odd thing to be doing. Who would plot *Johan*'s course and trim her sails while I was away? Going over the side might be the most magnificent and wonderful gesture in the whole universe . . . but I could not just leave *Johan* to her own devices. The issue hung there, in balance, for several seconds. Then I stepped back on to the deck. I shudder, even now, to think how close I came.

What, I have since wondered, could have gotten into me? I had not been drinking. I had, quite simply, become intoxicated with that great, luminous, roaring night. Out there, somewhere around 38°N, 52°W, I had for a moment experienced a total—and close to lethal—euphoria. Since that time I have read of several instances in which experienced ocean singlehanders were caught up in a similar exhaltation. One trailed along behind his boat on a thin rope, holding on by a single finger! The chief thing, it seemed, that prevented me from jumping was my reluctance to desert *Johan*, the stout-hearted Rosinante who had brought me so faithfully so far. If I had chartered a standard production boat for the race, the story might have had a different ending. Sometimes, even now, when I am seated before my hearth in Syracuse, I think of my doppelgang, the Man Who Jumped Over the Side, out there in 3,000 fathoms. In his way he was a better and more courageous person than I am. Somehow, though, I don't think he had much prospect of making it to Valhalla.

*   *   *   *   *

By the afternoon of the next day, Sunday, July 1, it was blowing hard. Streaks of foam, turned to white lace in the sunshine, marched in long columns down the wind. I had reefed just before breakfast and had steadily winched in the yankee furling line so that now *Johan* had little more than 150 square feet of headsail showing. The telltale waves, and the distant lightning of two days ago, had been signalling the approach of a major storm and it was clear that I would have to reef again in a little while. But such was the howling and the moaning of the wind on deck that I postponed the moment of stepping through the hatch.

Johan, so far as I could determine, had now passed under the tip of Newfoundland. St. John's, the easternmost city in North America, was now behind me. An hour or so earlier I had swung across the dial of the radio and picked up the Sunday church service from St. Paul's Anglican cathedral in Charlottetown, Prince Edward Island. This was the first transmission *Johan* had picked up from the New World. The sound of the singing boomed lustily above the storm. In my mind's eye I conjured up an image of the congregation lined up along the pews in their Sunday best. In time, the preacher spoke in what seemed to be a transplanted English accent. Each and every one of you, he told these near-blameless people, is a sinner. Your only hope for life everlasting is to be found in the Grace of Our Lord . . . Amen.

It was not my business what these folk said to each other in Charlottetown, P.E.I. But they were broadcasting their ceremonies, and if I could pick them up three quarters of a thousand miles away out here in the Atlantic then I had a right to participate. As the gale howled past *Johan*'s portholes, I tried to come up with a list of sins. I soon realized, however, that my efforts would not be too pleasing to the preacher in the cathedral. I had not murdered anyone nor had I stolen anything recently. Oh yes, sometimes I had not been the best husband and father in the world, but was that to stand between me and life everlasting? On such terms as

those, Heaven would be inhabited solely by celibates and clergy-
men.

It was an odd conjunction that brought this church service over
the air as *Johan* began to struggle against this growing storm. If
thoughts of sin and guilt could not dig my soul out of its shell, then
perhaps stark fear might do the trick. The wind, as it grew
stronger, was veering, and the best course that *Johan* could expect
to carry was above west. At 20:08 GMT I got a fix from my faithful
satellite No 11 that put me at 39°34'N, 54°34'W, or another forty
nautical miles further north. This eddy was pushing me in to the
main eastern flow of the Stream and, incidently, shoving *Johan* into
the middle of the major commercial ship lanes. She must get further off to the south. But the gale clearly had other ideas.

Every hour the wind seemed to be strengthening. The seas
were now significantly bigger than the ones *Johan* had encountered on her way to the Grand Banks. I was worried about the
control lines on the Aries, which were now making a creaking
sound that could be heard throughout the ship. If they broke, I
would have to steer the boat by hand, at best until daylight when
I might be able to effect some repair. I knew I should get out on
deck and reef again, but the world beyond the cabin seemed to be
inhabited by banshees.

Each new gust of wind pushed *Johan*'s starboard rail further
down, and it was clear now that the caprails, the strip of teakwood
lining the top of the bulwark, was leaking badly; the incoming
water had filled *Johan*'s bilges and was now beginning to slop over
the floorboards on the lee side of the cabin. I did not want to go
into the maelstrom and use the cockpit pump. With some difficulty
I pulled a heavy duty hose out of its locker in the fo'c'sle and
unwound it across the cabin floor. I now had to connect it to the
"indoor" bilge pump bolted to the starboard bulkhead just forward
of the mast. I pulled the plastic seal off the pump and a stream of
saltwater gushed into my face and soaked two big shelves of books.
This is like one of those cheap World War II submarine movies,
I thought. Each time a wave struck the side of the boat, water was
forced back, the wrong way, through two rubber valves into the
pump. I struggled to plug the flow with the flat of my hand. I
waited for a lull. Then, with water spurting everywhere I wrestled
the long intake pipe on to the pump and secured it with a clamp.
I then began to pump steadily; 120 strokes later I looked into the
bilge. It was still more than half full; the water must be coming in
through the cap rail almost as fast as I could pump it out. The only

solution was to don my oilskins, brave the banshees out there on
deck, and put another reef into the main.

In a little while I was suited up, samurai style. In view of my
almost-overboard experience, I double-checked my safety harness.
As I waited for the moment and flung back the hatch, the howl of
the wind seemed to go up at least two octaves. There was real
venom in it. The U.S. Yacht Squadron ensign on the backstay was
snapping itself to shreds. I hooked up the harness and clambered
out. Then I hastily pulled the hatch shut.

I glanced forward as a wave broke over *Johan*'s bow and sent
a wall of spray back into the cockpit. The sky was blue and the
wind, thank goodness, was warm. But the waves were coming in
like moving houses. I made my way up the leeside deck to the mast
and hooked onto the stanchion. I was now inhabiting a different

I wrapped my arms around Johan*'s mast. For what we are about to
receive . . .*

world. The surf blew off the larger waves in flat streamers. The smaller seas came roaring over *Johan*'s rail, pouring solid water past my ankles even though I was standing on the cabin top.

"Banshees," I yelled at the top of my lungs into the wind, "Banshees, go home!" This was fun! *Johan* seemed to be bucking in every direction at once. I began the reefing drill by slackening her main halyard. The boom hit the gallows aft with a thump, but the noise of the wind was such that I could only feel the blow. A gust of wind dipped under the back of my sou'wester hat and blew it over the side. I grabbed at it as it went by but to no avail. Without the hat I could see a lot better, but the driving spray hurt the back of my head. An even larger wave than usual loomed up as I worked, and, most ominous of all, I could hear the water breaking along its crest when it was still fifty yards away. I wrapped my arms round *Johan*'s mast. For what we are about to receive . . . There was a pause, a period of relative calm as the wave hung between me and the wind. Then the deck I was standing on drove my legs up like piston rods through thirty feet in the span of two seconds. I found myself on the top of a mountain ridge. This was not like most storms. The visibility was superb. I could see perhaps twenty miles off to the southwest over tier upon tier of similar grey-blue ridges slowly heaving their way toward me. It was a scene from another planet; I might have been on Jupiter or Mars. One half second later I was nearly washed off *Johan*'s deck as the huge wave broke all around me.

For the next quarter hour I wrestled to get a second reef into the mainsail. Even as I worked the sun sank into the sea and it was plain that the wind was still increasing. This was turning into Survival Time. But I was reluctant to just drop all sail and lie a-hull. There had, in recent years, been several instances (notably the experience of the Smeetons when attempting to round Cape Horn) in which such a policy had resulted in the loss of the mast, the rudder, or both. And, apart from anything else, *Johan* was in a race. She must do her best to keep moving. I decided to ease the boat by rolling up the yankee entirely and go under reefed main alone. But such was the force of the wind that when I winched in the furling line it pulled out its last turn with three feet of yankee still showing. The tag end of the sail now began to flap thunderously on the forestay. I tried to tighten the yankee sheet but the fairlead was so far out on the beam that this proved ineffective.

Now what?

If I left it flapping, a $1,000 Hild sail would soon be in tatters.

I went out on to the bowsprit and struggled with the furling line for a while. After three total submersions, I realized there was no way I could get a couple more turns on to the drum without letting the whole sail out again. The only solution, I decided, was to slack off the drum a little and make the yankee into a little storm jib of about fifty square feet. To my surprise, this plan worked and the sail stopped flapping. After fiddling with the Aries for a while, I clambered back below just as it was getting dark. I stripped off my wet clothes and flicked on Channel 16. As I did so I heard an unseen cargo ship tell another " . . . there's supposed to be a 1,000 millibar low around here somewhere . . ." I could not hear the other side of the conversation.

I looked at *Johan*'s barometer. It read 1,038 millibars. I could expect the weather, then, to get quite a bit worse. The boat was now sailing due west at four knots. This was faster than I liked, but I had no choice. She was well balanced under this reduced rig but as the storm strengthened, the waves began to strike her with one-two punches. The first blow would knock her in one direction and then, before she had time to recover, the second would strike from another direction. *Johan*, to my dismay, would sometimes just sit there shuddering, unable to decide which way to go. I could feel the hull flexing under the various impacts. It was not difficult to imagine the next wave ripping the deck off and taking both of us to Davy Jones's locker. I resisted the urge to check the chart and see just how deep the water was in these parts.

There are supposed to be no atheists in foxholes. Under extreme duress, the experts tell us, everyone starts praying to some god or other. I'm not sure that's true. In World War II, my schoolmates and I often heard bombs falling close by. One night our backyard was laced with a neat line of high explosive craters. It seemed at the time as if the world was coming to an end. Then there were the V-1 buzz bombs, designed to hit fourteen seconds after the engine cut out. Every night in our school dormitory, as the strange clattering sound abruptly ceased, some of the boys would start to count. Others of us would just lie there, silent. Then the blast would come, nearby or further away, and we all knew we had survived long enough to at least begin the next count. In those fourteen pregnant seconds, few of us took the opportunity to pray. Either the bomb would hit us, or it would not. Only one boy, so far as I can recall, ever whispered a few holy words, and in our harsh, nine-year-old fashion we considered him wet.

Maybe it was such unsettling conditions as these that lent im-

portance to my experiences of sailing in the Thames Estuary in the
years immediately after the war. Though I enjoyed hoisting sails,
steering, and dinghy work, the finest moment of the day occurred
when my father's old gaff-rigged yawl came to anchor in one of a
score of barely charted tidal creeks. The hard day's sail was over.

Walter in Melanie's saloon, autumn, 1947.

The dinner dishes were washed and stowed. Walter would light his pipe and Nelson Keeble would have a Woodbine cigarette and all aboard would loll in the dusk around the saloon table and talk. In a little while the anchor light, after much ceremonious cleaning of wicks and pouring of kerosene, would go up on to the forestay. A little later I'd turn into the port quarter-berth and hear the tide running past *Melanie*'s wooden hull. Perhaps, before I drifted off to sleep, I might listen to the smoky drone of conversation among the adults. Sometimes it was my father and stepmother and their friends, speaking of art and abstractions over a bottle of brandy. Sometimes it was men like Jack Pittock and his crew—friends of Nelson Keeble—who'd rowed over from their Thames barge anchored nearby to yarn of bygone deeds in the Estuary, and of politics and ladies they had admired.

The aura of such moments never left me. But those days were long gone now, of course. During the prosperity of the 1950s, the Thames sailing barges found they could no longer compete with modern highways and cheap trucking. Commercial sail died in my late teens, almost as I watched. The East Coast of England became a backwater. Fewer trains ran out of Liverpool St. Station. Nelson Keeble, now in his 70s, retired, and there were no younger men to replace him; they believed, perhaps rightly, that work as a paid hand was both unremunerative and demeaning. The old ways— the good-humored acceptance of discomfort, the insistence on gear designed for all seasons, and, yes, the unspoken egalitarianism— were gone in a puff of social justice. The living link, the seafaring tradition that extended back through Horatio Nelson (who grew up in a Norfolk parsonage) to Drake and Grenville, was irretrievably snapped.

Without Keeble to keep an eye on things, Walter was forced to dock his boat at a modern marina at Hamble, on the south coast. The move sharply underscored the sea-change that was taking place in sailing in both Britain and across the Atlantic in the United States. Fiberglass was crowding out wood, racing was pushing aside cruising, and impatience and anger were smothering good humor. On both sides of the ocean a new generation, unchastened by the ancient verities, had discovered what they imagined to be the joys of yachting. The Solent—with its crowding, its brusque clubmanship, and its blank stares between passing boats—was particularly baleful, and Walter became increasingly nostalgic for the old times in the Estuary. He took my sister Nicola

and me to see the church pews in North Walsham and Walbers-
wick, where preceding generations of Hubbards had snored away
the centuries. Smuggling lace and brandy from the Continent had,
it seemed, been a greater source of consolation to them than the
Anglicanism that had been foisted upon their pagan souls only a
few centuries back. They were not land-creatures but sea-crea-
tures. The real hell for them lay in the desolation of the East
Anglian hedgerows and the monotony of life on a flat farm. If they
worshipped any gods at all they were probably to be found in the
evening call of the curlew and the peewit along the saltings and
in the flow of the tides through the mudflats of the Estuary.

Now, forty years after the end of World War II, I sat not in a
foxhole but in a damp sleeping bag and thought about all these
things. I recalled the morning's church service from St. Paul's.
Neither guilt nor fear seemed able to bring me closer to God. As
the waves bashed *Johan* and the winds howled in the night a thousand miles from anywhere, I concluded that my soul—such as it
was—must be made of baser metal than the souls of the men and
women in the cathedral. It didn't feel guilty. And it seemed, when
all was said and done, to have but a marginal interest in the life
everlasting. Heaven was a glass of grog with old friends in the
saloon of an anchored sailboat. This special moment of the day
was, for me at least, holier than all the mud in the River Ganges
and all the cathedrals in Christendom.*

* * * * *

The storm gathered in its fury about *Johan*. Her jerky movements and the crash of the seas against the hull and deck made it
hard to sleep. I discovered that it was difficult to be in mortal fear
of death for a period of much longer than about one and a quarter
hours. After that, the distractions creep in. Had I brushed my
teeth? Would the books doused in my struggles with the bilge
pump remain glued together? Was Susan surviving the summer
heat with her pregnancy? How was the garden in Syracuse looking
now? Eventually, I dozed. It was too miserable out there to keep
any kind of visual lookout. Every twenty minutes or so I reached
up to the VHF, pressed the transmit button and sent a little beam
of radio waves to warn any nearby freighter of *Johan*'s presence.

"This is sailboat *Johan*, transmitting on one watt. Come in any

*For a more detailed account of life on the Thames Estuary, see Appendix B.

vessel that can read this signal . . ." The radio hissed back at me. No takers. But once I overheard another one-sided conversation that brought me out of my bunk. The officer of a cargo ship, speaking in a heavy European accent, seemed to be in contact with a sailboat whose transmissions I could not hear. Was it an OSTAR competitor? At one point the cargo ship said ". . . our position is 30°03'N, 55°05'W . . ." I scribbled it down as he spoke. It had to be a wrong fix, because 30°N was 600 miles away. Should I butt in? The sailboat must have sounded confused because the freighter came in again with, "You are about 690 miles east of Nantucket. Good luck."

It *had* to be OSTAR!

My heart leapt. Who else would be out in this shit? Could it be Jack Coffey in *Meg*, or Vasil Kurtev in *Nord*, or maybe even Mike Richey on a very fast run in *Jester*? For a second I considered raising the cargo ship and asking the name of his interlocutor. But he was very faint and I reckoned about forty miles off to the northwest. Reluctantly, I decided not to confuse matters further. I returned to my bunk and caught myself grinning stupidly at the bulkhead. This was still a horse race. My friends-competitors were still out there, just a few miles ahead in this black night.

Johan Lloyde was no longer alone.

16

Kicking the Mast

*T*his was probably bad news for Nathaniel Bowditch and company, but the further I travelled at sea the more I became convinced that every region of the ocean had its own unique atmosphere, a special mood that was determined by the meteorological—and the psychological—weather of the region. The first phase of my voyage had been dominated, after *Johan* escaped the English Channel, by the frigid peaks of Labrador and Greenland. Though they were 2,000 miles away to the north, they sent us the winds, the waves, and the ice. Then there was *Johan*'s breakout into the sunshine and her cheerful stint bowling along in the Tradewinds. This, in turn, was followed by the passage through Coleridge's slimy sea and the discovery of Corvo. Then came the dazzling sameness of the Great Void. Each phase had its psychological tone and flavor that, in retrospect, was far more memorable than the numbers and lines on any chart or weather map.

Now the tropical storm, like a roistering village fair, had packed up and gone. It had been replaced by a prolonged and very flat calm. It was as if *Johan* had fallen off one of her weather staircases into a meteorological black hole. For a while it seemed she still had a chance of beating David White's time in her sister-ship *Catapha*. The calculations on a pad beside the chart table told the story of my fading hopes. By noon (GMT) on July 2, my boat had to cover the 740 miles to the finish line (640 to Nantucket Shoals Lightvessel, plus 100 up to Brenton Reef Light) in fewer than nine days, an average of eighty-two miles a day. By the same time on July 3, still no nearer to Newport, she had to proceed at the rate of ninety-three miles every twenty-four hours. At the merest hint of a zephyr a mile away on the water, I would paddle *Johan*'s stern around with quick stabs on the tiller and trim the sails to take maximum advantage of the puffs when they came. I even hauled up the little brown staysail inside the yankee in the hope of snaring a mite more wind. *Johan* might move at a half knot for a couple of minutes, then the puff would fade. Half an hour later a new zephyr would waft in from another direction. Just as I worked *Johan* round, and got the sails trimmed, the wind would fade again.

Sometimes, in my eagerness to get *Johan* moving, I'd climb up the maststeps to the crosstree where the Portuguese flag now hung limp as a dishrag. Through the binoculars I could see little cats-paws ruffling the water away to the north and off to the west and east and south. But they seldom seemed to come anywhere near the weatherless pocket inhabited by *Johan Lloyde*, with her 750 square feet of sail drooping in the air. No wind at all, I decided, would be better than chasing these little puffs of nothing. My wish was to be granted. Soon there was a flat calm as far as the eye could see.

Then came the rain, great curtains of it snaking in from the southwest. It was accompanied by tropical lightning and thunder, much of it—to judge by the proximity of the flash and the bang—right overhead. For all her elaborate survival equipment, *Johan* had no defense against lightning, and I was aware that her mast, the highest point in an otherwise empty seascape, presented a most tempting target. When the boat was under construction in 1974, I'd asked Westsail to install a grounding plate in the bottom of the boat. Then I got to thinking. Lightning, I reasoned, was surely more likely to be drawn to a mast that was well grounded; also, a strike would not only melt the spar, it would go through the ground plate and knock a hole in the bottom of the boat, thereby sinking her. Much better to insulate the mast, disconnect the ground plate, and make it neutral. This I had done, but I was not convinced that I had made the right move.

The storms never seemed to last more than an hour. When they were past, they left the surface of the water flatter, if anything, than before. To be becalmed at such a juncture in the race was one of the sternest tests that could be imposed upon any competitor in the Observer Singlehanded. I'd heard some of the veterans in Plymouth refer to such physical and mental doldrums as the time for "kicking the mast." Lurking in the back of the competitor's mind was the thought that no breeze would ever blow again in these parts. The logic was clear. If it can be a flat calm for three days, then what's to stop it from being a calm for thirty days, or 300 days? The thought that this was a race, and that other competitors in other weather systems were bowling along under full sail, often made the frustrations especially hard to bear.

My mood swings, I discovered, could be as violent as the summer rain storms. Yes, the finish line lay tantalizingly over the horizon. I would meet Susan, whom I had not seen in two months, in Newport. And little Kate. My impatience to get going again, to pull *Johan* out of this airless pocket, was palpable. Yet it was tinged with apprehension. For the last month or so society as a whole had placed almost no demands upon me. No telephones had rung, no administrative snarls had kept me late in the office, no stamped envelope had presented me with an overdue bill. For weeks I had dreamed of the moment when I would cross the line in Newport and fall into the cool brown arms of my wife. But now, as the time approached, I became alarmed at the idea of having to deal with other human beings. After a month of fighting down second reefs, shouting at the ocean, and dining like a pig, I sensed that my social instinct could not be relied upon to make the "appropriate" response. I would hesitate and have to think through situations that ordinary people would take for granted. I also realized that when my foot touched the dock, a score of problems, most of them long-postponed and financial, would descend upon my head. As I sat on the deck and looked at the flat sea a small part of me began to see a case for staying out in the Gulf Stream a while longer.

Though the temptation was great, I decided that whatever happened I was not going to end up kicking the mast, either literally or figuratively. Unfortunately many of my books had been ruined in the storm by the backrush of water coming through *Johan*'s bilge pump. I found I could dry out most of the hardcovers, but the paperbacks were generally reduced to a formless mush that ended up over the side. One book that survived the deluge was a slim volume on Homer's *Odyssey* by a noted classics scholar at Cambridge. The prose was sleek and the scholarship (one presumes) immaculate, but I could not escape the thought that the insights might have carried far more weight if the author had himself, like Homer's hero, pushed his prow beyond a sunset or two. After a while I tossed the slim volume aside. In many ways it epitomized an aspect of British life, the preoccupation with an almost airless *petit point*, that had more than anything inspired me to emigrate to North America in 1956. In the autumn of that year I booked a flight to New York and crammed my personal belongings into one very heavy suitcase. My father came to the airport to see me off. We lifted the suitcase out of the car and, our hands touching on the handle, carried it into the air terminal together.

Without the aggravation of that intellectual *petit point* I would not, in all likelihood, now be drifting around in the doldrums trying not to kick the mast. For a while I sought to distract myself by playing all the tapes in my collection many times, at steadily increased volume. When I could stand it no longer I returned to my sodden bookshelves for a volume that did not hold bad memories and whose pages I could turn. I was stuck, it seemed, with the *Holy Bible* and the *Manual of Marine Diesel Maintenance*. Then I had an idea. If I could not read a book, then perhaps I could write one. I had bills to pay the moment I touched shore. I pulled out a pencil and an old exercise book. After a moment's reflection I began to scribble. My hero would be a man called Guy Tabac, the debonair skipper of the 60-foot trimaran *Phippp* . . . named after a French furniture polish. Like all heroes, Tabac had a problem. Furniture sales were way down, and his sponsors were anxious to reposition their product as a cocktail aperitif . . .

My pencil flew over the pages. The hours passed, and I still had not kicked the mast. Every now and then I'd pause to try and coax another fix out of the Walker Sat-Nav. As *Johan* drifted in her circle of windlessness, the Gulf Stream continued to play its games. So far as I could figure it, in one two-hour period Jormungand shoved the boat nearly seven miles to the south, the exact opposite of the direction he was supposed to flow in. I would have been able to plot these shifts and changes with even greater accuracy if the Sat-Nav itself had not been so whimsical. I'd heard in Plymouth that the U.S. Navy had a new navigation system and was letting the present system of satellites run down. Perhaps that explained why, though there were supposed to be four or five satellites up there, I kept getting No. 11. In ten years all the old satellites would have dropped out of the sky. Then the expensive equipment on *Johan* and thousands of other ocean-going boats would be moribund.

Surely there was a simpler, cheaper system than either Sat-Nav or Loran C, which did not reach into the larger oceanic spaces and was very expensive to run. Loran, also, was subject to distortion.

It was strictly a Zone tool; if you put it under another master beacon it had to be recalibrated.

If they put their minds to it, the micro-wizards ought to be able to design an "electronic" sextant. Like most of us, I had marvelled at the ability of the electronic eyes at supermarket checkout counters to read the price and nature of each item, even when the code lines were run by at speed and at almost any angle. Surely it would be possible to devise an electronic eye that, at the pull of a trigger, could transmit the precise angle between sun and horizon down a cable to a black box running on GMT. The navigator would get an instantaneous Line of Position. Do it an hour later, and he'd get a full fix. This electronic eye, like a supermarket scanner, should be able to snatch the correct angle even if the boat was bouncing every which way.

Refinements could be added. I looked through *Johan*'s skylight at the masthead. Why not place the eye of an electronic sextant up there? When programmed to the sun and certain stars, it could provide the navigator with a continuous running fix. Sensitize it to infrared light and it could find the sun in the heaviest overcast. I was aware that Tony Lush, now skippering the 35-foot sloop *Survival Technology* in OSTAR, had once used the lightmeter on his camera to obtain a crude fix through heavy cloud while sailing across the Indian ocean. A specially designed eye could, surely, be many times more precise. Such an electronic sextant would be both cheap and reliable; then we'd be able to kiss off Loran with its spooky distortions and Sat-Nav with it lame and moody satellites.

When not fiddling with the Sat-Nav and diverting myself with the adventures of Guy Tabac, I fought the doldrums by producing flamboyant new dishes in the galley. The Log notes the recipe for one creation called "Super Pud." It consisted of a cup of Alpen breakfast food, a cup of canned rice pudding, a spoonful of cocoa powder, a big spoonful of strawberry jam, all brought to a gentle simmer with a tot of Navy rum. This was the food of the future, I decided as I gave it a final stir, the kind of all-purpose paste that many astronauts would be proud to serve. An annotation made beside the recipe in a later, shakier hand chose to differ. "I can now say, unequivocally, that the final brew tasted even more disgusting than the sum of all its parts. Back to corned beef stew!"

* * * * *

At dawn on July 5, I went on deck to find faint airs blowing in from the west. By breakfast *Johan* was sailing northwest at three knots. At 2 in the afternoon, she sighted a freighter, hull down and derricks a mere blur, far off to the north. It was the *Walter Rice*, on her way from Holland to Virginia. I asked over the VHF for a weather forecast.

"For the next twenty-four hours," said a cheerful American voice, "winds will be west-south-west at twelve to seventeen knots, then backing to southwest at fifteen to twenty knots."

"That's my wind," I said jubilantly. "It's got my name on it." Inside, I felt as if some scholar of ancient documents had, casually, handed me a signed original of the *Magna Charta*.

"Good luck," said the unseen deck officer. "And keep a good look out. With the ice up north the Navy has routed commercial ship lanes further south than usual."

"Thank you, and have a good voyage. Out."

Johan Lloyde was on her way. Maybe the Left Hook strategy would work after all. I kept the staysail up, even though it gave the boat a slight lee helm. During my sojourn in the doldrums, I had figured a Rube Goldberg system of pulleys that enabled me to replace certain parts of the guide ropes on the Aries steering gear. It seemed to work as well as the original. By late that evening *Johan* was seventy-five miles west of the windless box in which she'd been sitting for close to three days. I put the ship's clock back another hour; now it was running only one hour ahead of Eastern Standard Time. By the evening of the following day *Johan*'s keel had passed between the submerged mountain ranges of Rehoboth and San Pablo. Though the sun was shining and the boat was bounding along at five knots on the port tack, such underwater phenomena still managed to spook me. Many eons ago, according to the geologists, when prehistoric monsters tramped the earth and before the submerged plains sank and the waters rose, these under-water ranges had formed a grand chain of midocean islands. No doubt, prehistoric birds sang on well-timbered hillsides, much as their relatives did today on Corvo and Flores. Then the floods came and the promontories became smaller and smaller and finally sank below the waves. Sat-Nav showed Nantucket to be bearing 284°True at a range of 480 miles. The distance between this and the previous fix was seventy-nine miles, but the electronic log in-dicated only seventy miles through the water. My plan to fight my way back south—doldrums notwithstanding—had been correct, and now even Jormungand had emerged from his lair amid the peaks of Rehoboth to help my boat upon her way!

Just before dark, three white birds with very long-feathered tails appeared and began to circle *Johan* as if about to land. I pulled out Roger Tory Peterson's magnificent guide to birds east of the Rockies, ungummed a few pages, and identified the newcomers as Whitetailed Tropicbirds, native to Bermuda, which now lay about 400 miles due south. What were they doing so far from home? Maybe their navigation had been crossed-up by the storm? Or perhaps they were on some prehistoric programming, seeking to return to the ancestral homelands than now lay 500 fathoms deep under *Johan*'s keel?

The tropicbirds circled for more than an hour. They had pretty black chevrons on their backs and wings. I enjoyed the company and I would have chummed them down with a few crackers, but they seemed to be quarrelling amongst themselves in what Peterson described as "a harsh ternlike scream."

In the early hours of July 7, I switched on the radio and for the first time picked up a throng of stations in the AM frequency range. Except for the brief transmission from Prince Edward Island, when *Johan* lay much further to the north, I had got almost nothing during daylight hours. But the ionosphere had formed in the darkness and was reflecting down all the sounds of a giant murmuring to itself in sleep. The stations were not always easy to identify. One, playing classical music and claiming a "temperature of twenty-six degrees downtown," I identified as Halifax, off to the north. Strong jazz seemed to be coming out of Boston, and a very powerful country-and-western station was booming out of Virginia on 1410. I heard scraps of all-night talk shows from New York and Philadelphia.

I had emigrated to North America nearly 30 years before. Now I was sailing toward this awakening continent in a boat I'd built myself and I felt as if I was making a second emigration. In many ways it was more real than the first. On this voyage, I had acquired a direct sense of the trials the early settlers must have endured before they could set foot upon the docks of Boston, Philadelphia, or New York. Travelling under sail from Europe to America, I had come to see that the ocean was much bigger than the antiseptic view normally presented to us from the airplane window. But I also realized that the two continents were more intimately connected than I imagined. It did not require an airline's supersonic technology to bridge this gap. The two colored patches in the atlas were connected by a permanent and very fluid umbilical cord which life in the airport—with its plastic counters, body searches, and loudspeakers—did much to obscure.

English children used to play a card game with their nannies in which anyone with a certain combination of cards could collect everything on the table by uttering the words "I claim." As I listened to the sounds of the hillbillies, the jazz, and the argumentative talk-hosts coming out of the ether in the predawn hours of July 7, I found myself saying with considerable emotion the magic words "I claim. Mine."

What had taken me so long?

Part of it, I suppose, was due to an odd kind of deference. Though I'd lived in America for more than one quarter of a century, and all my children had American mothers, I had never applied for citizenship. I did not want to seem, even to myself, like the guest in a house who comes down one morning and declares himself part of the family. Some bartenders believed this indecision to be subversive, or at best the act of an ingrate. Love it or leave it.

But for me, the equation was more complicated than that. Though the door stood open, I was uneasy about stepping through it; I felt unqualified. It seemed to me that the steady improvement in transportation over the years had brought with it a parallel deterioration in the commitment of new arrivals. Nowadays, emigrants could zip across the ocean in a morning. If they didn't like what they saw they could zip back again in the afternoon. Such casualness had even persuaded some low-life elements to pack their gelignite feuds and their syndicates into their trunks along with their personal effects. Often the traffic seemed so brazen that I came to wonder if I, too, might not be carrying unworthy baggage. With my loyalties to special places and special people, perhaps I was just another tribalist incapable of demonstrating true loyalty to the principles outlined in the U.S. Constitution.

In the old days, things were different. A different kind of commitment and a different kind of determination were needed to embark on a square-rigged ship and endure the perils and discomforts of a voyage across the North Atlantic. When Thomas Paine sailed into Philadelphia on December 5, 1774, after a two-month voyage from England, the ship had to be placed in quarantine for "putrid fever," a kind of typhus that often brought about internal

bleeding, delirium, coma, and, finally, death. Paine, who thought
his end had come, was so weak that he could not turn in his bunk
without help. In those days the simple act of arrival qualified the
traveller, implicitly, for warm acceptance by the inhabitants. In
any event the middle-aged schoolteacher must have felt himself
right at home, for within a couple of years he had contrived to set
the whole colonial empire aflame. Things had not changed much
by the time my paternal grandfather sailed into New York Harbor
more than a century later, in 1888. The ship, due to severe weather,
came in ten days after its advertised arrival time. Alfred John
Buxton Hubbard, aged twenty-two, stepped off on to the dock and
discovered a nation of adventurers and volunteers. During his
lengthy sojourn on this side of the Atlantic, he met and conversed
with Mark Twain and nailed down his share of railroad track in
California. In those days there were no immigration officials and
no paperwork. Nobody said love it or leave it. Just to *be* there was
enough; the exigencies of arrival eliminated the piranha fish and
the faint of heart. *That* was my America. And that was the special
America that reached out to *Johan* across the radio waves in the
early hours of July 7, 1984. I claim. Mine.

   Dawn came, and the sun soon dissolved the sounds of a nation
rising to meet another day. I was not interested in politics and
crime. But I would have given my last bottle of Iceberg gin to
receive a really detailed traffic report. I did not care from which
city it emanated so long as it had a helicopter hovering over the
worst jams. I wanted to hear how the people were doing.

17

Laughter in Valhalla

I poured myself a glass of Dewar's scotch, and went over my charts one more time in the pink glow of the cabin night-light. For the last five days now, *Johan* had been steadily climbing out of that deep, windless hole off in the Atlantic and tonight she stood on a navigational mountain top, about 400 miles due east of Richmond, Virginia. Though it was a black night, the view was splendid. This was as close as she would ever get to Waypoint Virginia. Just as planned, the Nantucket Shoals Lightvessel lay under her starboard bow, 180 miles to leeward. *Johan* heaved and swooped through the night like one of Horatio Hornblower's frigates. I savored the moment. Down the center of Chart 14003 ran a wavy hatched line with the inscription "Approximate Position of Axis of Gulf Stream, 1.7 knots." It curved round about fifty miles over *Johan*'s present position. I put my finger on the spot and felt quite bloodthirsty: this was where I was going across to cut old Jormungand's throat for good. I'd make my move in a few minutes. I sipped my drink and once again marvelled at the unused potential of sea power. If a fleet of British warships had occupied *Johan*'s present position in 1778 or in 1813, they could, in the space of four days, either have turned left and landed an army of 10,000 men in Charleston, or turned right to place that same army in Boston. How was it that the brass hats had failed to exercise such vast tactical possibilities to keep the American armies hopping all over the map? It would, in fact, have taken the colonists ten times four days to move an army of that size between those two cities by road. Instead of waging a war of maneuver (for which they were so well equipped), the generals had let their own lack of imagination—and the pleas of the American Tories—draw them into a war of fortified positions that, praise be, virtually assured the independence of the colonies.

Now *Johan* sat on the top of this uncharted ridge. And, psychologically speaking, Newport occupied a little gulley of safety amid all the misty canyons down below. In the time ahead I must sift through the navigational data, much of it conflicting, to bring her safely past all the precipices and blind alleys to the little stretch of channel, one mile wide, that awaited her. As I reviewed my final plans I did not know, of course, that coming down the wind toward *Johan* was a long chain of petty misfortunes that when put together would come close to scuppering my whole Left Hook strategy.

I drained my glass, pulled on my oilskin, and put the helm up to bring *Johan* on to a broad run at 325°True. By midnight local time the wind had increased and she was rushing downhill at seven to seven and a half knots. From time to time she yawed up badly as the mainsail stole the yankee's wind. For a while I toyed with the idea of reefing the main, but then decided to drop it altogether. *Johan*, steadier now, continued to roar through the night at six knots. First light showed heavily overcast skies with hotel-size rollers coming at the boat from the southwest. Even under the yankee alone, the boat was up to seven knots and occasionally touching eight knots. I should really put a few rolls into the yankee, but this was *Johan*'s big move.

As I sipped my first cup of hot coffee, laced with rum, I stood in the main-hatch and began my search for the two storm petrels that had swooped and fluttered in *Johan*'s wake for the last three days. The little black birds had a white stripe at the root of their tails, and long spindly legs. They were the vagabonds of the sea, flying into the North Atlantic each year from their nesting grounds in Antarctica, often without once sighting land. First I caught sight of one, about 150 yards dead astern. I threw out some crackers. Then I spotted the other through the binoculars, about a mile to leeward, swooping through the wave troughs.

Throughout the morning the wind continued to build. Soon, it was knocking the tops off the rollers. Some broke just before they reached *Johan*, and the broken cap of the wave blasted across the deck like a bucket of pebbles. Others broke as they reached the rail, and substantial quantities of water came swirling over the port bulwark into the cockpit. This was, I decided, *Johan*'s kind of weather. A little later I got out my 8 mm movie camera and tried to film one of these giants on its way in. As the camera whirred, I held my ground right through the deluge and got about 100 gallons of water down the main-hatch. I pumped out the bilge, which was now also getting its share of contributions from the starboard caprail, in 240 strokes. How fast were we going? Eight knots plus down the front of that last monster? I glanced at the electronic log, which had a needle to indicate the boat's precise speed. It read zero. I went over and tapped the glass. The needle bounced up, then returned to zero.

I cursed. How was I going to negotiate my way through the shoals off Nantucket and Martha's Vineyard without a log? I had a back up, of course, an old Walker Patent Log, but that meant trailing 300 feet of line astern with a bronze spinner. I dug out the plastic lunch box that contained *Johan*'s electrical tools, and took the log off the panel over the chart table—no easy task given *Johan*'s violent swooping motion. I tested the incoming wires with the voltameter. The log was getting the full twelve volts from the battery. Then I switched on the Sat-Nav to see if it was getting power. Yes. Idly, I programmed it for date and time. Maybe I'd pick up a fix. Then I unscrewed the back of the log and cast my eye over the maze of soldered transistors. The circuit diagrams, I decided, meant nothing to me. I blew on the transistors. Nothing seemed to be loose. Then I slowly packed the device back into its

Wilson's storm petrels.

watertight box and screwed it into its place over the chart table. I switched on; it still read zero. The whole procedure, I noted, had taken me more than two hours.

I put my tools away, and peered out the hatch. It was getting worse, and I decided to pull a few rolls into the yankee. The little Portuguese ensign, straight as a board at the starboard crosstree, was beginning to fray out. When the slimmed down yankee was sheeted home, I returned below. *Johan* roared on downhill. The big cross-waves were hitting with new force. As the bigger ones struck, she staggered, lost her footing for a moment, and then was up and running again. I apologized silently for pushing her like this, but we could not afford to slop around out here along the Approximate Axis of the Gulf Stream. I went forward to dig out the Walker log. It was an unknown quantity. Unless Sat-Nav suddenly started working on a regular basis, my only reliable source of information would be the Husun sextant—if the sky cleared anough for me to get a shot. I found the rope log and walked aft on my way to stream it. As I did, I glanced at the Sat-Nav. Turned on randomly, it had not snared anything, and I reached up to switch it off and try again later. As I did so, I glanced at the chronometer.

I experienced a long stab of apprehension.

The clock's second hand was no longer moving. What was going on? The chronometer had its own internal battery; it could not possibly have been affected by my work on the electronic log. I unscrewed the instrument. One of the beam seas must have struck *Johan* with such force that it banged the battery out of its stainless steel bracket inside the chronometer. I returned it to its place and secured it with some sail-repair tape. But how was I going to reset the time? Four seconds off either way would mean an error of one mile in a sunshot. I'd have to get a time-tick on the radio, but reception from Colorado would not be good until after midnight.

How was I going to navigate? With both the log and the chronometer out, and the Sat-Nav sulking, my lovely *Johan Lloyde* was going blind. There seemed to be a gremlin loose in her electronics. Why was this happening at the precise moment when she needed all the help she could get? Nantucket Shoals, a moonscape of rock and surf thirty miles across and 100 miles deep lay under my lee bow. I was not sure how much the Gulf Stream was going to push me around. For a moment I thought I had it; why not let *Johan*'s faithful storm petrels lead her into land? It took me a few seconds to realize I was getting the logic backwards—it was they who were following *Johan*. And anyway, I reminded myself, the birds hated land.

Now was the time to stay cool. I climbed on deck and streamed the Walker log and noted that the wind, if not moderating, was at least no stronger. I returned to the cabin and tried to figure the solution. There was always RDF once I got inside the 100-mile range of Nantucket Lightvessel's radio beacon. As a last resort I had the depth-sounder. It's no sweat, I told myself. We'll just go back to basics. A little while later, I looked at the electronic log. Seven knots! It was working again. I tapped the glass. The needle shivered a little, but it stayed at seven, then flipped up to seven and a half knots. I listened to the Walker log rumbling away on the taffrail; it was going to stay there, at least for tonight. As dusk settled in, the little green letters on the front of the Sat-Nav began to show up more brightly. "No Fix, No Fix."

I wanted to reprogram it, but without the chronometer to give me Greenwich Mean Time, that was impossible. Then the penny dropped. There was the Sat-Nav purring away at my elbow. It might not have been able to produce a fix, but since the electronic log blew out it had been sitting there with the chronometer's own time programmed into it. I pressed a couple of buttons for a read out, and restarted the chronometer, correct to the second.

Whew!

But my troubles were not yet over. In the next two hours I discovered that my last packet of macaroni cheese, saved as a special treat, had acquired a veneer of mildew. I tried to eat it anyway, but it did not taste good. I also discovered that *Johan*'s running lights had been on most of the day and had nearly drained Battery No. 2. I must have inadvertantly clicked them on during my attempts to get the log working again.

After dark, the wind seemed to back slightly and I climbed into the cockpit to slack off the yankee sheet. As the rope went out it rolled up upon itself and jammed solid in the winch. Kicking it in the dark with a sea-boot only made things worse. In the end I brought the windward sheet on to the lee side and led it through a trunnion block on the windward winch. I was not sure what happened after the sheet was cleared, but I suspect that I rove it incorrectly through the headstays and shrouds. In any event, as the wind moderated toward midnight, and I released some of the rolls in the yankee the whole sail turned into a great thumping sack of dacron and tangled line.

I switched on the foredeck light, but I could not figure out what had happened. The wire fairlead for the furling line had, among other things, contrived to wind itself halfway round the drum. Clipping on my harness, I went out on to the bowsprit and bent it straight. As I tried to unravel the mess, *Johan* sunk her bowsprit, with me on it, six feet into a chilly wave. To untangle the ropes, I struggled to make a little slack in them, but every time I got an inch or two of play the sail above me in the darkness would twitch and pull everything taut again. Sometimes it was only with great difficulty that I could extract my fingers from the mess. This was getting dangerous. The tangled sail was now shaking the whole mast about. I stepped in off the bowsprit, unrove the two yankee sheets, coiled them together and passed them around the forestay. One, two, three, four times. This seemed to give the yankee a new lease on life and it pulled both sheets out of my hands. Christ, I thought, they'll wind up round the propeller. It even now was spinning briskly in *Johan*'s wake. That's all we need. I hastily hauled the sheets back in again and rerove them through their fairleads back to the winches in the cockpit. Then I pulled a flashlight out of my oilskin pocket and looked aloft. The mess above was worse than ever; I had been winding the sheets the wrong way!

I was furious. First the log, then the chronometers, then the navigation lights, then the macaroni cheese, and now this! A huge sail was flogging itself to pieces up above, it was pitch dark, and I was soaked through. *Johan*'s triumphal march down to the finish line was turning into a fiasco. The present scene was just too outrageous to be true. I opened my mouth to utter a stream of profanity, but a different sound came out. It was the noise of a great gust of laughter. Yes, I did curse a little. "Well, you bastards," I told the trickster fates, "what else have you got in store for me? You thought I'd take the bait and get really mad. But I'm on to you. I've got your number." Then I sat down on the foredeck and chuckled until the tears ran down my cheeks. This was, I realized, the authentic Valhalla laugh. It was unconquerable. I was privy to the game being played by the fates, with their cute crescendo of provocation, and I was just *not* buying it. At that moment, even if they'd arranged to have the flailing sheets tie me in knots, I think I would still have continued to laugh.

As academic readers will be quick to point out, my mood was

one of gross anthropomorphism, with its attribution of thought and motive—and cunning—to insensate forces. But at the time it did seem to provide the only plausible explanation of a disastrous day. Certainly the laughter came from a far deeper part of my spirit than the preceding anger. And, so far as I could hear, it had hardly any resignation in it.

"Fuck you," I shouted to the winds with amiable vehemence. "That's my bloody yankee you're tearing apart." I'd fix these mothers. First, I hauled up the mainsail to get *Johan* moving again and to give some slight lee to the tangled sail. Then I brought *Johan*'s 200,000-candlepower Q-beam searchlight forward and tied it, face forward, to the base of the mast. I lashed the furling drum of the yankee to the bowsprit with several lengths of cord. Trussed up like a turkey, it could no longer move in either direction. I brought the yankee sheets forward again, coiled them carefully, and put a lashing on them. Then I systematically threaded them around and around the forestay. The lines, and the sail, gradually became less tangled. One hour later the searchlight was switched off and stowed, and the yankee was sheeted home. The fates and I retired to our separate corners for the night, and *Johan* was, more or less, back on course.

18

The End Game

What strange first impressions the European skippers must have of the United States . . . In the early hours of July 12, *Johan* had crossed over the line on to Chart 13006, West Quoddy to New York. The chart showed almost every submarine canyon on the Atlantic shelf to be stuffed with discarded military hardware. All the way from Sandy Hook to Georges Bank, warnings in purple letters read "unexploded bombs," "unexploded depth charges," "unexploded torpedoes." First, steamy jazz and combative talk-show hosts, and now a minefield of explosive toys that the Pentagon had cast aside like a bored child.

At first light, 4 A.M. local time, *Johan* was plugging along about forty miles southeast of Nantucket Shoals Lightvessel, close-hauled on the port tack. The two storm petrels, I was pleased to see, still swung gracefully in her wake. These spirits of the deep were taking their chances coming so close to land, but they made good company. The wind had moderated since the previous day, but the Gulf Stream had pushed me ten miles further east than I had anticipated, and I was now wondering if, for all my elaborate strategical planning, *Johan* might not end up tacking her way around Nantucket. I switched on the depth-sounder. Still no reading. In the next ten miles, if my calculations were correct, the bottom of the Atlantic would shelve up from 1,000 fathoms to sixty fathoms. The maximum depth that my Brooks and Gatehouse could record was sixty-four fathoms.

Just as the sun came up over the horizon, I picked up some radar beeps off the starboard bow. Eight miles away I saw, through the binoculars, a low-slung white motor cruiser emerging from a

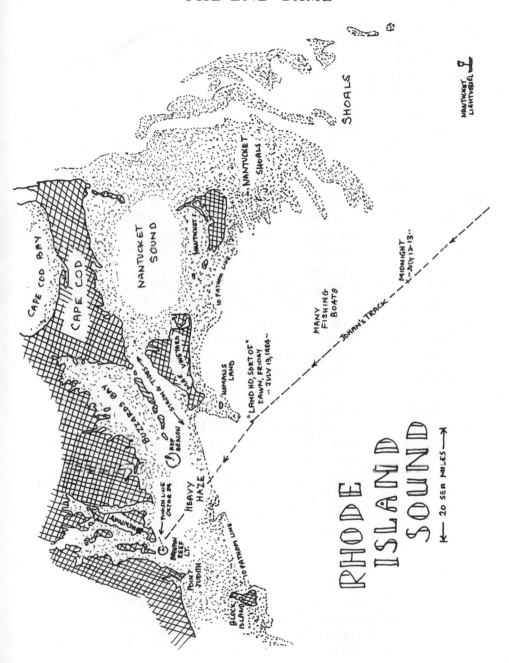

bank of morning mist. My first native boat! Great. Maybe I could have a chat and get a local weather forecast. I tried to raise him on VHF, but there was no answer. Strange. If he had radar, he must have VHF. I called again.

"Sailboat *Johan* to white cruiser about fifty-feet long at position approximately 39°50′N, 69°10′W. I am receiving your radar. White cruiser come in please, over."

Nothing. I went on deck and looked through the binoculars. The boat was turning to port back into the mist. The radar blips on the Pernicka by my right foot ceased abruptly. He must have switched off his radar. Hmmmm . . . Then I twigged. Probably a drug-runner, waiting for a shipment. Or, then again, maybe he was one of the good guys out looking for some bad guys. Either way, it must have had a chilling effect when I put his position and description out on Channel 16.

Good guys, bad guys. I decided I wanted nothing to do with any of them. In future, *Johan* would just lope on by and be more careful about talking to strangers. But I had a chuckle on one count. Despite the white cruiser's sophisticated equipment, I was pretty sure that *Johan*—with her "stealth" profile and her ineffective radar reflectors—could have gone on tracking him for quite some time without being spotted herself.

Things were happening fast now. An hour after the white cruiser vanished into the mist, I looked forward and saw a great churning in the water. One hundred yards ahead it changed color in a sharp line from deep purple-blue to dark brown. Rocks? In half a second I reviewed my navigation; perhaps *Johan* was going on Nantucket Shoals. I glanced through the binoculars. The line of dark water extended to the horizon on both sides. *Johan* was almost into it. I switched on the depth-sounder again. Sixty two fathoms! First soundings in almost a month. The sharp line in the water must have been where the Gulf Stream met the muddy tidal waters of the coast. A little later I hitched up the Locator RDF receiver and tried to take a bearing on Nantucket Lightvessel, now only thirty miles ahead. Nothing. Then I tried using it in conjunction with the crystal tuned Vecta RDF. The latter would identify the frequency and the transmission, while the Locator with its Sestral compass would give me its bearing. This combination had worked miracles at extreme ranges in the past. At one point I pulled in a flicker from Seal Island, 200 miles away on the southwest coast of Nova Scotia. But despite its far greater stated power, Nantucket remained mute.

After a brunch of sardines, crackers, and a can of stale Whitbread ale, I sat down to work out, as best I could, an advance schedule of satellite passes. I had luck with No. 11 and got a hint that No. 48 might be around if I could trap it into a fix. This was what the chess players call the End Game. With all the shoals and all the traffic I could not expect to sleep tonight; it would be like that first night in the English Channel, run backwards. At least now there was some wind. And it wasn't raining. As I worked, I could hardly suppress my excitement. This was it. I was actually arriving, engaged in a task that a part of me had imagined impossible. I tried to take a nap, but it was hopeless. I climbed back into the cockpit.

CRACK! CRACK!

It was the sound of two rifle shots, fired in quick succession. I slumped to the floor of the cockpit. The drug boat was back. They were shooting at me. I lay on the floor of the cockpit, my heart pounding. Welcome to America! Then, with great care, I bobbed an eye up above the rail. Nothing. I grabbed the binoculars and surreptiously scanned the horizon. Still nothing. Then it came to me. The twin explosions must have been the sonic booms of the Concorde coming in to New York. Its passengers must have left Europe about the time I started brunch. And here they were. After a while I returned below and pronged the last sardine in the can with a fork. When all was said and done, it tasted pretty good!

I never did see Nantucket Lightvessel, though *Johan* passed within seven miles of it. A heavy haze lay on the water as I began to cross the east-west shipping lane at about 3:45 P.M. First I saw the outgoing vessels, running east. Then, a little later, the incoming vessels running west (see chart p. 0). Nantucket's radio beacon on 286 kilohertz had come in about ten miles out. Even then, it was faint, though it was supposed to be effective for ranges up to 100 miles and audible even further than that. Why was it so much quieter than the less powerful Canadian stations?

I had noticed this same disparity cruising on Lake Ontario, where American and Canadian stations were linked on the same chain. The Canadian stations always boomed through, though the American ones were feeble at best. If anyone complained, the U.S. Coast Guard just told them their equipment was no good. But now

I began to suspect a deeper plot. Perhaps running the radio beacons on low power was a cute ploy by the Coast Guard brass to push the boating public toward the far more elaborate and far more expensive Loran C network. Later I was to query other OSTAR skippers. Their judgment was unanimous: Nantucket Shoals Lightvessel—one of the most critical RDF beacons on the eastern seaboard—was virtually dead in the water.

By evening the steamer tracks were twenty miles astern. *Johan* was close-reaching on the port tack at five knots, just weathering Brenton Reef Light sixty miles to the north. This, I realized, was her last night at sea. I had never sailed on this coast before and I was apprehensive about taking *Johan* through a tangle of strange shoals in the darkness. Twenty miles or so off the starboard side lay Nantucket Island and Martha's Vineyard, but so far as I could determine there were no off-lying markers to help me gauge *Johan*'s progress or her distance off shore. Looming somewhere off my port bow lay Block Island, and beyond it the rocks of Point Judith jutting more than five miles out into Rhode Island Sound. From the almanac, I knew three-knot east-west tides sluiced in and out of Vineyard Sound; I had also heard that several competitors in previous Observer Singlehandeds had sailed into Sakonnet River, under the impression that they were moving through the Newport channel, where the finish line lay.

Johan's log had this entry for 8:30 P.M. local time:

> Dusk. Sailing into Rhode Island Sound. My instruments are primed, and clicking away—RDF, radar alert, log, depth sounder, Sat-Nav—and seem to confirm each other's data. No bed tonight. Will I be able to spot the lights right? Though the sun set a while back there's still pink pastel in sky to west. The full moon has just risen out of the sea fine on the starboard quarter. It, too, is mellow pink—almost a harvest moon. My Wilson's storm petrels are flitting back and forth in its glow. For their own good they should say goodbye soon . . .

Walter, my father, would have relished that night, with its softness and the hint of perils in the darkness up ahead. He would also have been amused by the idea that *Johan* was attempting to make her transatlantic landfall in the early hours of Friday, July 13. He'd been in on much of the planning of *Johan*'s first Atlantic crossing and he'd approved of my attempts to wangle my way into the Observer Singlehanded. In one of my last conversations with him he had waved vaguely at the hospital equipment and nurses and said; "I don't want any of this to get in the way of your Atlantic thing . . ."

"Fair enough," I said, after a long pause. "But it will be lonely out there." Often, in years gone by, we had sensed each other's presence in the cockpit even when we were separated by an ocean.

"You should take a crew," Walter had said with a smile. He knew, of course, that the race was singlehanded.

"Perhaps I shall." This was my roundabout way of acknowledging that we might meet out there. Since I began the Observer Singlehanded I had known Walter's spirit, if it had any say in the matter, would not have missed it for anything. But now the voyage was over and I had not sensed the merest flicker of his presence aboard *Johan*, either in my waking moments or in my dreams. He had not come, and I was hurt. Then I realized how preposterous and how childish my hopes had been. I must learn to see that this was it. This was the chasm, the finality. He was gone.

I went down below into the cabin and retrieved a box of English Swan Vestas pipe matches that Walter had inadvertantly left aboard on his visit to *Johan* the previous summer. I returned to the cockpit and looked aft. The storm petrels were still there, flitting in and out of the moonshine. In a while I climbed up on to the stern, opened the box, and scattered the matches into *Johan*'s wake. Then I stood back and threw the box as far as I could into the darkness. I had not wanted to scare the petrels but when I looked back a little later they, too, were gone.

* * * * *

Many small power vessels, probably fishing boats, were moving down channel toward *Johan*. A few, also, were coming up astern and slowly overtaking her from behind. I tracked the lights and radar beeps of each carefully. It wasn't clear if they were using some kind of trawl or running lines. Just after midnight, one outgoing vessel came straight at *Johan*. I altered course to starboard, and the vessel's lights altered so that he was once more coming right at *Johan*. I studied him through the binoculars for a moment, then switched on the 200,000 candlepower Q-beam and aimed it at his chart house. I held it there for three seconds, then turned it away on to *Johan*'s mainsail. The boat swerved away sharply, and we passed about 150 feet apart. What, I wondered, could he have been heading for?

Earlier I had switched on Channel 16, in the hope of hearing some word from other OSTAR competitors. But all I got was laconic exchanges between the fishing boats. I sat on the engine box, my elbow on the chart table, and tried to say awake. By 3 A.M. I was very tired, but I was also filled with excitement at the prospect of making my landfall. I was particularly concerned about the effects of the tide. Despite my continued efforts to make Sat-Nav produce a fix, it had not come up with anything since 7:30 the previous evening. Just before daylight I took an RDF bearing on the radio beacon on Buzzards Bay Light. Though *Johan* was way beyond its twenty-mile limit, the line of position showed that she had, as yet, not been pushed significantly by the tide.

The first hint of light brought a kind of misty pink glow to the surface of the water. As the illumination grew brighter, I stood in the hatch and swept the horizon very slowly with the high-powered binoculars. Nothing. I looked again ten minutes later. Then I saw them, some small hillocks of land broad on the starboard bow, range about five or six miles. They appeared to be fringed by some kind of bushes or trees. "Land Ho," I said, "sort of."

But what on earth was it? I took a bearing. Was it an island off Martha's Vineyard, or a distant cape of a bigger piece of land? If my dead reckoning was correct, it should be a rock called No Man's Land, off Martha's Vineyard, but since I had not been in these parts before, I had no obvious way of confirming this. As the light became better, I spotted a buoy on the starboard beam. I timed the light. Flashing red, every four seconds. I'd got it; it must be a float designated R2 three miles due south of No Man's Land.

After all that ocean space I was still most uneasy about having land so close by in the mist. I reprogrammed the Sat-Nav yet again, but after half an hour, got nothing. After a fifteen-minute cooling-off period I tried again and almost immediately got a tentative fix from faithful No. 11. It was to be her swan song. The satellite had flipped up only ten degrees above the horizon. Indeed, it had passed so low that the Walker advised me to reject it. But when I plotted the fix at 41°9.34'N, 70°53.23'W, it came in right on the money, within 200 yards of my dead reckoning. No. 11, with her snapshot across the horizon was worth all the other satellites put together, high in the sky.

By now it was daylight. I checked *Johan*'s course to go across the line between Brenton Reef Light and Whistle Buoy No. 2. After setting my alarm-clock and two egg timers to go off in half an hour, I turned in to the starboard berth. Some time later I awoke with a start and looked at my watch. It read 7:11 A.M. I had overslept by nearly two hours! As I threw aside the blanket, I had a vision of *Johan* piling up on some rock at any second. I scrambled for the deck. As I passed the chart table I read the depth-sounder out of the corner of my eye. It was at eighteen fathoms. The horizon was, as before, empty. No Man's Land had vanished into the mist astern. On checking the compass I was relieved to see *Johan* exactly on course, and my heart began to beat a little more slowly. I returned below to brew a big mug of black coffee, but it took me quite a time to see the funny side: if I'd slept a little longer I might have become the first Observer Singlehanded competitor in history to go over the finish line feet first, snoring.

I put a tot of rum into the coffee and carried it back into the cockpit. It was, in truth, one of the most luminously beautiful mornings I had ever witnessed. In a while I clambered forward to the mast and hauled down the little Portuguese ensign that had come so far and hauled up in its stead the yellow quarantine flag over *Johan*'s long white racing pennant. I returned to my watch through the binoculars. I knew the cliffs around Newport were steep-to from a visit Susan and I had made to the city just before we were married. I should have spotted those great mansions an hour ago. Yet, all I could see on the horizon was pink mist. The wind began to fade and soon *Johan*'s speed was down to three knots. At about ten o'clock a big white ketch with a large crew motored across *Johan*'s bow. She was, presumably, going east to Martha's Vineyard. When the skipper saw the big black "11"s on *Johan*'s flanks, he came on over.

"Are you racing?"

"Yes," I replied. The man, a distinguished looking gent from Wilmington, Delaware, looked impressed.

"What race?"

"The Observer Singlehanded."

"That was over weeks ago," said the skipper, with an edge of disbelief in his voice.

"Not for the guys back in the pack."

"How long have you been at sea?" The skepticism was stronger in his voice now. He turned aside to talk to a crew man.

"About six weeks . . ." I replied to no one in particular.

This statement was greeted by the Delaware crew in silence. Then they waved, and started to put the engine in gear. I picked up the voice trumpet.

"Do you have Loran?" I asked.

"Yup." I was clearly wasting his time, now.

"Could you give me a bearing on Brenton Reef Light? That's the finish line, you know?" Was I being too chummy, I wondered.

For a moment the skipper hesitated, then he said "Okay." Perhaps he believed my request to be a violation of the race rules. He went below and returned in a few seconds and yelled out the bearing.

"Magnetic or true?" I asked.

"Magnetic." The tone was now quite abrupt. In his eyes I had fallen from Mount Olympus. I was no longer a Chevalier of the Deep but a piece of flotsam, a petty grifter who seemed to have trouble navigating his way across Buzzards Bay. Without another word, he slammed his engine into gear and drove off toward Martha's Vineyard. I waved farewell, but he and his crew did not wave back.

The ketch's Loran bearing dovetailed pretty well with my dead reckoning. Soon the breeze freshened up again, and *Johan* was moving across Chart 13218 at four, five, six inches an hour. By now I could not be more than six miles from the line, but the horizon was still wrapped in heavy white haze. I lifted the binoculars from the surface of the water by a few degrees and saw what looked like a distant gangway hanging between two clouds of mist. I could make nothing of it. The gangway gradually changed its position and got longer. Then I saw a line that looked like a horizontal pencil stroke emerge from the white wool off the starboard beam. I looked again. It must be the cliff tops off Newport Neck. And there was the side of a mansion. . . .

LAND HO!

The gangway between the clouds, I realized, must be a section of the tollbridge that crossed Rhode Island Sound several miles behind Newport. Everything began to fit together, and soon land loomed off the port bow, and Brenton Reef Light (I had expected a lightship) must be that platform on spider's legs right ahead. I emerged from the blanket of haze less than a mile from the line. I'd better alert race headquarters for a boat to tow *Johan* into the dock. I went below and switched on Channel 16. The air was filled with the babble of people making lunch appointments and dock reservations and trying to locate their children. I waited for a pause in the radio traffic, but none came. At one point a distraught voice shouted ". . . on the rocks, on the rocks . . ." Another voice, presumably the Coast Guard, tried to clear the channel but nobody seemed to take any notice. In a few seconds the babble of lunch dates resumed—as if this were a death in an anthill, to be accepted without remorse or curiosity. There was no place for *Johan* to get her oar in. Finally, I found a small niche and blasted out.

"Goat Island Yacht Club this is OSTAR competitor *Johan Lloyde*, come in Goat Island Yacht Club, over."

". . . Pete, did Ruby go with you in the whaler . . ."

". . . Zebra Nine-ah, this is *Rough Rider Two* . . ."

Johan crosses the finish line.

I repeated *Johan*'s call two more times, to no effect. I looked out the hatch. The wind had freshened, and *Johan* was reaching down at five knots. The finish line was about 300 yards away. I tried again, and then a voice came out of nowhere . . .

"Hey *Johan*, yer know there ain't no such place as Goat Island Yacht Club . . ."

I stared at the VHF set dumbly. Then I snapped back, only half in jest ". . . You mean I came all this way for nothing? . . ."

". . . Joanie, we'll be on the dock at 4 . . ."

I checked the telltale compass on the overhead above. *Johan* was right on course. We are born alone, we die alone, and we go over the finish line alone. I'd have to record *Johan*'s time myself. I clutched the radio and waited for another chink in the social chatter. Then, floating over the ether came the magic phrase I'd been waiting for. The voice was low-key, authoritative, and vaguely familiar.

". . . Okay *Johan*, we gotcha . . ."

That was all. The babble resumed instantaneously. Yet those four words were enough. I held up my shirt sleeve and wiped my face. For some reason it was wet.

The finish line was coming up fast. This was going to be done by the book. I laid a winch handle on the bridge deck forward of the cockpit and made it as parallel as I could to the finish line. *Johan* was crossing the line at a slight angle. When the length of the winch handle lined up with Brenton's Reef's spider tower, I quickly looked down the handle from the opposite end and found it lined up on the whistle buoy. *Johan* was over the line, and I pressed the stopwatch. I went below and stopped the watch again when the chronometer's second hand came straight up. It read fifteen hours, thirty-nine minutes, and zero seconds Greenwich Mean Time. The stop watch read twenty-eight seconds. If I deducted this from the chronometer time I'd have the instant *Johan Lloyde* crossed the finish, which was 15:38:32. Just to prevent any back-talk down the line, I rounded it out to fifteen hours and forty minutes. Since the race started on June 2 at 11:10 GMT, this gave a total time of forty-one days, four hours and thirty minutes elapsed since *Johan* crossed the line beyond the breakwater at Plymouth, England.

I started up from these computations. *Johan*, under full sail, was zooming on to the rocks of Beaver Neck, less than half a mile to leeward. I ran up on deck, rolled up the yankee entirely, then gybed the mainsail over and set a course to run clear of Ram's Head on Newport Neck. Several boats were tacking out of the Sound toward me. Among them was a green launch with a bow wave so large that I could barely see its pilot house. In a little while it passed by 100 yards to windward and then circled back on course parallel to that of *Johan*. It was the *Prowler*, one of the chase boats used most frequently in the America's Cup races. Slowly its course converged with that of *Johan*. A gang of half a dozen people stood in its cockpit aft.

"Hello."

"Hi."

"Congratulations on making it in one piece."

"Thanks." I recognized the faces of Tony Lush, skipper of *Survival Technology*, and Mac Smith of the 44-foot cutter *Quailo*. Rex Williams, a retired group captain in the RAF, was representing the Royal Western Yacht Club. "Where did I come?" I yelled over the roar of *Prowler*'s engines. There was a brief consultation in the aft cockpit.

"We're not sure."

"Who's still out?"

"Jack Coffey in *Meg*, Goos Terschegget—he broke his bowsprit on a berg—Mike Richey, Jack Hunt . . . We'll take you in tow the other side of Rams Head, there's a good lee in there." I signalled agreement. Several cameras were clicking aboard the *Prowler* now, and I was becoming self-conscious. Soon a blue cutter, about sixty feet long, headed straight for *Johan*, close-hauled. She sheered off at the last moment. As she went by the air was split by the wail of several air-horns. What was going on? Then I realized that this cacophony was a salute to *Johan* for Making It. After so long away from other human beings I was shy. All I could manage by way of a response was a brief wave of the hand. Soon the rest of the sailboats came tacking up to *Johan*, several of them bearing OSTAR numbers on the hull. The horns began to blow from every direction, and in a short time I overcame my timidity and was standing as high as I could on *Johan*'s afterdeck, exuberantly waving my sunhat in the air. *Johan* might be very far back in the pack, but she had made it across the North Atlantic on her own, something that many of these huge hefferlump motor cruisers now churning around probably could not do.

Soon *Johan* stowed her mainsail, and was towed alongside *Prowler* past fleets of yachts moored in Newport's outer harbor, into B Dock of the Goat Island Marina. A crowd of Dutch skippers and their wives stood on the dock and waved. Tony Lush and Mac Smith now came aboard and helped pass the mooring lines ashore. I could not believe that this was happening, that the race was over. Smith and Lush were doing a most seamanlike job with the warps and fenders, but it was difficult for me to relinquish the responsibility that I had had to exercise, night and day, for the last six weeks. Hour in and hour out, I had been *totally* beholden for everything that happened aboard this boat. Now, rejoining human society, I must learn to release my grip. Mac and Tony had been Out There, too, and well understood the miniature crisis in command that was now taking place. Lush, adjusting a bow spring, turned to me and asked, "Is this okay, or you want it off some more?"

"Slack her a bit. That's fine. Thanks."

In a little while, I swarmed up the tarred piles of B Dock and stood on the planking. This was not solid ground yet, but close to it. I must call Susan to find out if she was okay and to tell her that I was okay.

"Where's the phone, please?"

Lush, a burly fellow with a big brown beard, pointed to a kind of clubhouse a couple of hundred feet away at the base of the dock. "There's a good restaurant, the Marina Pub, there, too. Want to get a bite in a while?"

"Yes. Maybe I'll see you there in about twenty minutes?" I felt like a soul newly arrived on the far side of the Styx. Lush, it appeared, was to be my Guide. I started to walk off down the dock and my legs crumpled beneath me. I clung to a wooden pile for a moment, then I moved on carefully down to the clubhouse and found an empty phone booth. I had waited so long for this moment, and now it was happening. Susan's voice sounded almost as dazed as mine must have done. She and Kate would fly down from Syracuse the following morning. We said goodbye, and I tottered on down the dock to the big sunny office in which the Observer Singlehanded had its headquarters. A middle-aged, grey-haired woman sat behind a desk talking on the telephone. This must be OSTAR's Chief Coordinator in Newport. Eventually she hung up.

"Yes?"

"I'm Tim Hubbard. I just came in on a boat, *Johan Lloyde*. Can you tell me where I came in the race?"

"You'll have to wait 'til after lunch." The Chief Coordinator started packing stuff into a sizable handbag.

"I mean, just give me a hint," I persisted. "Which boats came in just ahead of me?"

The coordinator stopped packing stuff into her handbag.

"After lunch." She arched her eyebrows, as if making a point to a retarded child.

"After lunch," I said slowly, as if I were memorizing the words. The Chief Coordinator then pointedly locked the drawer of her desk and marched out. I found my way to the Marina Pub where Tony Lush was seated at a table with Chris Butler, skipper of the 27-foot *Swansea Bay* and Dr. Dick Huges, skipper of the 34-foot *Gladys*. I ordered a big stein of beer and something called a Blue Max sandwich. A few minutes later I was relating the story of my ineffectual attempts, after six weeks at sea, to have the coordinator reveal how *Johan* had placed. Soon our table was rocking with a reasonable facsimile of the Valhalla laugh.

"I came in two days ago," said Dick Huges, "and *Gladys* was rated fifty-ninth. *Nord* came in last night, so you must be sixty-first. Congratulations." Everyone took a peg of beer, and the stories began to flow. Huges, becalmed off Nantucket shoals, had been forced to anchor *Gladys* in seventy fathoms of water. Less than 100 yards away the surf was breaking on the rocks. "When the wind returned," said Huges, "there was so much chain out I could hardly lift it with the windlass."

In Chris Butler, a stocky fifty-two-year-old English boat-builder, the OSTAR had a new candidate for the title of Iron Man. His three self-steering devices had broken, and he'd steered the last 1,000 miles of the race by hand to make *Swansea Bay* the first boat home in Class V. His time was thirty days, fifteen hours. Lloyd Hircock, I heard, was also in Newport somewhere trying to get *Moustache*'s engine fixed. After breaking two backstays and overcoming many other troubles, he had come in five days after *Swansea* to take seventh place in class. Alan and Margaret Wynne-Thomas were off touring a boat-building plant in Massachusetts. Bill Homewood, nursing a badly abscessed tooth, had brought *British Airways II* up Rhode Island Sound at seventeen knots to take first place in class. Mike Richey and *Jester* were up around Sable Island, off Nova Scotia. Perhaps the most poignant casualty of all, I learned, was that of Rachael Haywood's 35-foot sloop *Loiwing*. On the night of July 7, Haywood had momentarily confused the lights outside Newport and piled up on the rocks of Point Judith. The boat was a total loss but her skipper, miraculously, survived unhurt.

The talk turned to ice. Several boats that had gone down the rhumb-line saw "growlers," low flat pieces of ice almost level with the water. José Ugarte, on the 45-foot Spanish cutter *Orion Iru*, came on deck after a long radio conversation with friends back home and found himself in the middle of an icefield. He extricated his boat with some difficulty, then ran off more than 300 miles to the south. Kai Granholm, whose 40-foot cutter *Patricia of Finland* was first monohull home in Class III, spotted several icebergs on his radar, one so big that it filled the entire screen. And Goos Terschegget, still tacking back and forth beyond Nantucket, had collided with a chunk of ice in the dark and lost his bowsprit off the 44-foot ketch *De Volharding*. For the final line-up of boats and times, see Appendix C.

The party in the Marina Pub was beginning to gather momentum. The official tally placed *Johan* sixty-first in the fleet of ninety-two starters, and tenth monohull home in Class IV. But I was having my share of sober thoughts. For all my elaborate strategical planning, very few boats seemed to have been outflanked by *Johan*'s great dash down from Waypoint Virginia. Perhaps if she had not been stuck for so long in the pocket north of Bermuda she might have done a lot better. And she might have done better still if she'd not stopped off in the Azores.

But then *Johan Lloyde* was the boat that found Corvo, and as a result I had met Umberto Augusto and Kurt Eriksen. Nothing on my homemade vessel had broken that I had not been able to repair myself at sea; fill her tanks, and bung a case of corned beef aboard, and she could sail for England, or the Madieras, tonight!

Most important of all, of course, she had arrived. The 12-ton *Johan*, with her snug all-weather accommodations, had used the force of the wind alone to find her way from one geographic dot on the globe to another geographic dot thousands of miles away. It was, come to think of it, a miraculous achievement. I looked across the tables of the Marina Pub; I was, in fact, surrounded by miraculous achievers, who had, mindful of Sir Francis Drake's prayer, continued unto the end. Therein lay the true glory. I looked at the faces, so much leaner and so much more sunburned than they had been in Plymouth, and decided that none of them really belonged in this century. They were travellers in time, popped out from some previous epoch. There was no torpor, no fashionable *angst* to be found amongst these grinning countenances. Every normal man or woman, they seemed to say, would jump at a chance to cast aside mortgage, family, and regular job for a hazardous adventure in which one's life hung on the turn of a winch or the force of a bicep. Their talk and laughter in the Marina Pub that night slowly grew to a great surging roar of sound.

In a while, I turned in to *Johan*'s starboard berth for my first good night's rest in weeks. I awoke, two hours later, to a mighty crash. My watch read 1:15 A.M. I went on deck in my clean white pyjamas to find *Meg of Muglins* coming alongside *Johan*'s starboard rail. There were floodlights everywhere and Jack Coffey, clad in salt-wet oilskins, stood in a cockpit full of ropes.

"Well, Timothy, now tell me just how *are* you?"

"Pretty good, Jack." I said, still half asleep. We shook hands.

"Well, you look like a terrible white ghost standing there in your pyjamas. Back to bed with you." As he spoke, a very wet rope snaked out of the darkness and slapped me in the ear. I made it fast to a cleat and and retired below. I was probably asleep again before my face hit the pillow.

Next morning I put on a work shirt and jeans and scrubbed *Johan*'s decks and tidied up a lot of the loose lines. I had my head down in the cockpit when a soft voice behind me said "Hello." Puzzled, I looked up. Susan! I scrambled up the piles on to the dock and fell into her cool brown arms.

The Last Leg

*E*ach morning in Newport I braved the baleful glare of the Chief Coordinator and pushed my way past the front desks of the Royal Western's American headquarters. Pinned to a wall-length partition in the back was a ten-foot-long plot of the North Atlantic. The Argos satellite equipment was now printing out only one fix a day for the tail-end Charlies. Each boat had been given a little colored button with its name tag. With each new fix, Rex Williams would take a huge pair of dividers and plot each competitor's position. Then he'd connect it with a pencil line to his previous position. By now the wall plot was filled with spider-tracks that crossed, recrossed, and crossed again to present a jagged summary of all that had passed since the ninety-two boats had left Plymouth on June 2. This was the view from the top, the Observer Singlehanded as perceived by the Race Committee and the big effendis of the media. It was here, in this well-lighted room, that officials had initiated and supervised the rescue or retirement of nearly a third of the OSTAR fleet. Like admirals in a gigantic sea battle, they had resolutely kept their minds on the big picture. The wind's howl and the icy seas had been no more than an abstraction for them. As I examined the plot in the morning sunshine, I realized that its portrayal of the race was almost as misleading as it was punctiliously accurate.

By now most of the lines of the expanded universe had coalesced at Brenton Reef Light. Goos Terschegget had just brought his 41-foot ketch *De Volharding* in with her broken bowsprit lashed to the port bow rail. Terschegget, an alderman of the city of Nijkerk, had been appointed to represent the Dutch people at the 150th birthday celebrations of Schenectady, New York. Time was short, and *De Volharding* had to leave on her mission up the Hudson River before a new bowsprit could be found. Now the only two boats still Out There were John Hunt's *Crystal Catfish* and Mike Richey's *Jester*. Hunt, just a hundred miles off Nantucket, was moving up fast and would probably make it within a day or so. But according to the wall plot *Jester* seemed to be zigging and zagging around in the channel between Nova Scotia and Sable Island.

"What's up with *Jester*"? I asked Rex Williams as he worked away with his giant dividers.

"Oh, he's having the time of his life," said Williams briskly. "He's been all over the North Atlantic." He pointed to *Jester*'s pencilled track over the last four weeks. The junk-rigged sloop, it seemed, had sailed south, then roared off north, and then came charging south again. Her progress toward Newport appeared to be almost incidental. I recalled Mike Richey's remark that *Jester* could not sail too close to the wind.

"Do you think she'll make it under the fifty-day limit," I asked. Williams, a brusque, athletic man stood back and looked at the plot.

"Not much chance, I'd say."

"This is probably Richey's last race," I said. "It'd be nice if *Jester* could be rated as an official finisher. Could the limit be pushed back a couple of days?" The retired group captain looked at me with genial contempt.

"Can't do that," said Williams. "Can't change the rules in the middle of the race." There was a long silence as we studied the map some more. For many skippers, the little green *Jester* embodied the spirit of the Observer Singlehanded. From the start, Mike Richey had known there was no way he could come in first, or even fiftieth. Yet, like the Lord of La Mancha and the rest of us back in the pack, he raced. Here, beyond the icy precision of the wall plot and beyond the immediacy of those cockpits waist-deep in water lay a third, more profound, version of the race. This deeper actuality, I realized now, could be perceived only indirectly, by tacking up to the mark at an angle just as *Jester* was now tacking her way across the North Atlantic. This actuality could not be filmed and interviewed any more than the human spirit itself could be filmed and interviewed.

I looked at Rex Williams again. If this was Mike Richey's swan
song, then surely the rules could be bent just a little. "The only
people to be affected are the other skippers," I said, aware that for
Rex my idea must carry with it a strong odor of mutiny. "I think
everyone on B Dock would be happy to see the limit extended for
Jester. Perhaps we should petition the Race Committee . . ."

"No, no. It would be quite pointless," said Williams in a military voice. "Look, that man's a professional navigator." He gestured toward *Jester*'s wavy track. "Half the fun of it for him is
trying to get in under fifty days. See,"—he pointed to several huge
zigs and zags on the plot—"Richey's just sailing around for the fun
of it . . ."

"I'm not so sure. He may be in trouble." I studied the chain of

Johan *chastely moored at B-Dock, Goat Island Marina, Newport.*

fixes, each with its time and date and tried to marry them up with my recollections of the weather on those days. "It's like a detective mystery," I said. "See here, if I had to put money on it, I'd say *Jester*'s having trouble going close-hauled on the starboard tack. Perhaps something's gone on the rig, or maybe the steering can't take the load . . . look, here and here . . . he'd be better off on the starboard tack, but he's on the port tack or running off."

But then, again, maybe there was nothing wrong with the boat. Much of *Jester*'s jagged progress might be explained if Richey himself had been in some fashion incapacitated. But Mike was a tough old coot. It was hard to imagine him being so badly hurt that he could not somehow make his way forward to press the Argos panic button. He had *not* pressed the button. Therefore he was okay. It was at this point that I was struck with an even more disquieting thought. Perhaps Richey had gone overboard weeks ago, leaving *Jester*, a riderless horse, to make her own way across the Atlantic!

I turned away and refrained from mentioning my fears to Rex Williams, who would doubtless view them as alarmist in the extreme. Richey must be all right, I told myself. He had come this way so many times before. But it was such a pity that his valiant efforts should be crowned with disqualification. I left race headquarters and walked slowly back to B Dock, where Susan and Kate were finishing breakfast on *Johan*. This, I decided, was clearly a case for the Half Crown Club. Go for broke, baby. A few hours —and quite a few tankards of beer— later, nearly a dozen OSTAR skippers had signed the following petition:

The undersigned OSTAR 1984 competitors would like the Race Committee to consider the following proposal: permit *Jester* to be rated as a bona fide race finisher, even though she has exceeded the 50-day rule. Here are some points the Committee might care to consider in its deliberations.

1) Mike Richey has probably entered more OSTARs than any other competitor. How many more will he enter?

2) *Jester* was a qualified finisher in 1968 and 1972 before the imposition of the 50-day rule. (Her times were 57 days and 58 days, respectively.) Since the imposition of the 50-day rule she has not qualified.

3) *Jester* is the only boat in the original race to be consistently re-entered. There is something incongruous about a situation that almost assures such a boat will no longer rate as a "qualified" finisher.

The petition's signatories included Dick Huges, Hans van Hest, Jack Coffey, Mac Smith, BOC Round the World contender Guy Bernardin, Bruno Fehrenbach, and Jack Hunt when *Crystal Catfish* made port.

* * * * *

Even as *Jester* drifted through the fogs off the coast of Nova Scotia, the Observer Singlehanded Transatlantic Race for 1984 was winding down. Two months earlier the clans had gathered in Plymouth. They had come from Glencairn in South Africa, from Wellington, New Zealand, from Birmingham, Alabama, and from Llwendendy Llanelli in Wales. They had sailed in to Plymouth Sound at any hour of the day or night from New Orleans, from Rome, from Dublin, from St. Croix, and from Sofia, Bulgaria. A few, of No Fixed Address, had just come gliding in off the ocean. Now the race was over and the boats were returning home or moving on to new adventures. Those of No Fixed Address vanished again, like the wind, into Nowhere. Hail and Farewell! See you in 1988!

Jack Hunt brought *Crystal Catfish* in just before dawn on July 16. Soon it would be time for *Johan Lloyde* to move along. In a little while, the only trace of OSTAR 1984 would be a couple of tables of statistics in the record books, and a few broken hulls lying under 2,000 fathoms of salt water.

Susan and I decided to return to Lake Ontario and the Thousand Islands the short way, round Long Island, up the Hudson and then through the Erie Canal to Oswego, New York. On the eve of our departure I walked into race headquarters and someone thrust a phone at me with the words, "Here, you're a finisher. Speak to this reporter."

Fame at last!

"Hello," I said, taking the receiver.

"I'm a reporter from the Jamestown paper," said a female voice. "Are you an OSTAR skipper?"

"Yes, I am," I said.

"We're doing a kind of wrap-up on the whole event. Could you talk a moment?"

"Sure." The reporter asked my name and the name of my boat. "How long did you take?"

"Forty one days and five hours," I said.

"Did anything go wrong?"

"No, I'm afraid not." I sensed this was not a helpful response.

"Did you experience any big storms?"

"Oh yes, one or two. But they were probably the same storms the other competitors went through."

"Then, where did you finish?"

"I came sixty-first and tenth in class."

"Out of how many?" There seemed to be a further cooling of interest in the reporter's voice.

"Ninety-two starters. But," I prattled on, "that's not so dramatic as it sounds. Twenty-seven retired or sank so I came fourth, maybe fifth, from last . . ."

"Are there any other skippers there?" asked the woman.

"Let me see." I looked around the office. "There's Jack Hunt here, but he came even further back in the pack than I did. Do you want to speak to him?"

"Errr . . ." The reporter seemed momentarily at a loss. "What I mean is," she said finally, "are there any winners there?"

"Winners?" I said. "No. The winners have all gone home. There are only losers here now, and I can tell you they're in a pretty mean mood."

"Oh." The voice now carried with it a gratifying hint of apprehension. "Well, thank you very much. Goodbye."

"Bye." I hung up. Jack Hunt, who'd heard the tail end of the conversation, let out a great bellow of laughter. The Chief Coordinator, whose phone I must have been using, treated us to one of her frostiest stares. In her book of nautical protocol, late arrivals like ourselves should be seen and not heard.

Later, a crowd of us were sitting around the Marina Pub. "Look at it this way," said Hunt, the leading and sole exponent of the Deep South Strategy, "at least we can say we came ahead of all the guys who sank. We beat boats like *Fury*, and *Crédit Agricole* and *Tyfoon*. We beat *Jet Services*, the transatlantic record holder."

"I dunno, Jack. We didn't beat them. The weather, or misfortune, beat them."

"No. WE beat them. That's what this race is about."

Though I continued to argue with him, I knew Hunt had a point. We had followed Sir Francis Drake and continued unto the end. We had finished and in consequence would receive a handsome brass plaque from the *Observer*. Though the idea clearly ran counter to the journalistic wisdom of the media, it struck me that there was in fact quite a story to be told about the nameless ones who sailed back in the pack. We were more than just colorful backdrop at the start, foils for the speed machines to race against and defeat. Our doings and our achievements stood in their own right. I took a sip of the Marina Pub's specially imported English ale. One thing I'd learned over the last few weeks was that the obstacles confronting the small amateur entrant were in many ways much more formidable than those facing the sponsored professional. The winners took sixteen days to get to Newport. Totally unmodified cruising boats like *Meg of Muglins*, *Crystal Catfish*, and my own *Johan Lloyde* all took over forty days, or at least twenty-four days longer. In those twenty-four days, we small cruisers were still Out There, grappling every vagary of weather, while the speed queens were chastely moored to B Dock in Newport. The skippers back in the pack found themselves yarning of gales and fogs, challenges and setbacks, wholly beyond the frontrunners' ken. As the winner Philippe Poupon would be the first to agree, this was a truly different race.

The psychological equation was also different. The leaders were alone on the ocean for a little more than two weeks, while the skippers of the smaller monohulls found themselves talking to the dolphins for six weeks or more. This was not necessarily an unpleasant experience, but it did represent a different kind of test. Insurance rates for unknowns, if insurance could be obtained at all, were prohibitive and most opted to sail cold turkey. While the highly sponsored professionals seemed to abandon ship at the drop of a spar, most of us were determined to bring the ship in, come what may. Some of the professionals' reasons for withdrawing were beyond our ken. One 60-foot tri retired with a broken main halyard. Another retiree had his mainsail "ripped off." Several boats called it a day when they "lost their electrics." While still in Plymouth, I had become confident of one fact: *Johan Lloyde*, much of which I had built myself, was coming home.

All in all, *Johan* had not done too badly. Despite her stop in Santa Cruz, she had taken only one day longer than had Francis Chichester in *Gypsy Moth*, when he won the first Observer Single-handed (and Blondie Hasler's half-crown) in 1960. There were other precedents. More than sixty years before, in 1923, the celebrated French singlehander Alain Gerbault had taken no fewer than 101 days to sail his 40-foot cutter *Firecrest* from Gibraltar to New York. In ancient times, Odysseus and his men had taken twenty years to return from the battlefield of Troy to their ancestral island of Ithaka. Early in June, *Johan Lloyde*, sailing far out beyond the Pillars of Hercules, had covered that same distance in slightly less than three days. She did not, of course, have to grapple with the wiles of Circe, or the beguilements of Scylla and Charybdis. But she'd had her own adventures beyond the sunset and the baths of all the western stars. She had flirted with the Grand Banks, that icy, fog-flecked Atlantis of the north. She had been caught for many days in the coils of the giant serpent Jormungand. And she had been lured by Aeolus himself into visiting the mountainous paradise of the lotus-eaters, where men sometimes forgot their homes and families and where it was almost always afternoon.

* * * * *

On July 19, six days after her arrival in Newport, *Johan* said her goodbyes and set off for Block Island. The partings were not easy. By and large, the OSTAR skippers were the happiest group of people I had ever met. They walked with a bounce. And when they stood still, they seemed to own the ground beneath their feet. Out there, alone with the sun, the stars, and the wind, they appeared to have discovered something that eluded the freeway philosophers and many of the born-again *religiosos*. They hardly spoke of it, but I sensed they had found within themselves what can only be described as a sense of awe. It was clear that they did not imagine themselves to be the center of the universe. Yet it was also clear that they knew themselves to be part of a larger whole.

Johan said farewell and sailed out to Block Island to anchor for the night. Next day she proceeded along the southern shore of

Long Island in heavy haze. Peter Dunning, the manager of the Goat Island Marina and a fellow East Anglian, had warned me about anchoring in Shinnecock Inlet on the eastern end of the island. But we did not relish the idea of a night out in the traffic lanes, and Shinnecock seemed the only possibility. We studied the large scale chart carefully, but a warning note said, "depths through the inlet are subject to frequent changes and may differ appreciably from the charted depths. Buoys are not charted."

Dusk was falling, and *Johan* was still two or three miles from the entrance. We decided to call Shinnecock Coast Guard station on Channel 16 for an update on the buoys and the location of the channel between the breakwaters. It was to be an encounter worthy of the Archdruid himself.

"Sailboat *Johan* to Shinnecock Coast Guard, how much water is there in the entrance?"

"Coastguard to *Johan*, we are not at liberty to say."

"Your station is right by the entrance. You must know how much water's there."

"I'm sorry," said the voice of the radio operator, "but we are not at liberty to say how much water there is."

"Let me get this straight," I said with a touch of impatience. "Are you telling me you know how much water there is but you are not at liberty to inform me of that depth?"

"Affirmative."

"I love it . . . This is like a TV game show. I have to guess it, right? Is there less than eight feet?"

"We are not at liberty to reveal that information."

"Is it less than six feet?"

"Revealing such information is contrary to our instructions."

I was beginning to get the picture. They must be apprehensive about lawsuits for putting out allegedly "misleading" information. It seemed to have escaped the individuals who formulated those instructions that, by gagging the Coast Guard and withholding information, they were thrusting boats like mine into jeopardy. Then I had an idea. If I came in gently on the flood I could probably haul *Johan* off if she touched bottom. But I needed the answer to a noncontroversial question.

"*Johan* to Coast Guard, let's keep it simple. What time is High Water at Shinnecock?"

"We are not at liberty to reveal that information."

I was stunned. Then I laughed. What was the point of having a Coast Guard if it could not reveal such basic information? Before I could think of any more leading questions, a noisy, new voice broke into my Kafka-speak with the Coastguard.

"This is *Sharpshooter* for sailboat *Johan*."

"Come in, *Sharpshooter*."

"Hey, there's eleven feet of water all the way through if you stay one-third out from the port-hand shore."

"Thanks a million, *Sharpshooter*. We're going in now."

"My pleasure. Take it easy, *Johan*."

"Wilco."

By now it was dark. I took the helm and headed *Johan* past the flashing green and red lights while Susan watched the depthsounder. Fifteen, fifteen, fourteen, thirteen, twelve . . . The radio squawked back into life.

"Shinnecock Coastguard to *Johan*. We cannot advise you to enter at this time . . . Repeat, we cannot advise you to enter at this time . . . " We let the VHF burble on to itself. Soon *Johan* was anchored out of the seaway, and a nice hot supper was on the stove. We had a good laugh, but we were sad, too; the Druids had plainly taken over a magnificent service and forced it to speak in tongues.

Johan Lloyde proceeded on down the shore by easy steps—Fire Island, Sheepshead Bay, then past Manhattan, and up the Hudson to Haverstraw. Two days later we pulled into Castleton-on-Hudson to take the mast down prior to entering the Erie Canal just north of Albany. Shortly after *Johan* had docked, *De Volharding* pulled in with her crew of Dutch celebrants on their way back from Schenectady. Many hands make light work. *Johan*'s mast came down as *De Volharding*'s went up. For her voyage back to Holland, the ketch had acquired a spanking new bowsprit of five-inch steampipe, courtesy of the mayor of Schenectady.

Five days and twenty-eight locks later, *Johan* emerged from the canal at Oswego, on Lake Ontario. Some of these locks were more than one hundred years old, and we had the strong impression that *Johan* was being hoisted back into the nineteenth century. Susan, now eight months pregnant, stepped ashore with Kate at Brewerton, New York, to keep a long-overdue doctor's appointment while I went on through the remaining locks to Oswego. Then the mast went up and *Johan* became herself again. After a night an-

chored in Schoolhouse Bay at Main Duck Island, she sailed her
way back into the Thousand Islands of the upper St. Lawrence.
She finally ran alongside our dock off Clayton late in the afternoon
of Monday, August 6, 1984. The circle was complete.

After securing the lines and stowing the sails I walked up to our
old island house. It had not been inhabited for two whole summers
now, and the path up through the rocks was overgrown. I switched
on the electricity in the house and placed *Johan*'s more perishable
food supplies in the fridge. The Husun sextant would stay aboard
where it belonged, but I unlashed Blagdon's Oar from the starboard rail and carried it in triumph up through the long grass to
the house. I swept out a couple of rooms. Then I unlocked the door
on to the front porch and pulled a folding chair out to my favorite
spot. After pouring myself a long drink, I put my feet up on the
porch rail and gazed off to the south across three miles of open
water to where Clayton lay in the afternoon sunlight. I could not
believe I was back. Since *Johan Lloyde* had sailed away from this
dock one crisp afternoon in May more than fourteen months ago,
she had travelled a total of 8,547 sea miles.

In those fourteen months, *Johan* had been a lone keel off many
headlands, both bright and drear. I had met many unusual characters along the way. Almost always we spoke from the heart; *Johan*
would pass that way but once. In the space of little more than a
year, I had proven that a home-completed boat could survive a
double ocean crossing without mishap. And I had also proven—
at least to my own satisfaction—that the old-style seamanship I'd
learned as a boy had not been superceded by the new plastic ethos
of waxed hulls and speed without joy. Now sunshine sailors could
lecture me all they liked about the merits of nylon rodes, alcohol
stoves, and weathered teak. I'd take it all in stride and smile and
quietly murmur, "Yes, yes, you have something there."

I sat on the porch and filled my glass a time or two. Late
afternoon turned to dusk and the lights of the village began to glint
upon the water. A big freighter slid past, on its way to the sea. For
years I had sat here with my feet on the balustrade and wondered
from whence these vessels came and to where they returned. I had
wondered what lay round the next bend in the river, and the next,
and the bend after that.

Now I knew.

I had sailed through every twist and turn, and down every

reach of this river to the sea and beyond. As I sat there in the
gathering darkness, I hoped this knowledge would help me appreciate my own corner of the world more for its own sake and less
as a shimmering highway to somewhere else. In a little while I
could see the stars reflected in the surface of the St. Lawrence.
Then I stood up and slowly walked back into the house.

Reprinted by permission of *The American Neptune*,
(Peabody Museum, Salem, Mass.), July 1977, pp. 157–63.

' . . . *En Otros Tiempos* . . . '
Did the Men of Bristol Discover
Newfoundland in 1481?

Much evidence has accumulated in recent years to suggest that the fishermen and merchants of Bristol anticipated Columbus's discovery of America by more than a decade. Though the name of the ship and the names of the men who made the discovery are debated by geographers and historians, there is compelling evidence to suggest that Bristol men, as a result of the restrictive measures of the Hanseatic League, struck out across the Atlantic and discovered some part of southeastern Newfoundland in the period 1480–1483. Thereafter they seem to have organized annual fishing expeditions to the shores of Newfoundland, or Hy Brasil, as they called it.

This claim is based primarily upon three documents. The first is a letter, not discovered until 1956, from an English merchant named Johan Day to Christopher Columbus describing Cabot's first expedition to Newfoundland in 1497. The letter, written in Spanish five years after Columbus's initial discoveries, contains the statement 'It is considered certain that the cape of the said land (sighted by Cabot on his 1497 voyage) was found and discovered in other times (en otros tiempos) by the men of Bristol who found "Brasil" as your Lordship knows. It is called the Island of Brasil and it is assumed and believed to be the mainland that the Bristol men found.'[1]

Who were these men of Bristol? And what is meant by the phrase 'en otros tiempos,' which clearly implies a discovery preceding that of Columbus in 1492?

The priority of the Bristol claim is substantiated without equivocation by the second document, Francis Bacon's celebrated biography of Henry VII (reign: 1485–1509). Though Bacon wrote a century after the events he described his family had been closely associated with the Tudors, and he presumably had access to many documents now lost or destroyed. Bacon is categorical. 'And there had been before that time

(1492) a discourie of some Lands, which they tooke to be Islands, and were indeed the Continent of America, towards the Northwest.' Bacon then asserts that 'some Relation' of this discovery may have reached Columbus to give him 'better assurance, that all was not Sea from the west of Europe and Africke unto Asia.'[2] It is interesting to note that, at his brother's request, Bartholomew Columbus arrived in England in 1488. Though Bartholomew boasted 'of no Latin learning' he was 'practical and prudent in sea matters and was well able to make sea charts.'[3] Just the man, it would seem, to check out the rumor of a discovery to the northwest.

The discovery of Newfoundland is further documented in the secret dispatches of Pedro de Ayala who, while serving as Spanish envoy to the English court, wrote a report on Cabot's discoveries. His letter, written in cypher, is dated 25 July 1498, and declares 'For the last seven years the people of Bristol have equipped two, three (and) four caravels to go in search of this island of Brazil. . . .' Ayala believed the 'cape' visited by Cabot belonged to the Spanish, and remonstrated with the English king 'several times on the subject . . . I told him the Islands were those found by Your Highnesses and although I gave him the main reason, he would not have it.[4]

Ayala's dispatch and Johan Day's letter are significant because both clearly indicate that the Spanish accepted, without dispute, the priority of some kind of transatlantic discovery by the mariners of Bristol. Day's phrase—'It is considered certain'—is especially provocative.

If the fact of a Bristol discovery is acknowledged even by England's chief territorial competitors, then one is brought to the question: by whom was that discovery made, and when?

The question has allure. It appeals not only to the intellect but also to the romantic in us much, perhaps, as the search for Prester John, the legendary Christian king of Arabia, intrigued the men and women of renaissance Europe. Several Popes sent forth ambassadors to seek out the monarch in his elusive mountain stronghold somewhere amidst the sands of Abyssinia. Many brave men departed on this holy mission; none ever returned. The same aura seems to cloak the discoverers of Bacon's lands 'towards the Northwest.' But the annals of the city of Bristol go far in transforming these wraithes into substance. According to F. R. Forbes Taylor, who has made a detailed study of Bristol's customs records, a significant voyage was made by a ship called *Christopher*. She departed Bristol, under the command of a certain Morris Targat, on 17 November 1479 ostensibly bound for Ireland. *Christopher* did not return for 115 days, time enough for a rival vessel to make three trips to Ireland and back.[5]

There are many possible explanations for *Christopher*'s absence. She may have been damaged in some winter gale and lain in Ireland for repairs; her master may have subverted the Hanseatic League's monopoly with a clandestine trip to the fisheries of Iceland; or she may have engaged in a little freebooting. Forbes Taylor, however, suggests that her listed destination was a 'cover' for a transatlantic voyage to Newfoundland.

Such an explanation is possible. But Professor D. B. Quinn disputes it. Writing in the London *Times* he argues that though 115 days would be sufficient time for a voyage to Newfoundland, 'the season offers difficulties.'[6] Veterans of the submarine war in the North Atlantic would tend to agree. *Christopher* would have to fight her way to windward into the teeth of the winter westerlies, and then return into the brisk spring easterlies. Square-rigged vessels, despite their poor windward ability, have made such voyages. But surely an experienced skipper would hardly *select* that season to initiate a pioneering venture across the Atlantic, as Targat is alleged to have done.

The Bristol records, in my opinion, reveal a far more likely candidate for the discovery. A three-year charter was granted by Edward IV on 18 June 1480 to Thomas Croft, a customs official, and three Bristol merchants to explore and trade 'to any parts' without restriction.[7] The granting of such an open charter may well have been the direct result of Hanseatic attempts to monopolize the Icelandic fisheries. In this fifteenth-century version of the cod war, the English king may well have decided that new fisheries must be discovered. Though communications between Europe and the Norse communities of Greenland had terminated more than a century before, British sailors in the Iceland trade may well have heard rumors of land to the west—Greenland, Labrador, and perhaps Newfoundland itself.

One month after the granting to the charter, on 15 July 1480, the Latin diary of a William Worcestre states that a ship of eighty tons— about sixty feet overall—left Bristol to seek the 'Island of Brasylle' under the command of Johan Lloyde, who was described as 'the most knowledgeable seaman of the whole of England.'[8] The expedition lasted nine weeks, and while no discovery was reported, it is possible that Lloyde sounded on the Newfoundland banks, or even glimpsed a shadow of land on the far side of a rainsquall. In any event Worcestre writes that Lloyde, upon returning to the coast of Ireland, began to prepare for another expedition into the Atlantic.

Was Lloyde, on this second expedition, successful?

In his history Bacon asserts simply that the discovery of land to the northwest was made before 1492 and Day writes of it as occurring 'en otros tiempos.' In recent years there has been some speculation among historians as to the precise meaning of this phrase. There are some things, though, which Day could *not* have meant by it. Presumably the discovery cannot have been made before 1480, for it is improbable that Edward IV would issue a license to search for land that had already been found. True, some part of Newfoundland may previously have been perceived by a wandering vessel, pushed off its normal course. But unless the position of the land were accurately recorded, so that others might return to the spot, the sighting could hardly be termed, in Bacon's phrase, a 'discourie.' On this evidence, then, we may reasonably conclude that the formal discovery by the men of Bristol was made some time in the twelve years 1480–1492. Ayala himself puts it back, at least, to 1491. And Bartholomew Columbus's long-delayed arrival (he was captured by pirates en route) in 1488 suggests that the substantial North Atlantic discovery referred to by Bacon had been made some time before that year.[9]

If we examine the context of Day's phrase 'en otros tiempos' the possibilities are narrowed still further. This phrase was written in the winter 1497–1498. At first glance the notion 'in other times' might be used to characterize events occurring in the distant past. But Day's phrase does not refer to an event that took place in 900 A.D. or 1200 A.D. but one which must have taken place less than twenty years before he wrote. How, then, can he speak of 'other times'? The phrase itself implies some kind of discontinuity between the occurrence of an event and the present moment. True this discontinuity, this break in the flow of circumstance, can happen with the passage of a great period of time, as when we say 'in other times men wore steel armor into battle.' But this discontinuity can also occur with a cataclysmic upheaval in the social order over quite a small span of time, as in the case of white Southerners who, even while Lincoln lived, might have referred to antebellum society as having existed 'in other times.' Such cataclysmic discontinuity may well have influenced Johan Day when he wrote of Cabot's voyage to Columbus.

Geographical historians, in analyzing the significance of Day's letter, have given slight weight to the fact that in 1485 the Lancastrian faction finally vanquished the Yorkist faction in the house of Plantagenet, and terminated the Wars of the Roses in the battle of Bosworth. The two years preceding Bosworth, that is from 1483 to 1485, were particularly unsettled, with no less than *four* kings seated in turn upon the English throne—Edward IV, Edward V, Richard III and Henry VII. A transatlantic discovery prior to such upheavals could well be characterized as occurring 'en otros tiempos.' Perhaps the discovery was carefully suppressed. In an era of acute civil strife, the Bristol merchants may have been reluctant to announce a Yorkist discovery to a Lancastrian monarch. Indeed, Croft and his associates may have kept their discovery secret—for commercial reasons—from their fellow merchants, and have contented themselves with the dispatch of a few vessels each spring to the fisheries of the Newfoundland banks. Thus it seems likely that Hy Brasil was discovered during the period for which Thomas Croft held his charter for exploration, 1480–1483.

Unless the successful expedition was launched amid the spring gales of 1483 (the charter expired 18 June of that year), the only possible years become 1481 and 1482, since Johan Lloyde drew a blank in his venture of 1480. On balance 1482 seems the less probable, since it requires a group of hardheaded Bristol merchants to pile the expenses of a third possible failure on top of two known failures. The unlikelihood of an expedition in 1482 is further substantiated by the fact that Thomas Croft got into legal trouble as a direct result of the 1481 expedition. Thus in addition to the cost, the Croft syndicate could logically expect further legal harassment if they organized a third expedition in 1482. Significantly, Croft's pardon was not granted until January, 1483.

The lawsuit is interesting. In the latter half of 1481 Croft was charged with illegally loading forty bushels of salt into two small balingers, *Trinity* and *George*. King Edward subsequently pardoned Croft, who argued in his defense that the salt was not for trade or profit but, according to the bastard Latin of the court record 'causa scutandi et inveniendi quandam insulam vocatam le Ile of Drasile.' This was rendered into English in 1483 as 'to serch & fynde a certain Isle called the Isle of Brasile.' But the English version is equivocal; it gives no indication as to whether Brasile had, or had not been found. Professor Quinn suggests that it is possible to translate the bastard Latin into legitimate English as 'on account of searching for and finding an island called the Isle of Brasil'— a wording that definitely points to a successful discovery.[10]

Despite this ambiguity, however, the motives of those who brought the charges deserve scrutiny. It is clear that the ships returned to Bristol without their forty bushels of salt. This suggests, in itself, that *Trinity* and *George* may have been successful in their mission. At least it implies that their crews must have used salt to fill their holds with new cured fish. Could the fish have come from the Newfoundland banks, and been cured and salted (a process requiring a lengthy sojourn upon land) in some protected anchorage on the far side of the Atlantic? This possibility is supported by an intriguing fact: since time out of mind the largest gulf on the east coast of Newfoundland has been known as Trinity Bay.

The evidence, given the certainty that a discovery was made, all points to 1481. The probability is underscored by the very fact that charges were laid against Croft, and event that bears all the claw marks of having been instigated by envious competitors, irate at being cut out of what looked like a profitable piece of business. Putting it another way, it is most unlikely that such charges would have been brought against Croft if Johan Lloyde had returned to Bristol empty-handed after weeks of buffeting around the North Atlantic. The charges clearly suggest that Lloyde discovered something, and that it was big enough to arouse the envy of less adventurous men.

Thomas Croft's subsequent history is almost as equivocal as the description of his discoveries. But then, perhaps he had become soured by his experiences in court. In any event, one year after his pardon, in the reign of Richard III, he transferred his loyalty to the Lancastrian usurper, Henry Tudor. Croft seems to have fought bravely for the future Henry VII at Bosworth, and enjoyed a modest portion of royal esteem until his death three years later. Is it credible in such ambiguous political circumstances that Croft would not seek to ingratiate himself with his new master by divulging the secret of Lloyde's transatlantic discoveries? Such revelations would have piqued Henry's curiosity, and his patriotism. And they might well have formed the substance of the preemptive assertions made by Francis Bacon more than a century later.

All in all, it seems clear that the men of Bristol had the courage and the skill to make a transatlantic discovery more than a decade before Columbus set sail. Johan Lloyde's achievement, however, in no way belittles that of Columbus, who kept his vessels moving westward in face of depleted provision lockers and mutinous crewmen, haunted by the thought that they were about to fall off the edge of the world. But one is left to wonder if Columbus would have held so resolutely to his course if it had not been for the previous discovery by the men of Bristol that 'all was not Sea from the west of Europe and Africke unto Asia.'

[1]Archivo General de Simancas, Estado de Castilla, legajo 2, fol 6.
[2]Francis Bacon, *The history of the reign of King Henrie the Seventh* (1622) p 188.
[3]James A. Williamson, *The Voyages of the Cabots* (1929), p. 199.
[4]J. A. Williamson, Argonaut Press Edition. *The Voyages of the Cabots* (1970), p. 39.
[5]London *Times*, 15 April 1976, p. 14.
[6]Ibid., 30 April 1976, p. 17.
[7]J. A. Williamson, *The Voyages of the Cabots* (1929), p. 20.
[8]Ibid., p. 188.
[9]Ibid., pp. 199–200.
[10]David B. Quinn, *England and the Discovery of America* (1974), pp. 74–75.

APPENDIX B

Life in the Estuary

The Thames barge evolved from the old scoop-bowed sailing lighters of the eighteenth century. By the 1850s the spritsail barge had become an integral part of the economic life of London. This was the imperial city of Charles Dickens and Queen Victoria. Yet it was set amidst the countryside of Thomas Gainsborough and John Clare. The barge, with its rust-red sails and its mighty 60-foot sprit angling out from the mast, was the unobtrusive link that bound city and countryside together. It was in this service that Nelson Keeble received his apprenticeship in sail.

In all, the barges were about 100 feet long and 80 feet on deck. Their slab-sided hulls were built for capacity, but a sharp bow and a beautiful wine-glass stern gave them a pretty turn of speed. Their hard chine and leeboards made them surprisingly effective to windward. The spritsail rig, which enabled the heavy canvas to be brailed up and stowed aloft, could be worked by two men and a boy. Indeed, by the 1880s the craft had proven themselves so handy and so seaworthy that they were carrying cargoes out of the Thames Estuary to the coasts of Holland, France, and even Portugal. But their true metier lay in working the maze of tidal swatchways that laced the east coast of England. A barge's 20-foot beam and 6-foot draft—laden—enabled it to carry cargoes of 150 tons or more in and out of the little rural creeks of Suffolk, Essex, and Kent. Typical cargoes to London Pool might be brick, coal, cement, wheat, flour, and, for a city that still ran on horsepower, hay. With a ten-foot rise and fall of tide along the entire coastline, the barge could glide into the most remote river hamlet on the flood and dry out while her crew and local farm hands unloaded and loaded her again. Then she could ease her way out on the next high tide. Without that flood tide, isolated farming communities like Wivenhoe, Mistley, Tollesbury, and St. Osyth would be all but cut off from the world.

Nelson Keeble, born about 1885, first went to sea as a boy of twelve on the *Bluebell*, skippered by his father, Benjamin Keeble. It was his job to perform all the most uncongenial tasks aboard the barge. Surprisingly, he was also responsible for all cooking while the barge was underway. For these duties he was paid four shillings (or about $1) a week, with grub and berth included. Later he became mate on several other barges, including the *Emma* and the *Memory*. The net income generated by the barge was divided into sixths. The owners took three-sixths, the skipper two-sixths, leaving the mate with one-sixth. This generally amounted to about twenty to twenty-five shillings a week for Nelson. If a barge remained at anchor due to bad weather, the crew was not paid for time lost.

This meager income was partially supplemented if the crew undertook to load and unload their own cargoes. Today, it is hard for us to comprehend the rigors of such work. On one occasion, Keeble, with four young children to feed and his rent in arrears, off-loaded two thousand 140-pound bags of flour from *Memory*'s hold in a single day. He had, working entirely alone, shifted 126 tons of flour. For this he was paid the princely sum of fifteen shillings and ninepence (about $4), or exactly one and a half English pennies per ton of flour landed. When he finally staggered home, his pretty young wife asked, "What do you want to do tonight?"

"Go to bed."

"That," she replied tartly," is all you think about."

In the summer of 1939, my father wanted to take my stepmother, Barbara, on one last sail to Europe before Adolf Hitler made good on his threat to change the world. *Melanie*, then lying at Pin Mill on the Orwell River, was too much for them to handle alone. Walter dreaded hiring a paid hand. He'd encountered them on the big Solent yachts. "They were so discreet, and so deferential," he later noted, "that there seemed to be nothing left for the owner and his party to do." Walter sought out old Harry King, Pin Mill's preeminent boatbuilder, and with some misgivings asked him to recommend a man.

"I know just the fellow," said old Mr. King, and a few days later Nelson Keeble moved into *Melanie*'s fo'c'sle. The first hint that the East Coast version of a paid hand might be neither discreet nor particularly deferential came on Barbara and Walter's initial night aboard. After supper had been cleared away, Barbara looked out into *Melanie*'s cockpit and beyond it to the dark cliffs of the Orwell.

"How beautiful," she said. "There's a new moon."

"Then, ma'am, you must turn your money over."

"I don't have any," laughed Barbara in reply.

"And neither do I," said the new hand a trifle grumpily.

Melanie sailed across the Estuary and down the Channel to Calais. Then she moved on to Dunkirk and Ostend. It was now late August 1939.

To avoid spoiling this enchanted cruise, Walter resolutely refused to buy a newspaper or listen to the radio. One tidbit of news, however, came over the air as they were listening to the BBC weather forecast. With the deteriorating international situation, said the announcer, the Duchess of Kent had decided to close up her French chateau and return to the safety of England.

"Ooo, I *am* glad," said the deferential paid hand from his corner in the saloon. So much for the aristocracy.

The acceptance of Nelson Keeble as a full-fledged member of the family was sealed when Barbara chanced to cut her finger on one of *Melanie*'s door latches. Walter painted the finger with iodine, and the sting on the wound caused Barbara to hop around the cabin. After enduring her cries of agony for a while, the new paid hand advised her to try blowing on it, which she did.

"That doesn't do any good," said Barbara, somewhat aggrieved. "It still hurts."

"Yes, I know, ma'am," replied Nelson, "but it's a lot quieter now."

The next morning, Walter went ashore and noted a lot of commotion in the streets of Ostend. With great foreboding he bought a Belgian newspaper. Hitler had invaded Poland. The summer dream was over. That night, *Melanie* sailed for England. As they cleared the Belgian coast, Barbara began to prepare supper. Walter, perhaps distracted by the news, was in the cockpit at the helm. Barbara passed him a can of corned beef to open. He handed her back the coiled metal lid and threw the beef over the side into the darkening waters of the English Channel.

"Sometimes," observed Nelson when he came on watch, "you country people amuse me."

Back in England, *Melanie* anchored off Southend but the customs officials, usually so punctilious, failed to appear. By the time she reached Pin Mill, England was at war.

In the years that followed, all recreational boating was forbidden by law. Nelson worked aboard *Memory*, which had her masts pulled and her hull filled with electrical equipment for degaussing vessels so they would not trigger the magnetic mines laid by the Germans in the Estuary. Barbara became a reporter for the *Woodgreen Observer*, and Walter—with his master's ticket in sail—taught seamanship and navigation to those intending to infiltrate Hitler's Europe. I was evacuated to a boarding school at Flint Hall Farm in Hertfordshire. On the rare occasions that we were all at home together we played a board game invented by Walter. In it we had to correctly name all the shoals, channels, buoys, and lights on an unmarked map of the Thames Estuary.

As World War II came to a close, Walter was able to lease an isolated farmhouse on the banks of the Orwell River, one mile down from Pin Mill. Clamp Cottage stood just behind the dike on the very edge of the saltings; it had neither electricity nor running water. We paid three shillings and ninepence a week in rent. The back half of the house was subleased to Nelson Keeble, and for several winters *Melanie* was brought ashore in a mud berth in a nearby creek. From this remote base, Walter, Barbara, Nelson, my kid sister, Nicola, and I sailed forth to every little creek and anchorage in the Estuary. In those early post-war days, hundreds of barges still plied the waterways. Most of the crews knew Nelson, and when *Melanie* entered any anchorage she generally received a chorus of Hulloos. After supper, when the riding lights had been hoisted into the growing darkness, the ship's boats would ply back and forth and the yarning would begin.

Gradually, the barges became fewer. London, and the little riverside communities, no longer needed them. Many were reduced to hauling cow dung and garbage. Of this dwindling flock Nelson could identify every one from afar. From *Melanie*'s deck we'd just catch the glimpse of a topsail over the horizon and he'd say "That's the *Audrey*" or "That's the old *Wolsey*." Though we were all anxious to score a point or two off him, we never once found him wrong in these matters.

APPENDIX C

Yachts and Contestants in OSTAR 1984

Classification: Class I, 45ft to 60ft; Class II, 40ft to 45ft; Class III, 35ft to 40ft; Class IV, 30ft to 35ft; Class V, 25ft to 30ft.

Yacht	Time Days:Hours	Crew	Nationality	Class	Type
Umupro Jardin V (1)	16:06	Yvon Fauconnier	French	I	T
Fleury Michon (2)	16:12:25	Philippe Poupon	French	I	T
Elf Aquitaine II (3)	16:12:48	Marc Pajot	French	I	C
Paul Ricard (4)	16:14	Eric Tabarly	French	I	T
Travacrest Seaway (5)	16:17:23	Peter Phillips	British	I	T
Nantes (6)	16:17:51	Daniel Gilard	French	I	T
Region Centre (7)	16:19	Olivier Moussy	French	II	T
L'Aiglon (8)	16:20	Bruno Peyron	French	I	C
Ker Cadelac (9)	16:21	Francois Boucher	French	I	T
Thursday's Child (10)	16:22	Warren Luhrs	U.S.	I	M
Kermarine (11)	17:04	Vincent Levy	French	I	T
Mainstay Voortrekker (12)	17:22:02	John Martin	South African	I	M
Lessive St Marc (13)	17:22:17	Denis Gliksman	French	I	T
Destination St Croix (14)	18:12	Jack Petith	U.S.	III	T
Côte Basque (15)	18:13:34	Didier Munduteguy	French	II	T
Idenek (16)	18:13:49	Yves le Cornec	French	II	T
Gespac (17)	19:07	Philippe Fournier	Swiss	III	T
Sebago (18)	19:10:38	Walter Greene	U.S.	II	C

Yacht	Time Days:Hours	Crew	Nationality	Class	Type
Chica Boba III (19)	19:10:41	Edoardo Austoni	Italian	I	M
City of Birmingham (20)	19:22	Tony Bullimore	British	III	T
City of Slidell (21)	20:23	Luis Tonizzo	U.S.	IV	M
Carteret Savings (22)	21:01	Jack Boye	U.S.	I	M
British Airways II (23)	21:05	Bill Homewood	U.S.	IV	T
Cenet (24)	21:06	Patrice Carpentier	French	II	M
Region de Picardie (25)	21:08	Alain Petit-Etienne	French	I	C
Patricia of Finland (26)	21:13	Kai Granholm	Finnish	III	M
Biscuits Lu (27)	21:18	Guy Bernardin	French	II	M
Survival Tech Group (28)	22:02	Anthony Lush	U.S.	IV	M
Orion Iru (29)	22:15	José Ugarte	Spanish	II	M
Ntombifuti (30)	22:16	Ian Radford	British	III	M
Big Shot (31)	22:18	Jim Bates	U.S.	IV	M
Vingt sur Vannes (32)	23:13	Alain Veyron	French	IV	C
Ms Patty (33)	24:14	John Shaw	British	III	C
Alcatel (34)	24:13	Olivier Dardel	French	III	M
Royal Leerdam (35)	24:18	Wijtze van der Zee	Dutch	III	M
Douche Champion (36)	25:03	Bruno Fehrenbach	French	IV	M
Betelgeuse (37)	25:05	Simon van Hagen	Dutch	II	M
LDS Sailor (38)	25:09	Henk Jukkema	Dutch	IV	M
La Baleine (39)	25:15	Colin Laird	Tobagan	II	M
Lone Eagle (40)	26:06	Tom Donnelly	U.S.	III	M
Jemima Nicholas (41)	26:18	Alan Wynne-Thomas	British	III	M
Abacus (42)	27:11:11	Jerry Freeman	British	II	M
Sherpa Bill (43)	27:11:50	Alan Perkes	British	III	M
Gladiator (44)	28:04	David White	U.S.	I	M
Gamble Gold (45)	29:15	Brian O'Donoghue	British	IV	M
Quailo (46)	29:23	Mac Smith	U.S.	II	M
Olle P2 (47)	30:04	Hans van Hest	Dutch	III	M
Summer Salt (48)	30:12	Spence Langford	U.S.	III	M

Yacht	Time Days:Hours	Crew	Nationality	Class	Type
Swansea Bay (49)	30:14	Chris Butler	British	V	M
Timpani (50)	30:23	Michael Serge de Petrovsky	British	V	M
Phagawi (51)	31:07	David Ryan	U.S.	V	M
El Torero (52)	31:08	Albert Fournier	U.S.	V	M
Lands End (53)	31:23	Robert Scott	U.S.	III	M
Sea-Beryl (54)	32:14	Bertus Buys	Dutch	IV	M
Shamrock (55)	32:15	Jan van Donselaar	Dutch	V	M
Mitsubishi Electric (56)	32:20	Alan Armstrong	British	V	M
Free Bird (57)	35:04	John Howie	U.S.	IV	M
Moustache (58)	35:15	Lloyd Hircock	Canadian	V	M
Gladys (59)	39:06	Dick Huges	Dutch	IV	M
Nord (60)	40:16	Vasil Kurtev	Bulgarian	V	M
Johan Lloyde (61)	41:04	Tim Hubbard	U.S.	IV	M
Meg of Muglins (62)	41:16	Jack Coffey	Irish	IV	M
De Volharding (63)	41:20	Goos Terschegget	Dutch	II	M
Crystal Catfish III (64)	44:14	John Hunt	U.S.	IV	M
Biotherm II	Ret	Florence Arthaud	French	I	T
33 Export	Ret	Gilles Gahinet	French	I	C
Marches de France	Ret	Michel Horeau	French	I	T
Colt Cars GB	Ret	Jeff Houlgrave	British	I	T
Crédit Agricole	Ret	Philippe Jeantot	French	I	C
Fury	Ret	Hugh McCoy	U.S.	I	C
Jet Services	Ret	Patrick Morvan	French	I	C
Lada Poch	Ret	Loick Peyron	French	I	C
Aliance Kaypro	Ret	Monique Brand	French	II	M
Roger & Gallet	Ret	Eric Loizeau	French	II	T
Tyfoon VI	Ret	Gustav Versluys	Belgian	II	M
Marsden	Ret	Frank Wood	British	II	T
Batchelor's Sweet Pea	Ret	June Clarke	British	III	T
Dancing Dolphin	Ret	Bob Menzies	British	III	M

Yacht	Time Days:Hours	Crew	Nationality	Class	Type
Loiwing	Ret	Rachael Hayward	British	IV	M
La Peligrosa	Ret	Andre De Jong	Dutch	IV	M
Prodigal	Ret	Bob Lengyel	U.S.	IV	M
Double Brown	Ret	John Mansell	New Zealander	IV	C
Karpetz	Ret	Karl Peterzen	Swedish	IV	M
Jeremi V	Ret	Jean Jacque Vuylsteker	French	IV	M
Go Kart	Ret	David Duncombe	British	V	M
Quest for Charity	Ret	Geoff Hales	British	V	C
Refugee	NS (ill)	Douglas Parker	U.S.	V	M
Jester	Out	Michael Richey	British	V	M*
Race Against Poverty	Ret	Chris Smith	British	V	M
Rizla +	Ret	Thomas Veyron	French	V	T
Tjisje	Ret	Hank van de Weg	Dutch	V	M
Novia	Ret	William Wallace	U.S.	V	M

*Mike Richey arrived in Halifax July 28. A month earlier, several battens poked through the leech of *Jester*'s junk-rigged sail, seriously affecting the boat's windward performance.